Employment Opportunity

OUTLOOK, REASON, AND REALITY

Alan L. Moss

plus

Employment Opportunity Database

Donald G. Yale

Prentice Hall

Upper Saddle River, New Jersey 07458

Library of Congress Cataloging-in-Publication Data

Moss, Alan L.
    Employment opportunity : outlook, reason, and reality / Alan L. Moss.
      p.   cm.
    "Plus Employment opportunity database / Donald G. Yale."
    Includes index.
    ISBN 0-205-29800-1
    1. Vocational guidance—United States.   I. Yale, Donald G. Employment opportunity
database.

    HF5382.5.U5 M67 2000
    331.7'02'0973—dc21

                                              99-048716

Acquisitions Editor: *Sande Johnson*
Managing Editor: *Mary Carnis*
Production: *Holcomb Hathaway, Inc.*
Director of Manufacturing and Production: *Bruce Johnson*
Manufacturing Manager: *Ed O'Dougherty*
Assistant Editor: *Michelle Williams*
Marketing Manager: *Jeff McIlroy*
Marketing Assistant: *Barbara Rosenberg*

Printed in the United States of America

10 9 8 7 6 5 4 3 2 1

ISBN 0-205-29800-1

Prentice-Hall International (UK) Limited, *London*
Prentice-Hall of Australia Pty. Limited, *Sydney*
Prentice-Hall Canada Inc., *Toronto*
Prentice-Hall Hispanoamericana, S.A., *Mexico*
Prentice-Hall of India Private Limited, *New Delhi*
Prentice-Hall of Japan, Inc., *Tokyo*
Pearson Education Asia Pte. Ltd., *Singapore*
Editora Prentice-Hall do Brasil, Ltda., *Rio de Janeiro*

For Penny, David, and Jennifer

For Miriam, Richard, and Mark

Contents

CHAPTER 3   **WHAT'S IN A LABOR MARKET?**
(WHERE THE HUMAN AND ECONOMIC SIDES MEET)   **53**

Part B Keys to Career Decisions   69

CHAPTER 4   GUIDANCE KEYS TO CAREER DECISIONS   71

Part C Career Income and Investments   99

Part D Unlocking the Doors to Fulfilled Employment   129

Appendices

Preface

The *Employment Opportunity System* includes three components:

- This text, *Employment Opportunity: Outlook, Reason, and Reality*
- A CD-ROM, *Employment Opportunity Database* (included with the text)
- The Internet Website, *Employment Opportunity News Service* (www.prenhall.com/success/Moss)

The *Employment Opportunity System* provides you with knowledge, techniques, and data to find your career. As you will see, it is much more than the traditional career or jobs guide. It is a comprehensive and innovative program to improve career decisions, sharpen job search techniques, and ultimately enhance your chances of finding "fulfilled employment."

What is "fulfilled employment"? For many years, while teaching at the University of Virginia's Northern Virginia Campus, I used the term "fulfilled employment" to describe winning at careers. Quite simply, it means finding a career that takes full advantage of your capabilities and provides you with a satisfying worklife and lifestyle.

The road to fulfilled employment is often marked with unnecessary and disruptive detours:

- Instead of making investments in planning their future, some people avoid difficult choices by seeking immediate employment in the best job they can land at the time.
- Others put off career decisions by needlessly extending their education or by taking temporary opportunities outside the fields in which they are really interested.
- Still others accept employment requiring skills way below their capabilities, avoiding a true test of their competence.

Most of these people have faith that through a gradual process of moving from job to job, they will eventually find a satisfactory career. If you are one of these non-planners, keep reading. *Employment Opportunity* and your own good judgment could make the difference between success and failure in the world of work.

Employment Opportunity recognizes that selecting your career is a complex and challenging task that requires serious study. Therefore, the objective of this book is not to give you quick tips for a whiz-bang career. Books of that nature may provide some useful information, but they will not allow you to understand enough about the world of careers to find your way. Instead, this book's principal objective is to provide the knowledge and competencies necessary to guide you through the difficult process of defining your best Employment Opportunity. For you, working through this "curriculum" should greatly improve the odds of winning.

The *Employment Opportunity* text is organized into **four major sections:**

- Part A: The **two sides of careers,** human and economic.
- Part B: **Keys to career decisions,** guidance and economic.
- Part C: **Career income and investments,** rewards and requirements.
- Part D: **Unlocking the doors to fulfilled employment,** dealing with employers and a career plan.

Accompanying this book is a CD-ROM containing the comprehensive and powerful *Employment Opportunity Database* (also known as a warehouse or encyclopedia of data, where much useful career information is being stored for your use). The CD-ROM includes: (1) millions of data entries on industries, occupations, job requirements, current and projected employment, earnings, and job openings for the nation, and its 172 economic/geographic areas, and (2) a guide to help you relate your interests, skills, and potentials to appropriate occupations. Use of this unprecedented database is woven into the fabric of the book in a structured manner. As a result, the *Employment Opportunity* text enables you to learn important career concepts, while the *Employment Opportunity Database* facilitates immediate application of those concepts to the "real world."

You may also use the enclosed *Employment Opportunity System* to access the resources that allow you to readily identify many employers likely to hire workers in geographic areas of interest, in your chosen career field. Once you make your career decision and find the right job, the *Employment Opportunity News Service,* through its Internet website, will keep you informed of the latest labor market trends and developments, and the availability of new resources to help you advance your career.

The *Employment Opportunity* text, *Database,* and *News Service* should greatly improve your employment prospects, whether you are planning your path through school, entering or reentering the labor market, or seeking to enhance or change your current career. By understanding that your quest for a successful career will not be easy, and by taking action to learn about the world of careers, you are already on your way to fulfilled employment.

For many who face potential discrimination, *Employment Opportunity* materials and know-how can help you to penetrate workforce barriers. Career development competencies also may help you to compensate for the established networks and favoritism that provide some with significant advantages.

Although *Employment Opportunity* provides you with exhaustive resources, don't hesitate to supplement its use with additional support. For example, *Employment Opportunity* activities may be carried out under the experienced eye of a qualified career counselor. Also, be aware that family and personal problems can threaten your career, while problems with work can imperil your family life. In such situations, there is no need to face adversity alone; seek assistance from a professional career counselor. Your career development may be enhanced by using computerized career information systems designed to provide you with career options and useful information.

ACKNOWLEDGMENTS

The authors wish to express their gratitude to Jennifer and David Moss and Scott Ross for their diligent reading of numerous drafts, editing, and constructive ideas for improvement. The authors also gratefully acknowledge the assistance of those who provided much cooperation and support in furnishing and explaining data utilized for the *Employment Opportunity Database.* Special thanks to staff of the Bureau of the Census, the Bureau of Labor Statistics, and the North Carolina Occupational Analysis Field Center. The authors also honor those of the U. S. Employment Service who pioneered development of the Dictionary of Occupational Titles, the Guide for Occupational Exploration, and related products of their genius.

The authors also wish to acknowledge significant contributions of several academic reviewers, including Susan Ekberg (Western University), Robert L. Stanelle (Tulane University), Pat Jachim Kitzman (Central College), Mike Henle (University of Minnesota), Mike Stableton (University of Minnesota), Patrick Schutz (Mesa State College), Ellen Oppenberg (Glendale Community College); Michael Gooch (DeVry Institute of Technology, Long Island, NY); David A. Jepsen (University of Iowa); Michael S. Lavan; and Michael McTague (Provost, Technical Career Institute, NY).

Any errors or shortcomings that remain are the responsibility of the authors alone.

Employment Opportunity

OUTLOOK, REASON, AND REALITY

plus

Employment Opportunity Database

Introduction

Career Information and Employment Opportunity *Resources*

Overview

LEARNING OBJECTIVES * (Covers Preface and Introduction)

- Become familiar with the *Employment Opportunity* components.
- Define *fulfilled employment.*
- Become aware of common career detours.
- Understand the significance of careers and career decisions.
- Know why sound career decisions are often difficult to make.
- Become familiar with accessing data from the *Employment Opportunity Database.*

CHAPTER EXERCISES

Data-Speak: Use the *Employment Opportunity Database* to learn about the nation's 172 economic/geographic areas.

Career-Inquiry: Explore your current concept of a winning career, and learn about career turning points.

Few things in life are more important than your career. For the most part, your occupation determines the style in which you live, the amount of respect you receive, and the satisfaction you derive from your work. The job that you do determines how well you do, and how you are viewed. It should therefore go without saying that finding a career that matches your individual and economic needs is very important and worthy of serious examination.

*Learning objectives state what completing the chapter will allow you to accomplish.

Making sound career decisions is challenging in today's changing world. Globalization has swept over our economy, foreign workers threaten domestic jobs, rapid technological change speeds occupational obsolescence, and businesses rarely offer their employees the degree of security on which workers relied in the past. Even when the economy is booming and jobs are plentiful, identifying occupations that are right for you, and insulated from future downturns, remains a demanding assignment. When the economy is in a slump, your ability to find and land the right job may be a matter of economic survival.

Since careers are so important to an individual's happiness, and finding the right career is a difficult process, one would expect that expert assistance with this dilemma would be readily available. Unfortunately, nothing could be further from the truth. This is due to four unfortunate developments:

1. In the past, many young people preparing for the workforce could rely upon advice of parents, relatives, and friends. But today, with jobs becoming increasingly complex, those close to us usually don't know enough to provide good advice about the array of skills and occupations in which one might find a satisfying career. Job requirements, management styles, and shifting patterns of supply and demand fly by at the speed of light, defying the understanding of casual observers.

2. Often, teens are not ready to face the reality of having to prepare for a career and a lifetime of work. Even when high school career centers are loaded with job publications and provide access to computerized information systems, counselors find it difficult to attract students. Competing for grades, preparing for SAT or ACT exams, completing entrance applications, and participating in pressure-packed extracurricular activities are more than enough for most. Adding worries about career selection and preparation is often just too much.

3. There is a shortage of qualified school guidance counselors, relative to the number of students and their extensive demands. Also, since student concerns are typically short-run—e.g., determining courses to be taken for the next semester—information on careers is often unused, as class schedules, college placement, and personal problems expend 110 percent of counselor hours. The fact that career exploration should drive many class schedule and college placement decisions is rarely reflected in the guidance process.

4. The concepts that explain career outcomes are themselves complex, diverse, and not always well recognized by experienced academics, let alone the average jobseeker. Of all the markets for various resources, those for labor have the distinction of being the least understood. Moreover, elements that play an important role in career decision-making are not limited to a single discipline. For example, some are derived from developmental psychology (personality, interests, and values), some are drawn from sociology (social relationships), while others are economic (human capital, wages, and competition).

These four problem areas often lead graduating students to find that heavy educational investments in time and tuition do not necessarily lead to fulfilled employment. In fact, when the economy is not booming, a high school diploma or college degree is no guarantee of any employment. While such situations upset parents and students, professionals involved tend to be resigned to this result. In fact, many economists call the rate of unemployment in "normal times" the "natural rate of unemployment." In other words, there is something natural about jobseekers being without work because they lack the right skills or enough information.

For those willing to take on the challenge, *Employment Opportunity* resources will provide you with fundamental knowledge, techniques, and tools to maximize your chances for fulfilled employment. Deciding to invest hours in your future career now should lead to years of increased job satisfaction and rewards. Whether this is the first, second, or tenth time you review your career options, *Employment Opportunity* resources are ready. They may be used over and over to confirm your career choice or help you move in a new direction.

One positive development in recent years has been the growth of school courses that seek to improve career decision-making, planning, and development, and offer training in effective job search techniques. In addition, new orientation courses, targeted at students entering college and those about to graduate, often include valuable career/job search lessons. The *Employment Opportunity System* is an ideal resource for such classes.

The *Employment Opportunity* text is organized into four parts and nine chapters. At the end of each chapter (and this introduction) are exercises to help you understand and apply concepts covered. These Data-Speak tasks allow you to use the *Employment Opportunity Database* to describe, quantify, and personalize the material covered. For example, after reviewing your career interests and studying how labor markets operate, Data-Speak offers the immediate opportunity to go over the content of occupations in which you are interested, to see the extent to which employment in those occupations is projected to grow, and to gauge current occupational employment by industry and geographic area.

Career Inquiry exercises offer brief research opportunities to apply career concepts for your own use. For example, after you have focused on building blocks of effective job search materials, and a process for identifying employers likely to offer employment opportunities in your chosen occupation, Career Inquiry offers a structured approach for you to prepare each product required for an effective job search.

References

County and City Databook, U. S. Department of Commerce, Bureau of the Census, Washington, D.C. (Annual)

State and Metropolitan Area Databook, U. S. Department of Commerce, Bureau of the Census, Washington, D.C. (Annual)

Statistical Abstract of the United States, U. S. Department of Commerce, Bureau of the Census, Washington, D.C. (Annual)

Thomas, G. Scott, *The Rating Guide to Life in America's Fifty States,* Prometheus Books, Amherst, New York, 1994.

The World Almanac and Book of Facts, 1999, Primedia Reference Inc., 1998.

Data-Speak
LEARNING ABOUT ECONOMIC AREAS

The *Employment Opportunity Database* provides information on jobs within 172 Economic Areas, as defined by the U. S. Department of Commerce. Each Economic Area, such as the Boston-Worcester-Lawrence-Lowell-Brockton area, consists of one or more centers of economic activity and surrounding counties. In general, Economic Areas are formed based upon commuting patterns. Therefore, each Economic Area includes, as far as possible, the place of work and the place of residence of its labor force.

Now, turn to Appendix A in the *Employment Opportunity* text, to view a listing of the nation's 172 Economic Areas. They are arranged alphabetically within eight regions. Tentatively, select three areas of interest and note their titles. Initially, they will be the subjects of this chapter's Data-Speak exercises.

Now, use the *Employment Opportunity Database* CD-ROM to obtain information about the areas selected. Go to Data-Speak Introduction: *Learning About Economic Areas.* Select *Economic Areas* and review the alphabetic/regional listing to see if there are other areas that you want to investigate. Then, select *Economic Area Composition* to learn the towns and counties that compose each area of interest. Finally, select *Economic Area Profile* to learn each area's population, employment, and per capita income. Note that information on public sector employment, excluded from all subsequent screens, is provided here. After you have obtained information on the areas you initially selected, fully explore other economic areas of interest. (You may wish to supplement these data with information on climate, transportation, housing, etc. See the suggested references above.)

Complete Data-Speak Worksheets Intro.A and Intro.B so you may easily retrieve the findings of this database exploration at a later time. Worksheet Intro.A records a summary of information about the economic areas you explore. Worksheet Intro.B lists those areas that appear most attractive to you.

■ DATA-SPEAK GUIDANCE

You may wish to follow these four steps in evaluating Economic Areas:

1. Identify those area characteristics that mean the most to you, e.g. population size, employment, per capita income (wealth), projected growth, region of the country, climate, etc.

2. Gather information on these characteristics from the Employment Opportunity Database for areas under consideration, and enter that information on the corresponding worksheets that follow the Introduction.

3. For areas in the running, research additional information, such as climate, population density, and adequacy of transportation (see suggested references).

4. Weigh the information obtained, and identify those areas that best meet your selection criteria.

Career Inquiry
WINNING AT CAREERS AND CAREER ROADMAPS

Winning at Careers. As you progress through the *Employment Opportunity* curriculum, you will refine your perception of what constitutes a winning career for you. To begin this process, profile your *current thought* by describing the most important characteristics of what you consider to be a winning career. Record this information on Career Inquiry Worksheet Intro.A.

Career Roadmaps. Nothing in the world of careers is a sure thing. For the most part, planning and wise investments in developing skills and abilities pay off; but one can never be sure. Often, success goes to those who can take advantage of unanticipated opportunities, while minimizing the damage of unfortunate developments. To demonstrate the uncertainties of real world careers, and the benefits of planning and investment, interview an individual (not a relative) who has been in the labor force for 20 years or more. Through your questions, identify the most important career turning points for that individual. At each such juncture, did the interviewee steer the situation by his or her preparation, and/or action? Was the change in direction dictated by someone else, or by uncontrolled circumstances? In other words, was the individual proactive or reactive? What was the ultimate impact of each transition?

Use Career Inquiry Worksheet Intro.B as an interview guide, and to record your subject's information. Summarize the information gained on Career Inquiry Worksheet Intro.C.

DATA-SPEAK WORKSHEET INTRO.A
SELECTED ECONOMIC AREAS

Area Title	Region	POPULATION			PER CAPITA INCOME			EMPLOYMENT		
		2000	2005	%Chg	2000	2005	%Chg	2000	2005	%Chg

DATA-SPEAK WORKSHEET INTRO.B
ECONOMIC AREAS SELECTED

AREA TITLE	STRENGTHS	WEAKNESSES

CAREER INQUIRY WORKSHEET INTRO.A

WINNING AT CAREERS

Characteristics of Your Winning Career

CAREER INQUIRY WORKSHEET INTRO.B
CAREER ROADMAP INTERVIEW GUIDE & DATA COLLECTION FORM

(Remember to focus on turning points; forces responsible for turning; and impact.)

Individual Interviewed _____

Current Occupation _____ Industry _____

Age _____ Sex _____ Education & Training _____

Pre-Employment Investments in Education and Training:

Early Years Work Experiences:

Mid Years Work Experiences:

Later Years Work Experiences:

DATA SPEAK WORKSHEET INTRO.C

CAREER ROADMAP DATA SUMMARY

Turning Points

CAREER TURNING POINT	FORCE RESPONSIBLE FOR TURNING	IMPACT

PART A

The Two Sides of Careers

The Human Side of Careers

How human characteristics and feelings influence your view of careers.

Overview

LEARNING OBJECTIVES

- Understand that an array of human factors influences career choice.
- Be able to articulate how personality, values, interests and attitudes, aptitudes and abilities, and stage of development influence how an individual views careers.
- Understand those forces that form the early foundation for career preference: genetic composition, gender, and childhood environment.
- Be aware of the relationship between career and family life.
- Know the linkage between needs and careers, and childhood environment and self-concept.
- Comprehend the power of motivation.
- Discover the Interest Areas in which student career aspirations are classified.
- Understand the nature and extent of family influence on student educational and occupational perspectives.

CHAPTER EXERCISES

Data-Speak: Use the Employment Opportunity Database to weigh your career interest areas through a convenient checklist.

Career Inquiry: Develop a career genogram to gauge the extent to which your family's educational and work history has influenced your career interests.

Setting the Stage

NON-COMPETING GROUPS AND THE HUMAN SIDE

There are those who contend that competition and the drive for material wealth fully explain the economy and careers. Businesses act to maximize profits and workers seek jobs that deliver optimum income and satisfaction.

If life were that simple, career choice would be a snap—all workers would seek the jobs that pay the most. In that case, all workers would be pursuing a few high-paying occupations. Of course, we know that this is *not* the case. While some seek the monetary rewards of investment banking, others are perfectly happy with the modest salaries of elementary school teachers. Career choice involves more than money.

Reconciling the reality of the labor market with the theory of competition is nothing new. In 1874, John Elliot Cairnes, a British economist, felt "compelled" to recognize the existence of "non-competing industrial groups":

> what we find, in effect, is, not a whole population competing indiscriminately for all occupations, but a series of industrial layers, superimposed one on another, within each of which the various candidates for employment possess a real and effective power of selection.*

Cairnes and later economists explained these non-competing groups mainly on the basis of skill and geography. The unskilled laborer could not compete for a physician job vacancy, but could realistically qualify and compete for a number of low-level jobs. The blue-collar worker in Pittsburgh was not aware of jobs in Southern California, and wouldn't have the desire or the means to pull up stakes and trek out to the coast anyway.

While skill level and geography certainly play a role in determining occupational choice, today these factors only tell part of the story. Many human characteristics, such as an individual's personality, values, interests and attitudes, aptitudes and abilities, and stage of development represent the human side of careers. These factors, applied against the economic environment and its competitive forces, explain how career decisions are finally made.

The Human Context

You cannot realistically separate the world of careers from the rest of your life. Your personal needs and desires, and your self-concept will affect your choice of a career.

If you believe your capacities to be limited, view your potential as weak, and reject large groups of occupations out of hand, you restrict your own possibilities. On the other hand, if you have faith in your capabilities, view your potential as having few limits, and accept the challenge of many types of occupations, you have already taken major steps toward opening the doors to numerous career opportunities.

* John Elliot Cairnes, *Some Leading Principles of Political Economy Newly Expounded* (New York: Harper, 1874), pp. 66–67.

Your *personality* may lead you to jobs whose characteristics are compatible with your temperament. For example, an individual who thrives on social contacts may be drawn to politics. Or, the artistic personality may seek a career painting landscapes, composing music, or interpreting modern dance. In any case, individuals feel most comfortable in jobs that are suitable for their personality type, working with people who also are attracted to these careers and share likes and dislikes.

If an individual's strongest *values (needs)* are wealth and status, he or she may seek to become a corporate CEO (Chief Executive Officer) or professional athlete. If the individual needs to feel good about contributions to society, becoming a social worker or safety inspector may be the answer. The needs felt and the values held steer one into specific groups of careers.

If *interests* and *attitudes* reflect a preference for dealing with things rather than people, career choice may involve occupations in scientific research over those involving many personal contacts, such as sales. If the priority is to feel more secure with routine and organized work environments, a career within a large government bureaucracy, rather than a small innovative organization, may emerge. If interests are in creative thinking versus utilizing the ideas of others, composing science fiction novels, instead of systems operation manuals, may be the ticket to happiness on the job.

If *aptitudes* and *abilities* are characterized by a high intelligence level, advanced numerical operations, and superior spatial ability, architecture could be within reach. On the other hand, extraordinary motor coordination, finger dexterity, manual dexterity, and eye-hand-foot coordination may be elements in a successful career as a baseball player or professional golfer.

Just as physical development occurs over a number of years, awareness about personal needs and how they may be satisfied through work also takes time. If the *stage of development* is that of a child, the individual may seek attention, and be attracted to occupations that receive public acclaim, such as astronaut, professional hockey player, or fashion model. As a teen, individuals may recognize that their physical stature and skills will not permit realization of a childhood dream, and so they may become tentative about where to go from there. As an adult, armed with a clearer view of individual needs and abilities, the characteristics of occupations, and the economy in which jobs exist, individuals may be able to reconcile their doubts and make rational and satisfying career decisions.

How the Human Side Is Organized

What forces organize the way people feel about careers? Every human being is unique. Each is a distinct combination of physical and mental characteristics, reacting to situations and events. However, in most cases, the forces that determine career preference begin to form early, based upon: (a) genetic composition, (b) gender, and (c) childhood environment, as reflected in family cultural and socioe-conomic position and psychological profile.

GENETICS

Life begins with the *genes* that are inherited. Composed of DNA, they form the physical basis for transmission of inherited characteristics. Individuals enter life with traits that contribute to their make-up. Whether it is a strong physical stature, a knack for solving mathematical problems, or a tendency to contract diabetes, inherited genetic structure usually plays a role.

The influence of genetics on composition may be illustrated by clear-cut ex-amples, such as the extent to which an individual resembles one or both parents. Scientists also have traced certain sensory perceptions, such as the ability to de-tect the odor of a specific chemical, to heredity.

On the other hand, when it comes to personality, emotional traits, and intel-ligence, it has been very difficult to measure the relative influence of genetic con-tent versus environmental and cultural forces. However, research does conclude that environmental factors account for the great majority of variation in IQ. Forces that are particularly significant are socioeconomic status, language skills, and motivation.

Example THE AIR UP THERE

Nicholas Cesuski was born in Central Russia in 1972. As a child, he was very much like his father, very tall and very thin. In fact, he was always the tallest child in his class at school, just as his dad was the tallest man in town. As with very tall children anywhere in the world, the classic question always asked of him by the other kids was the universal crack: "How's the air up there?"

Nicholas didn't let the teasing bother him. His dad told him that one day he would use height to his advantage. Since many tall children grow up to have weak endurance, Nicholas began lifting weights and running track during his early teen years. By the time he was a junior in high school, he was strong, athletic, and 6 foot 9 inches tall.

That year, he was invited to play basketball in a summer league in Rome, Italy. When he dominated every game in which he played, collegiate scholarship offers started arriving from around the world. Today, the gift of height he inherit-ed from his father, and his own dedication have propelled him into a profession-al basketball career, a contract for many millions of dollars, and much enjoyment of the air up there.

GENDER

Even though most modern women who choose to do so are able to successfully pursue a career as well as a family life, *gender* has had a negative influence upon female employment. From a very early age, many children have been subjected to artificial concepts of what jobs are appropriate for each sex. For women, caring for others often was placed ahead of assuming power. Thus, some women rejected nontraditional roles and accepted stereotype positions in order to avoid being viewed as unfeminine or undesirable.

The result of this situation was a narrowing of choice, as women were discouraged from seeking many higher level positions. Gifted young women had lower career aspirations than gifted young men, and women overall demonstrated less interest in science, math, and professional jobs. Women commonly possessed lower self-esteem, underutilized their aptitudes, and failed to effectively follow their interests. Even though women generally achieved higher grades than men, they have been underrepresented in many prestigious occupations.

Example JAN'S UNLIKELY EQUATION

Jan Bolger grew up in San Diego, California, the only child of Richard and Susan Bolger. As a teenager, Jan recognized that her parents were a product of the 1950s. During those years, it was generally understood that to maintain their femininity, women must place home over career. If a career was an economic necessity, many felt that only occupations such as teacher (summers off and several shorter vacations to be with the kids), nurse (caring for others), or librarian (assisting students and intellectuals) were proper.

Although Jan's parents provided her with a warm and caring environment, and encouraged her to seek good grades in school, their scope of appropriate occupations for women reflected their own upbringings. But Jan had other ideas.

As a junior in high school, Jan elected to take a course in introductory statistics. To her surprise, her teacher was a young woman who made statistics fascinating. Jan quickly established herself as the best student in the class. Utilizing her teacher as a role model, Jan took several AP courses in statistics, and planned her further education with a concentration in statistical methods.

While Jan's parents were initially unfamiliar with statistics as a profession, they learned from their daughter, and admired her initiative and enthusiasm. With her parents' financial assistance, and scholarship money directed to women with strength in math and science, Jan eventually earned a Ph.D. in applied statistics. She is now vice president of a leading economic research-consulting firm.

CHILDHOOD ENVIRONMENT

Another important determinant of career perspective may be traced to *childhood environment.* What message does the family environment deliver?

Did the family culture reward achievement in educational accomplishments, or were the parents more impressed by hard physical labor? Did the family's social and economic dealings reflect a standard of living of the affluent, or did the family just make ends meet? Did the father/mother provide a successful role model in business or a profession, or were they in craft or service occupations?

Research indicates that the first set of circumstances encourages academic excellence and prestigious careers, while the second set may lead to more modest educational achievements and routine positions. Of course, there are numerous examples of children who have overcome very difficult beginnings to rise to academic heights and distinction in their careers, as there are examples of those with every conceivable advantage accomplishing little. However, breaking out of the family mold of cultural-socioeconomic values may not be an easy feat.

Example ANDY'S BIG APPLE

Andy Simms grew up in New York City. An only child, he received much attention and support from his parents, who adored his every move. Although New York City is possibly the toughest environment in the world in which to excel, Andy's father convinced his son that he could achieve great heights, especially if he followed his father and uncle into the investment banking industry. Affluent and educated, they offered him a business, and a network of clients and contacts through which Andy could maintain and advance the family's standing. After graduating from the University of Wisconsin with a major in real estate, he entered the firm as a low-level assistant. Today, some 25 years later, with his dad and uncle deceased, he is president of his own firm, worth 100 times the value of the family business that he entered.

Example RON'S LOST DREAM

Ron Burke spent many hours after school working in the family's clothing store. Beginning as a stock boy when he was in seventh grade, by the time he was a senior in high school he was a top salesperson. Ron's mom and dad, married when they were 19, went directly from high school to retail sales. They scrimped and saved over many years to buy their store. Now, they offered Ron a full-time job, with the promise of being assistant manager in five years and partner when advanced age reduced their work time.

While Ron enjoyed working in the store, his dream was to be in advertising. With little or no support from his parents, he obtained student loans and graduated from the state university with a major in business administration, and a minor in marketing. After graduation, in the midst of a severe recession, Ron had trouble finding a job with an ad firm. Rather than spending months searching for work, he postponed his advertising career and returned to the family store. Over the years, he often vowed to pursue his advertising dream, but never was able to break away. When his father suffered a heart attack, and had to quit working, the store was sold to a competitor, and Ron was let go. Convinced that he was too old to start anew, Ron's career became a succession of temporary sales jobs.

PSYCHOLOGICAL FORCES

Psychological forces in the family also exert a strong influence on personality and eventual career direction. For example, young children provided with an orderly, protected, and loving environment learn to trust those around them, encouraging an optimistic, open, and positive perspective. Success at early tasks, such as putting toys away, leads to development of self-confidence, self-reliance, and an assertive, independent, and task-oriented temperament. Identification with the same gender parent, and freedom to explore and imagine build self-confidence, leadership characteristics, and accepted behavior. On the other hand, the downsides of these psychological forces lead to negative behavioral counterparts that act to stunt healthy development and career potential.

MAC'S CHOICE

Ostell McNight was known to his friends as Little Mac. His grandmother raised him until he was 17 years old. That year, he moved in with his brother (Big Mac) and his brother's wife and two children. When he lived with his grandmother, she emphasized that he stay out of trouble, and pass his classes. If Little Mac graduated from high school on time, Big Mac promised him a job in the auto assembly plant where he worked for the past 12 years.

Over the summer, Little Mac worked as a counselor at a community center day camp. He was extremely popular among the other counselors, who admired him for his ability to enjoy almost every situation. They also admired his easygoing attitude about the future. While they were sweating grades and SATs, he seemed to have faith that the future would take care of itself.

But in fact Little Mac's future was in jeopardy. His grandmother died and his brother was laid off. With no realistic job prospects, he quit school and took a job as an insurance salesman. Working mainly on commission, he was unable to make a go of it and fell in with the wrong crowd.

But when he was confronted with the choice of illegal gain or trying to work his way back, Mac could make only the right choice. Thinking of his grandmother's love and concern for his well being, Mac could not let her down. Through his brother's best friend, he was able to enter an apprenticeship program in the construction industry, while he completed his high school diploma at night. After two years of long and difficult hours, Mac earned his high school diploma, as well as journeyman status as a professional electrician.

Impact on Workers and Their Careers

Your career choice goes beyond the walls of the work environment and into life at home. The career you practice and the occupation and job you fill dictate the length of your commute, the hours worked, the salary earned, the trips taken, the health care received, and the retirement afforded. Each of these considerations is likely to have a strong influence upon your home life.

At the same time, family life impacts progress in careers. A young married couple, each partner with a full-time job, initially may view travel as an adventure, and an indication of management's faith in their capabilities. They may treat business trips as a perk, and willingly go along. On the other hand, should that same couple have children, they may begin to view continuous travel as an obstacle to an orderly family life, and they could well resist trips at the expense of career advancement. They may even look for employment that better conforms to the interests of their children and life at home.

Needs and the extent to which they may be satisfied by an occupation influence the way people think about careers. As noted above, wants and desires flow from the genes inherited, gender, and life experienced as a child, including cultural background and socioeconomic position of the family. The stronger an individual's needs, the more motivated he or she is to satisfy them through careers.

Two important by-products of the combination of genes, gender, and childhood environment are self-concept and motivation. They play an important role in determining the success or failure of an individual's worklife.

Homes that provide attractive and positive role models, enforce reasonable rules, and place appropriate limits on activities often lead to positive self-concepts and high self-esteem. Such conditions also may lead to feelings of proficiency, kinship, and value. On the other hand, where respected role models are absent, and expectations are slight, inconsistent, or impossible to achieve, children tend to lose self-reliance, and may fail to develop high self-esteem. Positive self-concepts and high self-esteem often lead to career accomplishments, while negative self-concepts and low self-esteem discourage achievement.

All of the factors discussed above influence an individual's level of motivation, perhaps the most significant factor of all. Motivation determines the extent to which one is willing to strive for and commit to a particular career. Of all the elements considered, level of effort often is the most telling barometer of success.

Example WITH A FLICK OF THE WRIST

Rick Woodall was a true Texan, and a child prodigy. At 16 years of age, his artistic ability was recognized throughout the Dallas area. Although he loved to swim, painting was his life and his passion. One hot and muggy night in August, Rick and some friends cut through a field on the edge of town to get to an old swimming hole. As he had done a thousand times before, Rick grabbed hold of a rope tied to an old oak tree, swung over the pond, and let go. No one knew that the pond had been drained the day before, and Rick's fall resulted in complete paralysis. But Rick knew that he would paint again. After two operations and endless physical therapy, he began to move his wrist. Rigging brushes to his hand, and using a customized paint dispenser, Rick began to paint once more. Today, his quaint country scenes demand top dollar, and he has become a consultant to movie studios on innovative set designs.

References

Gysbers, Norman C., Heppner, Mary J., and Johnston, Joseph A., *Career Counseling: Process, Issues, and Techniques,* Allyn and Bacon, Boston, 1998.

Hartl, Daniel L., *Genetics,* 3rd Ed., Jones and Bartlett Publishers, Boston and London, 1994.

Holland, J.L., *Making Vocational Choices: A Theory of Careers,* Prentice-Hall, Inc., Upper Saddle River, N.J., 1973.

Osipow, Samuel H., *Theories of Career Development,* 3rd Ed., Prentice-Hall, Inc., Upper Saddle River, N.J. [year].

Seligman, Linda, *Developmental Career Counseling and Assessment,* 2nd Ed. Sage Publications, London, 1994.

Data-Speak
DOCUMENTING YOUR CAREER INTERESTS

Bearing in mind the just-completed review of forces that shape career selection, this Data-Speak activity allows you to explore your own career preferences. Turn to Appendix C, Interest Checklist. This tool should be used as an initial screening device to identify broad areas of work in which you may be interested. It lists activities found in a wide range of industries and occupations in our economy.

Read each of the statements carefully. If you think you would "like" to do this kind of activity, make an "X" under the "L"; if you "don't like" the activity, make an "X" under the "D"; if you are not certain whether you would like the activity or not, make an "X" under the "?". After you have marked each activity, go back and place a second "X" under at least five activities that you think you would like most to do. List those activities and the *Interest Areas* they represent on Data-Speak Worksheet 1.A. (You will utilize this information in more detailed career exploration activities at the end of Chapter 4.)

You may mark an activity even if you do not have training or experience for it, if you think you would enjoy the work. Mark the "?" only when you cannot decide whether you would like or dislike the activity, or when you do not know what the activity is.

Career Inquiry
YOUR CAREER GENOGRAM

A Career Genogram is designed to help you understand your educational and occupational heritage. Through this family history, you may be able to use the past to better understand your current view of educational and career accomplishment.

Turn to Career Inquiry Worksheet 1.A and complete your genogram. This involves filling in the name, year of birth, highest level degree earned, and primary occupation of your parents, you and your brothers and sisters, your two sets of grandparents, and any aunts and uncles you have. If a family member is deceased, place an X within the individual's circle or square, and enter the year of death under the birth year entry.

Once you have completed the above tasks, review your entries and answer these questions in the spaces provided in Career Inquiry Worksheet 1.B:

1. How would you describe your family's educational experience?
2. How would you describe your family's work experience?
3. How do your education/career aspirations fit in?
4. Is there a family member you most want to emulate?
5. Are there family conditions you need to overcome/take advantage of?
6. What educational, career, occupational behaviors form the most conspicuous parts of your ethnic/racial/socioeconomic heritage?
7. How does your family's cultural background serve as a strength/weakness for your career?
8. How does your family's socioeconomic background serve as a strength/weakness for your career?
9. If you could change the past, how would you change this genogram?
10. How might study of this genogram alter your career path?

DATA-SPEAK WORKSHEET 1.A
DOCUMENTING YOUR CAREER INTERESTS

Interest Check List

ACTIVITY SUMMARY	INTEREST AREA REPRESENTED
1.	
2.	
3.	
4.	
5.	
6.	

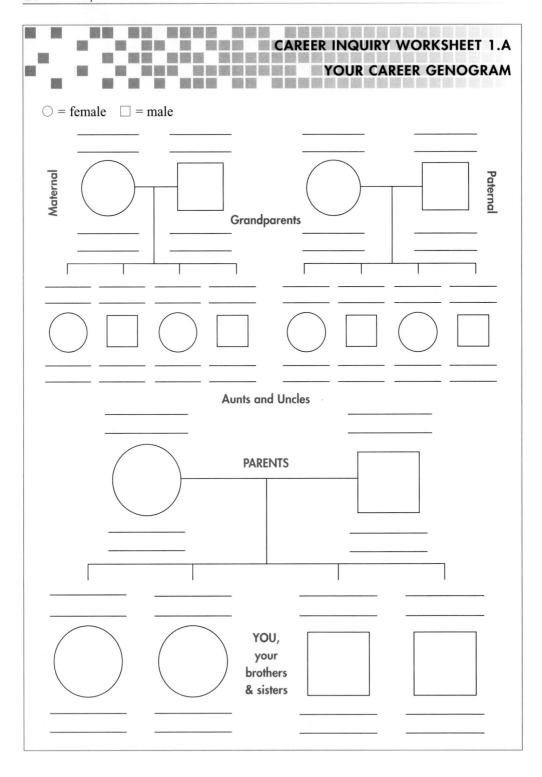

CAREER INQUIRY WORKSHEET 1.A
YOUR CAREER GENOGRAM

○ = female   □ = male

Maternal

Paternal

Grandparents

Aunts and Uncles

PARENTS

YOU,
your
brothers
& sisters

CAREER INQUIRY WORKSHEET 1.B
GENOGRAM ANALYSIS

1.

2.

3.

4.

5.

6.

7.

8.

9.

10.

The Economic Side
of Careers

An overview of the U. S. economy,

how it is organized, works, and impacts workers.

Overview

LEARNING OBJECTIVES

- Understand the economic roles of self-interest and competition.
- Be able to articulate the purpose of economic activity and why economic systems have difficulty meeting consumer expectations.
- Explain the business–household connection in terms of how the economy is organized.
- Define economic markets and their place in the economy.
- Know the determinants of demand and supply.
- Identify the chief motivators of businesses and households.
- Explain how the structure of the economy, its performance, demographics, and government policies impact workers and their careers.
- Understand the significance of the business cycle and its four stages.
- Explore characteristics of industries of interest and their total and occupational employment nationwide and for Economic Areas of interest.
- Understand the impact of changing technology on careers.
- Demonstrate the ability to research the major characteristics of a selected market.
- Conduct research to determine the current stage of the business cycle and its impact on selected careers.

CHAPTER EXERCISES

Data-Speak: Use the *Employment Opportunity Database* to explore characteristics of industries and their current and projected employment, both nationally and in areas you select.

Career-Inquiry: Investigate the impact of technology, labor markets, and the business cycle (performance of the economy) on careers of interest to you.

Setting the Stage
SELF-INTEREST AND COMPETITION

Employment Opportunity now turns to how a market economy, such as the United States economy, operates and relates to careers. We engage this subject matter because every career depends on the availability of suitable jobs. Regardless of how well your skills, abilities, and personal characteristics match occupational requirements, if the economy fails to generate a sufficient number of suitable jobs in your chosen career, the satisfaction you seek is likely to be stifled.

Becoming familiar with careers and the economy enables you to visualize how the work you will do fits into the larger economic picture. Moreover, to be prepared for the future, you must gain an appreciation for how our evolving economy is likely to impact your job, salary, and security.

Remember first that capitalist economies are marked by two distinct and dominating characteristics: self-interest, the chief motivator of most participants, and competition, the principle restraint.

From an economic perspective, men and women have careers because careers are in their material self-interest. By pursuing careers, people can assist employers to provide society with goods and services that consumers want. In return, workers are rewarded with pay that enables them to purchase food, clothing, transportation, housing, education, health care, and recreation. Recognition of this linkage is provided by freshman college students who often indicate that they are attending college primarily to get a better job, so they may be better off financially.

As each individual seeks to serve his or her self-interest, competition is born. For example, assume that 50 seniors at a local university decide that becoming lawyers would provide them with their highest potential level of job satisfaction and income. Their common decision creates competition . . . to gain admission to law school, then to obtain high grades, then to win attractive job offers, and finally to capture lucrative clients. Competition drives providers of goods, services, and resources (such as land, labor, and capital) to supply society with what it wants at reasonable prices. When prices are out of line, purchasers seek those willing to accept less or find another way to satisfy the need. For example, if a lawyer's billing rates are much higher than those of comparable lawyers, potential clients are likely to hire a lower-priced attorney.

What does all this economic jargon mean to you? It means that when you sit with a prospective employer, and you are asked about salary expectations, your response will not be evaluated in a vacuum. It will be weighed along with the salary desires of other available candidates, i.e., the competition. An assessment of your education, experience, and skills—relative to the rest—will determine the outcome. This is just one example of the role competition plays in our economy.

Therefore, throughout your quest for fulfilled employment, remember that our economy is driven by self-interest—the career motivator, and competition—the career limiter. Most people act in their self-interest, and this common action results in competition.

The Economic Context

The overall purpose of economic activity is to provide consumers with an ever-expanding array of goods and services. This is a difficult challenge because consumers are continually raising their expectations, while the resources needed for production are limited.

Assume you have just won $10 million in lottery money. Congratulations! For a while, you will be delighted as your newfound wealth raises your standard of living to unanticipated heights. After some time, however, the odds are that you will establish a taste for the finer things of life, some of which will even be beyond your expanded means. In other words, that "unreachable" BMW that now sits in your driveway has been replaced by dreams of a Rolls Royce. Human nature causes most of us to continually adjust our sights upward.

Progress in technology also raises our material wants. In the 1950s, RCA introduced a record player that became an instant success. It allowed one to stack several 45-inch records and play them, one side only, one at a time, providing continuous rock 'n' roll hits for half an hour or so. As the first record concluded, an arm housing a needle raised and swung to the side as the next hit record dropped on top, soon to be played by the returning arm.

Today, such a contraption would be viewed as a relic from the past. Serious music fans get hours of continuous enjoyment, specifying selections and the order of play from many CDs, as systems play recordings in surround-sound stereo. Anything less is considered subpar. And yet, given today's pace of new electronic developments, it probably will not be long before new technology renders CDs obsolete!

While the heights to which consumer wants may rise are limitless, the availability of resources needed to meet those demands is finite. There are only so many skilled workers, so much capital equipment, so much land, and so many ideas on how to combine resources to meet consumer expectations. For example, a shortage of skilled and highly educated computer professionals has moved the Congress to expand the number of foreign computer professionals that may enter the United States on a temporary basis. Such difficulties in meeting the needs of a continually expanding consumer demand represent the problem that economic systems are designed to solve.

How the Economic Side Is Organized

The American economy is composed of over seven million employers and close to 140 million workers. How do they all fit together to create an efficient and productive force?

One way to view the U. S. economy is as a constant flow of activity between households and businesses. Households furnish businesses with the resources needed to create output. For example, households provide businesses with workers who compose the employee workforce.

Businesses view the acquisition of such a resource as one necessary cost of transforming raw materials into goods, and knowledge into services. At the same time, households view the sale of resources as a way to earn income. An individual worker sells his or her labor for wages and benefits. Workers also provide capital in various forms in return for rent, interest, and profits. These earnings then are used to operate the household.

The result of businesses utilizing household resources is the production of goods and services. Households view the acquisition of these consumer goods as consumption expenditures, necessary to meet the material needs of the family. Businesses view the sale of goods and services as a way to earn revenue.

The magic of the free enterprise system is the manner in which the supply and demand for resources and consumer goods and services are expressed, and their prices established. Basic decisions about how much will be offered for sale, how much will be purchased, and what price will be charged are arrived at through markets, places which bring buyers and sellers together. These hotbeds of competitive force are a powerful source of honesty and efficiency in our economic system.

What exactly is a market? Stock exchanges serve as the classic example of free markets. The XYZ Company has a great year, reports record profits, and the demand for its stock and the price of XYZ stock soar. The next year, profits fall, demand for XYZ stock evaporates, and the price hits rock bottom.

In a broad sense, we may count many locations we visit every day as "markets"—the local supermarket, dry cleaners, corner gas station, or your favorite hair salon. At each of these locations, buyers and sellers of consumer goods and services express their preferences and observe established prices. At the same time, real estate offices (land), employment agencies (labor), and industrial equipment wholesalers (capital equipment) represent markets established for resource goods.

Figure 2.1 provides a simplified picture of the business–household connection. The couple in the illustration has just purchased a new home. While their income was high enough to qualify for the required mortgage, they have come to realize that they need higher income to live comfortably in this new environment. Since higher paying jobs are their most practical path to more income, they freshen up their resumes and visit the ABC Employment Agency. As they offer their services to employers who may be willing to increase their salaries, they enter the resource market for labor.

Coming off a good year, the XYZ Company is expanding operations and hiring additional workers. To the company, our couple represents one of several resources—labor—needed to produce its product or offer its service. Their salaries are just one of numerous costs of production incurred by XYZ. Our couple lands the jobs at their desired salaries because they have demonstrated advanced skills and relevant experience. At the same time, XYZ is willing to pay a premium wage in order to complete its expansion and acquire top-rated staff for the future.

At their higher salaries, the couple now is able to enter the consumer market and make those purchases that their previous income would not support.

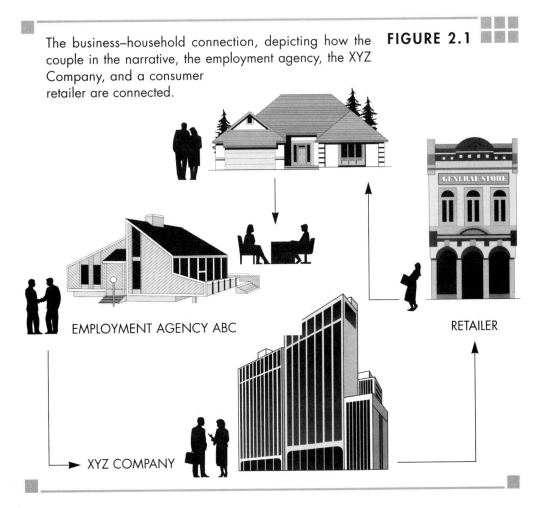

The business–household connection, depicting how the **FIGURE 2.1** couple in the narrative, the employment agency, the XYZ Company, and a consumer retailer are connected.

EMPLOYMENT AGENCY ABC

RETAILER

XYZ COMPANY

DETERMINANTS OF DEMAND AND SUPPLY

Demand for resources, consumer goods, and services is determined by their price, customer tastes and preferences, the number of customers, prices of related goods, expectations of future prices and incomes, and consumer incomes. All else remaining the same, lower prices mean higher demand, while higher prices reduce demand. (This is known in economics as the "law of demand.")

Common sense tells us that a price that has been reduced from its previous level makes it easier to purchase that good, service, or resource. Also, reduced prices allow us to make a purchase while holding on to more of our income. Such favorable conditions cause us to substitute a lower-priced item for a higher-priced good that is somewhat comparable. For example, as the price of the Ford Taurus goes down, consumers favor it over the Honda Accord, with a price that has not declined. Of course, a price increase in the Taurus, with no increase in the Accord, would have the opposite effect.

Figure 2.2 identifies each force that plays a role in determining demand. Each force is explained in terms of The Wonder Computer Company and its production of personal computers for the home. It is assumed that all the economic forces remain unchanged.

FIGURE 2.2   Forces that determine demand: Wonder Home Computers.

Price: Market research has shown that if the price of the basic home computer can be reduced to less than $1,000, many more families would consider buying one, increasing demand. This gives the Wonder Computer Company incentives to reduce costs and prices.

 **Customer Tastes and Preferences:** Not that many years ago, only computer professionals used computers; today, the average consumer sees the benefits of home computer use, increasing demand. It is this shift in consumer perceptions of computers (and technological gains that make computers easier to use) that has given birth to companies such as Wonder.

Number of Customers: As young people, very attuned to computer use, set up households, the demand for home computers is bound to rise. Given this near certainty, Wonder has developed plans for a slow but steady expansion.

Prices of Related Goods: Lower prices for computer printers and monitors (complementary goods) will further spur the demand for household computers. As the prices of complementary goods have fallen, Wonder has increased its sales forecasts.

Expectations of Future Prices and Incomes: If potential customers think that falling Asian computer prices will drive the cost of household computers down in three to six

(continued)

months, consumers are likely to postpone purchases until they see the lower prices, reducing current demand. If potential customers expect that their incomes will increase in the foreseeable future, they are more likely to buy a new computer now, increasing current demand. On the other hand, expecting higher prices later increases the desire to buy now, while anticipating lower income down the road introduces consumer caution and a hesitancy to make new purchases.

Consumer Incomes: Studies have shown that as family incomes rise, the family's likelihood of purchasing a home computer also rises, boosting demand. Although lower prices would likely create demand from more middle-income families, Wonder currently targets its advertising at families in the higher-income brackets.

The **supply** of resources, consumer goods, and services is determined by their price, the level of technology used to produce them, the price of raw materials required to obtain a resource or produce a consumer good, the level of taxes and subsidies, changes in the price of related goods, expectations of future prices, and the number of sellers/suppliers in the market. All else remaining the same, higher prices mean higher supply, while lower prices reduce supply. (This is known as the "law of supply.")

Figure 2.3 identifies forces that play a role in determining supply. Again, each force is explained in terms of Wonder Computers, assuming all other economic forces remain unchanged.

Forces that determine supply. **FIGURE 2.3**

Price: The higher the price of a computer the greater the incentive for producers to offer computers for sale. Higher prices mean higher sales revenues and higher contributions to profit (the excess of revenues over costs).

Technology: For the most part, new technology offers a way to produce output with fewer resources. Since fewer resources usually means lower costs, the use of new technology often means increased supply. Therefore, Wonder has increased its production as a result of adopting the use of new equipment that streamlines the process of computer assembly.

Resource Prices: A new supply of lower-priced computer chips reduces the cost of computer production. As a result, producers, seeing an opportunity for increased profits, boost supply. On the other hand, an increase in the price of computer chips would raise production costs and tend to reduce supply.

Taxes and Subsidies: Lower taxes on Wonder means reduced costs, which results in increased computer production and supply, and vice-versa. Providing a subsidy

(continued)

(e.g., the Federal government provides a grant to Wonder to develop less costly computers for schools) lowers costs and, therefore, increases supply.

Prices of Other Goods: An increase in the popularity (and therefore price) of laptops (making their production more profitable than home computers) leads to an increased supply of laptops, and a reduced supply of home computers.

Expectations: If Wonder expects computer prices to rise next year, they may postpone current production and wait for the higher price. Expecting lower prices in the future would encourage higher current production.

Number of Sellers: An increase in the number of home computer manufacturers increases the supply of home computers, and vice-versa.

___

Utilizing real life experience in resource and product markets, households and businesses are able to gauge demand and supply, and discover the going rates for what they need and what they will offer for sale. No individual planner or planning board determines how many home computers will be produced this year, or what their prices will be. Instead, manufacturers will evaluate their sales experience and forecasts and attempt to produce enough units to meet product demand at a reasonable price.

If too many computers are manufactured/supplied relative to demand, inventories will rise and producers may be forced to lower prices or reduce production. If too few computers are produced and offered for sale, their inventories will be too low and producers may increase prices or boost production.

EMPLOYER DECISION MAKING

The market forces of supply and demand compel economic decisions. When profits disappear, business incentives to produce also disappear. When profits increase, existing producers have added incentive to increase their output. Also, new producers are attracted to enter the business. This may lead to expanded output, lower prices, and even a moderation of profit levels. For the most part, businesses seek to boost revenues over costs to *maximize profits.*

Example

CELL PHONES AND PURE PROFITS

In the 1980s, the United States had only a few companies offering cellular (wireless) telephone service. At that time, base stations (transmitters/receivers) covered a small portion of U. S. populated areas, and cell phones were large and difficult to handle. Within 10 years, new technology resulted in cellular phones shrinking to pocket size, and coverage spread to every major population center.

As demand for cell phones grew sharply, companies that were in on the "ground floor" at first reaped huge profits. Once established, because of the limited competition, they were able to charge premium prices, and earn "pure" profits, i.e., profits well above what would be considered normal return on investment. However, these extra profits attracted new firms into the cell phone business. Over the years, the additional service providers have increased competition, lowered prices, and reduced profits to more normal levels.

Example
NO PROFITS IN 3-D

In 1955, Paramount Pictures released *The House of Wax,* starring Vincent Price, Frank Lovejoy, Paul Cavanagh, Phyllis Kirk, Carolyn Jones, and Charles Bronson. This movie became a top draw at the box office. A clever horror flick, it was the first major motion picture shown in 3-D. Once you put on a pair of cardboard-framed glasses with treated cellophane lenses, objects appeared to jump off the screen and into your lap. The high point of the film had a terribly scarred character swinging on a rope into the terrified audience.

Even though *The House of Wax* was a hit by normal standards, Paramount failed to make sufficient profits. This was because 3-D technology involved significant extra production costs. Although more 3-D movies were released in the 1950s, after a while, audiences considered the special effects to be a gimmick and the necessary glasses an uncomfortable and silly-looking inconvenience. By 1960, the company that manufactured 3-D technology and paraphernalia, lacking profits, went out of business, and further attempts at utilizing this technology were derailed.

As a means of maximizing profits, firms seek the least costly means of production, thereby promoting competitive edge. A firm producing a product at costs higher than those of competitors must charge higher prices or accept lower profits. Higher prices are likely to reduce sales, while lower profits depress stock prices and perhaps management's compensation.

Example
COMPETITION THROUGH TECHNOLOGY

Until the 1970s, U. S. carmakers generally had the American market to themselves. With the exception of the Volkswagen Beetle and a few Mercedes, auto imports were limited. The Japanese had been unable to penetrate the American market, as their autos, and most Japanese products, were considered low-quality goods.

To change this, the Japanese invested heavily in new manufacturing facilities that utilized the latest technology. In the 1960s and 1970s, while U. S. companies were busy making annual cosmetic changes to their cars, the Japanese were investing in technology, resulting in better constructed vehicles, faster assembly, and lower production costs. Innovations, such as the use of robotics for welding, put U. S. automakers at a competitive disadvantage with Japanese producers. By the 1980s, the Japanese producers had won a significant share of the U. S. auto market. However, by the late 1990s, U. S. producers had won back a share of what was lost, largely through their own introduction of new technology, improved quality, and management innovation.

HOUSEHOLD DECISION MAKING

Households purchase consumer goods and services offered for sale, while businesses purchase resources and technology. The usual objective of the household is to maximize its level of satisfaction, given income available for purchases. What the household can acquire depends on the price of what's being offered relative to the income of the prospective customer. In terms of households and family members, income level often may be traced back to levels of education and career selection.

Example TO BRICK OR NOT TO BRICK

The Smith household believes in low-maintenance housing. Moving into a new development in a suburb of Atlanta, Jerry Smith—a recent graduate of the University of Virginia Engineering School—chose to pay an extra $6,000 for brick all the way around. Bob Paris—an education major who teaches 10th grade algebra outside Atlanta—just moved into the same development and purchased the same model house. However, Bob just qualified for his mortgage and, consequently, purchased the base house (i.e., no brick). Both Jerry and Bob have accomplished much, and both are likely to enjoy their new homes. However, given the prices of these houses and their respective incomes, Jerry can afford the aesthetics and low maintenance of brick, while Bob cannot.

Impact on Workers

As we have seen, the U. S. economic system is in a constant state of adjustment. Supply–demand decisions are routinely made, refined, and changed based upon and reflecting changes in price. What effect do such decisions have on U. S. workers?

The economy directly impacts workers in two ways. First, the economy's structure sets conditions under which workers will be rewarded and penalized. Second, the level of performance of the economy affects workforce participants.

STRUCTURE

Under *structure of our economic system,* three points of impact with workers may be identified:

1. Competition (impact with other workers/job candidates) means that those in the labor force are rarely, if ever, alone. To succeed, an individual's skills and abilities must compare favorably with others seeking to gain income in the same or comparable ways.

Example KNOW YOUR COMPETITION

Gary Flannigan loves to write. He was editorial page editor of Denver West High's monthly newspaper. Also, he won three journalism awards in local competitions. Having graduated near the top of his class from the University of Colorado, he decided to travel to New York City to seek a job with one of the country's major publishing houses, or possibly one of the city's daily newspapers. After two months of being unable to land even an interview (and wearing out his welcome with an aunt and uncle in North Jersey), Gary decided to take the advice of one of the few publisher employees willing to talk with him:

> The competition for these jobs is so intense, you have to prove what you can do, in a professional journalism environment. Find a job on a small local newspaper or other similar publication first. Then, after you've developed an extensive portfolio, and made some respected contacts, try again. For the most part, new college journalism graduates can't compete effectively with those who have paid their dues working in this field.

2. Relevance to the needs of businesses is the foundation of the employment relationship (impact with business' drive to make a profit). Often firms have little or no loyalty to workers; their allegiance is to resources (land, labor, capital, and ideas for organizing production) that encourage lower costs and higher profits.

Example RELEVANCE IS THE TICKET

Sharon Fishkin and Maria Gomez have been fellow workers for a large computer firm for ten years. Caught off guard by the trend toward PCs, their company was forced to drastically reduce its mainframe business and lay off thousands of good employees. Sharon received her pink slip early. As a marketer of mainframes, she knew her relevance to the firm and her future employment was doomed. Maria, on the other hand, was a recruiter in the firm's Human Resource Department. When she learned of the coming problem, she suggested that she form a team to study how other companies with similar dilemmas helped those being laid off to find alternative employment.

She spent three months conducting thorough research and putting together a blueprint for action. Her report recommended company-sponsored counseling and job search assistance, as well as development of an automated system to keep track of those employees who might be high on a list of recalls, if and when demand for experienced workers were to recover. Based on her continued relevance, in spite of changed conditions, Maria was promoted and now commands enhanced respect within the company. Sharon was forced to begin again.

3. Markets are the locations where buyers (businesses) and sellers of labor (workers) meet to express their desires (impact with the reality of market conditions). If those desires fail to be realistic (e.g., requesting a wage far above the going rate), they will not be met.

Example

KNOW THE MARKET TO PLAY THE GAME

Clarence Sykes played halfback for a Division II-A school in the Midwest. He set every running back record for the school and conference. In his senior year an agent willing to represent him with the NFL approached. Clarence dreamed of a multi-million dollar signing bonus and millions more over the life of an NFL contract.

But Clarence's agent was inexperienced and didn't properly gauge his client's market value. After Clarence was drafted in a late round and received a contract offer well below his expectations, his agent was unable to negotiate a satisfactory deal. Clarence was forced to sit out his first year of eligibility and was branded "difficult to deal with." The rights for Clarence were traded to another team during the off-season. After reassessing his value, Clarence fired his agent and quickly came to terms for even less than he had been offered the previous year.

PERFORMANCE

Under *performance of the economy,* there are three further points of impact:

4. Economic growth rates vary as the economy passes through various levels of spending by business, consumers, and government (impact of the business cycle—see Figure 2.4). During most of the 1990s, U. S. workers, business, and federal tax, spending, and interest rate policies maintained the economy's growth. However, history teaches us that sooner or later we are bound to experience economic highs and lows that result alternatively in increased inflation (a general rise in prices), and unemployment (many seeking employment unable to find work). Also, as some problems are minimized, others emerge. For example, while inflation and unemployment were reduced in the 1990s, income stagnation (failure of wages to rise) and income inequality (a shrinking middle class) accelerated.

Example

THE BUSINESS CYCLE BLUES

Soon Pak graduated from the University of Illinois with a major concentration in Business Administration and Accounting. He went to the university to prepare to take over the family business, three major-appliance stores around Columbus, Ohio. Unfortunately, just as Soon graduated and entered the business, in 1981, the deep recession of the early 1980s hit the economy. Soon knew—from his Economics classes with Professor Vuglen—that when recessions occur, con-

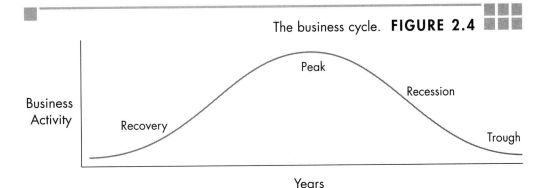

The business cycle. **FIGURE 2.4**

CHARACTERISTICS OF BUSINESS CYCLE STAGES

	Recovery	Peak	Recession	Trough
Spending	Rising	High	Falling	Low
Employment	Rising	High	Falling	Low
Prices	Rising	High	Steady/Falling*	Steady/Low*

*Note that even when production falls, unless recessions are prolonged, prices tend to remain steady, i.e., "sticky" in the downward direction. The sustained high level of economic activity through most of the 1990s, with little or no inflation, is not typical, and likely has been due to productivity rising faster than average wages, and the downward pressure on prices exerted by emerging global competition.

sumers tend to postpone large purchases, such as major appliances. Soon's dad knew that from hard experience, and he explained that they needed to "batten down the hatches," cut costs, and ride out the downturn.

But Soon also knew that during such periods, consumers don't restrict minor purchases. So he suggested that their stores introduce music departments where they could market compact disks, which were just beginning to catch on. He also reasoned that bringing music customers into the stores could result in increased sales of stereo equipment, especially after the economic recovery. Soon's idea not only compensated for reduced appliance sales during the recession, but led to a music franchise business in over 100 Midwest department stores. This new venture created revenue many times that generated by the company's best annual appliance sales.

5. Demographics affect the overall size and composition of the U. S. workforce, by age, sex, and race (impact of population trends). For example, the 1990s are producing the slowest growing U. S. labor force since the 1930s. However, new labor force entrants are more likely to be women, African Americans, Hispanics, and Asians, as a truly multicultural work force emerges.

Example

LIKE FATHER...NOT SON

Back in the 1960s and 1970s, children of the baby boom (those conceived directly after World War II) reached college age, and the age that most young people enter the labor market. Jonathan Birch was born in 1945, and entered Rutgers University in 1963. Huge annual increases in college applicants put a strain on university facilities. When Jonathan attended summer orientation, he was told to "Look to the student on your right, and look to the student on your left, because the odds are that one or both would not be there at semester's end."

During that period, most state colleges accepted more students than they could handle, and were forced to flunk out large numbers in order to reduce overcrowding. In addition to strain on educational facilities, the wave of baby boomers entering the labor market created unusually high rates of youth unemployment. Therefore, Jonathan felt much anxiety, not only about remaining in school, but facing a job market characterized by record high youth unemployment.

On the other hand, Jonathan's son, Jason, entered Rutgers University in 1990. With the opposite population trend, i.e., relatively few college-age youth, most colleges were working hard to recruit talented freshmen. Colleges made special efforts to reduce dropout rates, recognizing that their financial standing depends on full enrollments, in spite of the reduced numbers of traditional age students. In order to supplement student rosters, most schools initiated comprehensive extension programs, attracting those already in the labor market. Jason was pleased with the fine treatment he received, and was enthusiastic about entering a job market with record low rates of unemployment.

6. Government policies play a major role in setting the level of demand for workers in certain industries and occupations (impact of government spending and regulations). For instance, radical change in U. S. policies concerning deregulation of industries, such as telecommunications, has created thousands of new career opportunities. On the other hand, cutbacks in defense spending have significantly reduced the employment of military contractors.

Example

DON'T CALL ME

For 10 years, John Bellows had been a successful trainer with a large telephone utility. He had become a valuable resource, training managers in everything from quality techniques to customer relations. When the Federal Government's deregulation policy hit the telephone industry, John was transferred from Oregon to Washington. Since he believed that more change was in store, he left his family behind, not interrupting his wife's career and his two daughters' school.

As sales dipped, the training unit was reduced and John was laid off. With his job gone, John moved back to Oregon and contacted several similarly unemployed trainers. His idea was to form a consulting firm that would train employees of the many new firms in the industry. Within three months, John was back at work, utilizing his old skills, earning three times his previous salary, and experiencing the satisfaction of his own business.

Chapter Wrap

As we have seen, workers, representing households, look to businesses to locate career opportunities. At the same time, businesses look to households to provide needed labor. Supply and demand for labor, other resources, consumer goods, and services are expressed in markets where prices are determined. Businesses seek to maximize profits while households attempt to gain optimum satisfaction from income earned. Worker success is influenced by competition, relevance of skills, market realities, economic growth rates, demographics, and government policies.

References

Career Guide to Industries, 1998–99 Ed., U. S. Department of Labor, Bureau of Labor Statistics, BLS Bulletin 2503.

McConnell, Campbell R. and Brue, Stanley L., *Economics, Principles, Problems, and Policies,* 13th Ed., McGraw-Hill, Inc., New York, 1996.

North American Industry Classification System, United States, 1997, Executive Office of the President, Office of Management and Budget.

Standard Industrial Classification Manual, 1987, Executive Office of the President, Office of Management and Budget.

U. S. Industry & Trade Outlook '98, DRI/McGraw - Hill and Standard & Poor's and U. S. Department of Commerce/International Trade Administration.

Data-Speak
LEARNING ABOUT U.S. INDUSTRIES

Our study of the economic side of careers led to the understanding that workers look to businesses for career opportunities. A convenient way to learn about business is to study the industries in which they are organized. The *Employment Opportunity Database* provides information on more than 300 U. S. industries and their employment. Before entering the database, turn to Appendix B, in the *Employment Opportunity* text, for a listing of 309 industries in which most businesses may be found. Tentatively select three industries of interest, which will be used to begin your exploration of U. S. industries.

Now, turn to the *Employment Opportunity Database Warehouse:* Chapter 2. Select "Industry Titles" and review the industry listing to see if there are other industries you want to explore. Now, select "Industry Descriptions." It includes each industry title, along with detailed industry titles that indicate what these firms do. Select three or more industries of interest and then review the industry descriptions provided. List the industries explored and your impression of each on Data-Speak

Worksheet 2.A (for example, can you see yourself working in a doctor's office, steel mill, or research laboratory?). Before you settle on industries, you may wish to review copies of the three industry reference materials listed at the end of this chapter, under selected readings. They likely are available at your university/local library. Continue to explore and list your results until at least three "favorable" industries are selected. List those industries in Data-Speak Worksheet 2.B.

Now, utilize the *Employment Opportunity Database Warehouse* to learn about industry employment by Economic Area. Select "Employment by Economic Area" and then select the Economic Areas you identified during the exercise at the end of the Introduction. The system then displays the current and projected total employment of each industry in that Economic Area. Note the employment of the industries selected above and record those totals on Data-Speak Worksheet 2.C.

Next, select "Employment by Industry." Displayed will be total U. S. employment for that industry, and that industry's employment for each of the 172 Economic Areas. Record the nationwide employment data, and employment data for all areas of interest on Data-Speak Worksheet 2.D. (Note that some relatively small industry totals within specific areas are excluded due to government confidentiality requirements.)

Finally, choose "Occupations by Selected Industry Group." Highlight an area and industry, click "Enter," and the system provides the employment for each occupation within that industry and area. Record this information on Data-Speak Worksheet 2.E.

Career Inquiry

TECHNOLOGY, MARKETS, AND THE BUSINESS CYCLE

1. *Technology makes the job go round.* It is said that jobs are formed and shaped to fit available technology. . . and not the desires of workers. Select one of the industries in which you are interested and research the technology utilized 10 years ago, today, and likely to be employed 10 years into the future. Complete Career Inquiry Worksheet 2.A, based upon your research.

■ CAREER INQUIRY GUIDANCE

You may wish to follow this strategy in learning about industry technology:

Seek information from the appropriate industry association, a large firm within the industry, or a union that covers workers in the industry. Your library should have a directory of industry associations, and Dunn & Bradstreet listings of employers within specific industries. You may also request information from the U. S. Department of Commerce, Industry and Trade Outlook Division.

2. *Super labor market.* Identify a market for labor that you think offers super possibilities for your career. Define the market in terms of industry, specific types of employers, and geographic areas. Research supply, demand, and compensation for the market involved. Provide your findings on Career Inquiry Worksheet 2.B.

3. *Business cycle locale.* Research the current state of the economy: production (spending), employment, prices, and other economic indicators. From this information, indicate where the economy stands relative to the four stages of the business cycle. Indicate the location on the business cycle figure on Career Inquiry Worksheet 2.C, and provide justification for your conclusion. What impact is the current stage of the business cycle having on careers in which you are interested?

■ CAREER INQUIRY GUIDANCE

Research the current state of the economy by reviewing the following publications:

Economic Indicators

Department of Labor Monthly Labor Report

Recent editions of *Business Week, The Economist,* and other economic periodicals

DATA-SPEAK WORKSHEET 2.A
INDUSTRY DESCRIPTIONS

INDUSTRIES EXPLORED	OVERALL IMPRESSION		
	Favorable	Unsure	Not Favorable

DATA-SPEAK WORKSHEET 2.B
SELECTED INDUSTRIES

1.

2.

3.

4.

5.

6.

DATA-SPEAK WORKSHEET 2.C
INDUSTRY EMPLOYMENT BY ECONOMIC AREA

ECONOMIC AREA TITLE/ CODE	INDUSTRY TITLE/ CODE	EMPLOYMENT 1996	2006

DATA-SPEAK WORKSHEET 2.D
EMPLOYMENT BY INDUSTRY

Nationwide and by Economic Area

INDUSTRY TITLE/ CODE	EMPLOYMENT 1996 2006	AREA TITLE/ CODE	EMPLOYMENT 1996 2006

DATA-SPEAK WORKSHEET 2.E

OCCUPATIONS BY SELECTED INDUSTRY GROUP

OCCUPATIONS OF INTEREST

Area	Industry	Title	Employment

CAREER INQUIRY WORKSHEET 2.A

TECHNOLOGY MAKES THE JOB GO ROUND

Industry title and definition:

Selected technology utilized 10 years ago:

Impact on employment, education and training, and compensation:

Selected technology utilized today:

Impact on employment, education and training, and compensation:

Selected technology likely to be utilized in 10 years:

Impact on employment, education and training, and compensation:

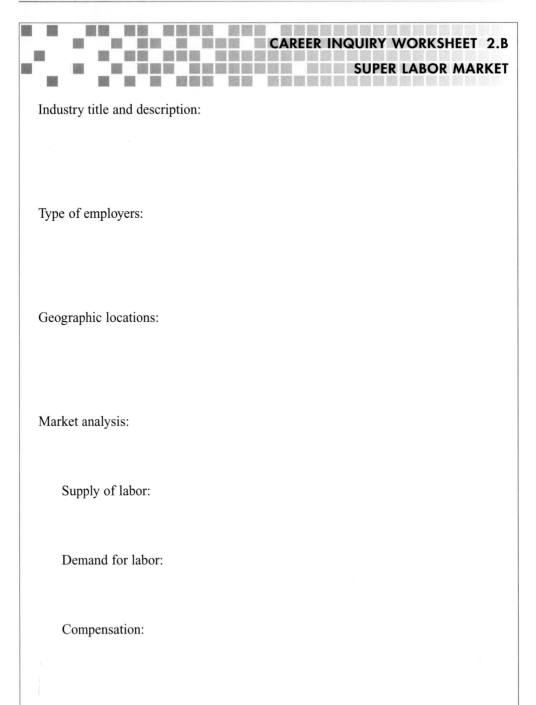

CAREER INQUIRY WORKSHEET 2.B

SUPER LABOR MARKET

Industry title and description:

Type of employers:

Geographic locations:

Market analysis:

Supply of labor:

Demand for labor:

Compensation:

CAREER INQUIRY WORKSHEET 2.C
BUSINESS CYCLE LOCALE

Mark today's business cycle location with an X.

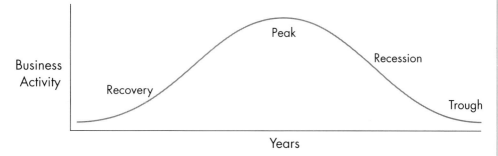

RELEVANT ECONOMIC DATA:

Production (spending):

Employment:

Prices:

Other indicators:

Provide a summary justification for the location you selected:

How has the current location of the business cycle impacted careers in which you are interested?

What's In a Labor Market?

(WHERE THE HUMAN AND ECONOMIC SIDES MEET)

The unique nature of labor markets, and their four stages of operation.

Overview
LEARNING OBJECTIVES

- Demonstrate the unique nature of labor as an economic resource.
- Articulate the four stages of labor market operations.
- Define "human capital."
- Define "wage differential."
- Understand the primary objectives of workers and employers in their attempts to establish an employment relationship.
- Explain why employment relationships are difficult to form and maintain over time.
- Understand the role of specific training in perpetuating employment.
- List alternative means employers use to motivate workers.
- Explain why today's employment relationships are often short-lived.
- Understand the serious implications of disemployment.
- Articulate the productivity consequences of division of labor and how this is related to the formation of occupations.
- Explore the major characteristics of occupations of interest, and their current and projected employment for the nation and for selected Economic Areas and industries.
- Analyze occupational data obtained from the *Employment Opportunity Database*.
- Inventory and assess your current stock of human capital in terms of its applicability to careers of interest.

■ Chronicle the job search experience of an individual who has obtained a new job in the past five years.

CHAPTER EXERCISES

Data-Speak: Use the *Employment Opportunity Database* to explore occupations and their current and projected employment, nationally and for industries and areas you select.

Career-Inquiry: Begin building a bank of information on occupations of interest, your human capital, and job search experiences.

Setting the Stage
THE UNIQUE NATURE OF LABOR

The challenge of understanding labor markets is the challenge of understanding both the economics of labor and the behavior of people, i.e., bringing together the realities of the labor market and human feeling. For many years, economists failed to recognize this fact. They treated labor markets as they would markets for corn, steel, or tobacco. The problem with this approach is that labor is a uniquely human commodity. In effect, businesses are not buying the individual, but the work that the individual is capable and willing to perform. Because the provider of labor is a human being, the labor provided is affected by factors that would fail to impact any other resource. Three characteristics of labor reflect its unique nature as an economic resource.

First, labor maintains a *sense of equity*. Workers have a sense of what's fair and what's not. If management fails to follow the often unwritten, but still potent code of equity, repercussions follow. For example, a new assembly line worker is hired. Even though the new employee is inexperienced and has no special education or training, because he is a relative of the foreman, he is provided a company car. In reaction to this injustice, most workers treat the new employee poorly and slow down assembly line production.

Second, the *level of compensation* may influence the productivity of labor. For example, a rookie quarterback signs with an NFL team for a modest contract. The starting and back-up quarterbacks are injured and the rookie takes the team to the playoffs. Even though he is under a modest three-year contract, the team voluntarily renegotiates his contract at a much higher level. The quarterback remains happy and continues to develop and lead the team. In the absence of renegotiations, his performance may well have suffered.

Third, workers establish and maintain a social sense of the labor market that they are very reluctant to violate. For many years, economists have pondered the existence of long-term unemployment. Why do some workers remain unemployed for so long? Their social conscience is the answer.

A large oil company decides to downsize by laying off 500 middle managers. Six months later, many of those managers are still unemployed. Why don't they return to the company and offer to perform their previous tasks at 75 percent of their previous salary? They refuse to take such action because it is socially unacceptable. Workers would prefer to protect salary levels and social mores at the cost of continued unemployment.

In summary, the behavior of labor as a resource is unique because it is influenced by its sense of equity, level of compensation, and social responsibility. Conversely, the output of resources such as machines (capital equipment) or parcels of land is unaffected by such variables.

Keeping the unique nature of labor in mind, we proceed to investigate those mechanisms that bring the buyers and sellers of labor together.

Labor Market Operations

From the worker's perspective, one might view labor market operations in four distinct stages: development, job search, employment, and disemployment. Each stage is discussed below.

Stage I—Development. *Development is accomplished as investments are made in providing future employees with new skills and abilities, often described as "human capital."* These investments take the form of education (grammar school through high school, community college, college, graduate school, and professional school); and general training (vocational courses and other institutional training that enhances the trainee's worth to a large array of possible employers). As the level of investment increases and individuals grow older, areas of specialization are emphasized to fit the needs of particular occupations and jobs (specific training).

These investments are justified because they provide returns (earnings) and job satisfaction that otherwise would not be realized. We know that those who graduate college earn an average of almost twice what high school graduates earn. Therefore, the investment in college (in the form of tuition, effort, and reduced earnings while attending college) usually pays high dividends. (While difficult to measure, high dividends are also earned in terms of the life experiences and appreciation of our surroundings engendered by a well-rounded education.)

Example
INVEST TO SPEND

George Martin has watched his dad, Ralph, age on a never-ending string of construction jobs. Although he's an intelligent man, Ralph Martin dropped out of high school at 16 when *his* dad passed away. To help the family make ends meet, Ralph worked as a laborer on a three-year project to build a convention center in town. Ralph relied on his physical strength and good hands to make a living in construction. But as the years went by, arthritis and a bad back have resulted in missed days on the job and short paychecks.

George is determined to avoid the fate of his father. George studied hard in high school and has graduated from college with a degree in accounting. He has invested in his human capital to earn the income and security his dad never had.

Stage 2—Job Search. *Once education and general training are considered sufficient, workers seek employment.* The labor market accommodates job search activities by providing services, information, and employment catalysts to workers and employers. Services facilitate the transmittal of resumes, employment applications, and recommendations, and the conduct of interviews. Information includes listings of job vacancies, resumes, employer directories, and advice on effective job search techniques. Employment catalysts include want ads, employment agencies, "head hunters," job placement offices, human resource offices, union hiring halls, and the Internet (including resources such as America's Job Bank).

Effective job search activities require knowledge of the occupation selected, skill and experience requirements, industries and geographic areas that employ such workers, and the employers within those industries and areas most likely to provide open jobs. The geographic scope of the search may be determined by the probable location of job openings, as well as applicant preferences.

From the applicant's perspective, the primary job search objective is to identify a number of open jobs that will offer a reasonable opportunity for fulfilled employment, i.e., compatible jobs that will fully utilize the applicant's skills and abilities, while providing the means for a satisfying worklife and lifestyle. From the employer's perspective, the objective is to attract a variety of candidates who offer realistic potential of meeting job requirements and justifying employer investments necessary to transform new employees into productive workers.

Example

KNOW ME

With his new accounting degree scheduled to be conferred in a couple of months, George's job search activities are well under way. Living in Northern Virginia (where he wants to remain), George is well aware of the size and security of the Federal Government. He has contacted the Office of Personnel Management, and has participated in two Federal job fairs. George has interviewed with the General Accounting Office (GAO) and feels that his prospects there are favorable.

In addition, George sent resumes to local offices of three of the nation's large accounting firms. After interviewing with each, two have asked him back for a second round of interviews.

Finally, through his own research, George identified 26 large area firms likely to employ a number of accountants. Sending resumes to each led to three interviews, one of which appeared hopeful.

In summary, George has invested much time and effort in his job search. Devising a strategy, networking, targeting employers, preparing finished written materials (resumes, cover letters, and follow-up letters), and preparing for (and rehearsing) interviews were all significant projects. But George reasoned that his previous investments in human capital were worth little unless prospective employers were made aware of his capabilities.

Stage 3—Employment. *Employment is attained when applicants and employers agree to terms.* This may be a difficult process because of the need to match applicant skills, abilities, and preferences with employer job requirements, pay (wages and benefits), and working conditions. In circumstances where employers are not able to attract an adequate number of applicants, because of problems such as an undesirable location, the employer may pay a wage *higher* than the going rate (the increase is referred to as a "wage differential"). Likewise, applicants unable to attract offers of employment may have to *lower* salary expectations.

The employment relationship is typically governed by understandings that are incomplete and presumed. For example, prior to employment, employers rarely indicate all the tasks they expect the employee to perform and rarely do employees and employers sign employment contracts. Moreover, company policies expressed orally, such as "promote deserving employees," are open to broad interpretation. Therefore, in the absence of a binding contract, maintaining the employment relationship requires that both the employer and employee feel that they gain more from continuing the relationship than from ending it.

One way that a steady relationship is encouraged is through the provision of training that has direct application to the current employer; e.g., Saturn provides assembly line training that applies only to its unique facility. Such specific training increases the productivity of the trainee when working at the Saturn auto plant, creating extra output. If the returns (revenue) from selling that output are divided between the employer and the employee, they represent both additional profits for Saturn and extra income for the employee. However, if the worker were to leave Saturn, the extra output, revenue, profits, and income would be lost.

In addition to making an effort to see that employment relationships are mutually beneficial, employers utilize supervisors, profit sharing, and piecework (pay for the units of output produced) as a means of motivating workers. However, in spite of employer efforts to keep workers happy and on the job, and employee convenience in remaining with the same firm, today's workers average 12 employers during their worklife. Globalization, rapid technological advances, and the drive to cut costs simply are not compatible with long-term employment relationships.

Example **PARTNERSHIP OR PART COMPANY**

George was offered and accepted a job with one of the two national accounting firms that expressed interest in him. Working with that firm for eight years now, he feels as though he made the right choice among job offers from the GAO, a large candy manufacturer whose headquarters is in Northern Virginia, and the other accounting firm. He has learned a great deal, has become an expert bank auditor, and is making twice the money he would have made in the Federal Service.

While he feels secure in the firm, George is unhappy that he has not yet become a partner, with added pay and prestige. Last year, he was promised a partnership if he moved to Chicago, where he would lead a team that regularly audits one of the nation's largest banks. After selling his house and moving his family from Virginia to a northern suburb of Chicago, his firm unexpectedly merged with another national accounting firm. Accommodating staff from the other firm prevented George from attaining partner status for at least a year, and he is considering offers from former clients who have attempted to woo him in the past.

Stage 4—Disemployment. *Disemployment occurs when, for whatever reason, the employment relationship is terminated.* Given the dynamics of the global economy, there is very little chance that a new worker will begin and end a career with the same employer. The worker may or may not be *unemployed*, but is likely to be placed in situations that require landing a new job. In the most common examples, new technology, an economic downturn, downsizing, foreign competition, mergers, or a change in the pattern of government spending cause employers to eliminate jobs. In such situations, there is a more efficient way for employers to get your work completed, if there is still the need at all. More subtle circumstances may see promotional opportunities disappear, salaries become depressed, or work schedules become unrealistic, leading to a search for alternative employment.

The implications of disemployment are far more serious than those attending the job search activities of entry-level workers. Those looking for their first real job typically have no dependents, often live with their parents or other relatives, and have few ties that narrow geographic scope. However, those with extensive work experience are likely to have several dependents, the financial obligations of running a household, and community ties that limit mobility. In addition to the financial hardship of job loss, there is often serious psychological trauma that follows the realization that one is no longer needed on the job.

Example

MOVE ON

George's position at the firm has become untenable. With so many new accountants from the firm with which his company merged handling bank audit tasks, there simply is not enough work to justify another partner in Chicago. Now the firm has offered to move George back to Virginia, where he could step back into his former position.

George is resentful that his employer of eight years failed to consider him and his family in the merger plans. With his expert auditing skills and a fine record of accomplishment on the job, he believes he can now "call his own shots."

Although it will mean further hardships for his wife and children—adjusting to new towns twice in two years—George is accepting a position as Deputy to the Chief Financial Officer of a rapidly growing firm that provides rental storage for homeowners in transition. While he is assuming some risks, his new position near the top should offer added opportunity and security.

Surviving the four stages of labor market activity often depends upon seeing what's coming, and taking steps to be recognized as a highly valuable resource. This thought is effectively communicated in William H. Whyte's *The Organization Man:*

> No one likes to be played checkers with and the man that the organization needs most is precisely the man who is most sensitive on this point. To control one's destiny and not to be controlled by it; to know which way the path will fork and to make the turning oneself; to have some index of achievement that no one can dispute—concrete and tangible for all to see, not dependent on the attitudes of others. It is an independence he will never have in full measure but he must forever seek it.*

THE IMPORTANCE OF OCCUPATIONS

Ever since the Industrial Revolution, economists have recognized that the work of individuals is more productive when it is organized into distinct occupations. Workers are most efficient when they learn and perform varied but related tasks. As a result, specialization of labor is a building block of advanced economies.

Doctors administer physical exams, diagnose illnesses, and prescribe medication, but do not ordinarily take time off from their medical practice to repair their automobiles. Teachers develop course curriculums and plans, instruct students, and advise parents and children, but do not build their own homes. And systems analysts determine automation needs and design computer systems, but do not teach their children geometry. Because we focus our labor on a single occupational area for which we are best suited, and avoid interruptions, our productivity is maximized.

Since occupation is a fundamental element in your choice of careers, it is necessary that you have at least a basic familiarity with the array of occupations that characterizes today's labor market. On the other hand, you need detailed information about those occupations that you are seriously considering as career possibilities.

References

1. *Dictionary of Occupational Titles,* U. S. Department of Labor, Employment and Training Administration, 1991.
2. Ehrenberg, Ronald G., and Smith, Robert S., *Modern Labor Economics: Theory and Public Policy,* 5th Ed., Harper Collins College Publishers, New York, 1994.

*Whyte, William H., *The Organization Man*, New York, Simon and Schuster, 1956, p. 167.

3. *The Occupational Information Network* (O*NET 98), U. S. Government Printing Office, 1998. (Free download available via Internet: http://www.doleta.gov/programs/onet/)

4. *Occupational Outlook Handbook,* U. S. Department of Labor, Bureau of Labor Statistics, January 1998, Bulletin 2500. (http://stats.bls.gov/emphome.htm)

Data-Speak
LEARNING ABOUT OCCUPATIONS

The nation's 140 million workers are grouped into a number of occupations, based on the primary tasks they perform. Turn to Appendix D to view a listing of over 600 occupations. Next, select three occupations of interest. You may wish to utilize occupations that correspond to your preferences expressed in the Interest Checklist presented in Chapter 1 Data-Speak.

Now, turn to the *Employment Opportunity Database* Warehouse, Chapter 3, "Learning About Occupations." Click on *Employment Opportunity Occupations.* It also includes each occupational title. Review this alphabetical listing to identify any additional occupations you want to explore. Now, enter Occupational Descriptions and review the descriptions provided for the occupations of interest. Also provided are related occupational titles from the *Dictionary of Occupational Titles* (*DOT*). The *DOT* provides a very comprehensive presentation of titles and definitions, and much additional occupational information for 12,000 occupations. It is generally available at public and school libraries and career centers.

The occupations you select should be those that might form the basis of your career. Continue to review occupational titles and definitions until you locate three in which you have a real interest. Record the title and definition of each on Data-Speak Worksheet 3.A.

Next, select *Employment by Economic Area.* Learn the employment for your occupations of interest in Economic Areas you select. Enter data you wish to retain on Data-Speak Worksheet 3.B.

Now, select *Employment by Occupation* and specify the occupations of interest. The *Employment Opportunity Database Warehouse* will provide that occupation's current employment for the nation and for each Economic Area. Enter the national totals and those for areas of interest on Data-Speak Worksheet 3.C.

Next, select *Employment by Area and Industry.* Find out—for a given area—industry employment in occupations of interest. Note that both current and *projected* totals are provided. Enter your findings on Data-Speak Worksheet 3.D.

Career Inquiry
OCCUPATIONS, HUMAN CAPITAL, AND THE JOB SEARCH

1. *Occupational information and your career.* Select one or more of the occupations that were included in this chapter's Data-Speak tasks. Utilizing the *Employment Opportunity Database* screens just reviewed, and the in-

formation recorded for this chapter's Data-Speak tasks, describe the labor market for each occupation in terms of employing industries and geographic locations. What is the expected growth in employment for these occupations in areas and industries of interest? Record this information, and explain how it might influence your career choice, on Career Inquiry Worksheet 3.A.

2. *Your human capital.* On Career Inquiry Worksheet 3.B, fully describe the human capital you have *already* formed. In addition to an overview of your educational and work experience, specify the skills and abilities you have developed that should assist you in one or more career fields. At this point in your career path, what additional education, work experience, and skills and abilities appear most desirable?

3. *Job search search.* Finding the right job isn't easy. Even in very favorable labor markets, the challenge of identifying and landing the best open job is very substantial. Find an individual who has found and accepted a new job in the past five years, and who is willing to tell you about his or her most recent job search experience. Record the information you obtain in the appropriate sections of Career Inquiry Worksheet 3.C.

DATA-SPEAK WORKSHEET 3.A

INTERESTING OCCUPATIONS

OCCUPATIONAL TITLE	DEFINITION
1.	
2.	
3.	
4.	
5.	
6.	
7.	

DATA-SPEAK WORKSHEET 3.B
EMPLOYMENT FOR OCCUPATIONS OF INTEREST IN SELECTED AREAS

1. Occupational Title: 1996 Employment

      Economic Area Title

   a.

   b.

   c.

2. Occupational Title:

      Economic Area Title

   a.

   b.

   c.

3. Occupational Title:

      Economic Area Title

   a.

   b.

   c.

DATA-SPEAK WORKSHEET 3.C

OCCUPATIONAL EMPLOYMENT

1996 Employment

1. Occupational Title:

   National Employment:

   Employment by Economic Area:

   a.

   b.

   c.

2. Occupational Title:

   National Employment:

   Employment by Economic Area:

   a.

   b.

   c.

3. Occupational Title:

   National Employment:

   Employment by Economic Area:

   a.

   b.

   c.

DATA-SPEAK WORKSHEET 3.D
EMPLOYMENT BY AREA AND INDUSTRY

	Employment	
	1996	2006

Economic Area:

Occupation:

   Industry

   a.

   b

   c.

Economic Area:

Occupation:

   Industry:

   a.

   b.

   c.

Economic Area:

Occupation:

   Industry:

   a.

   b.

   c.

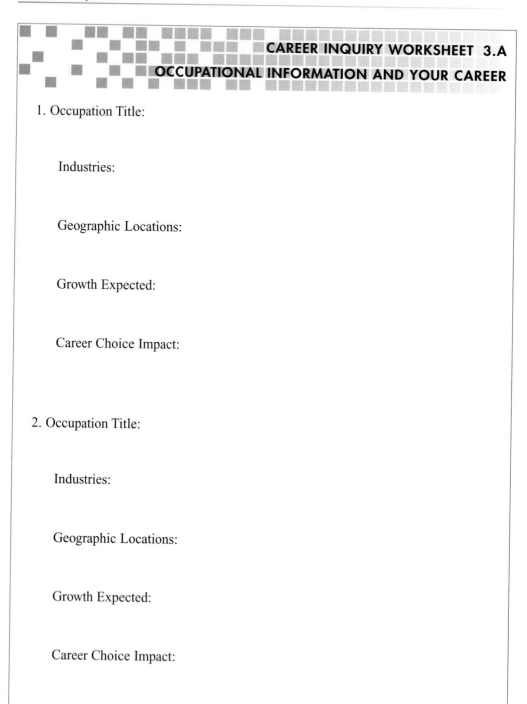

CAREER INQUIRY WORKSHEET 3.A
OCCUPATIONAL INFORMATION AND YOUR CAREER

1. Occupation Title:

   Industries:

   Geographic Locations:

   Growth Expected:

   Career Choice Impact:

2. Occupation Title:

   Industries:

   Geographic Locations:

   Growth Expected:

   Career Choice Impact:

CAREER INQUIRY WORKSHEET 3.B
YOUR HUMAN CAPITAL

1. Educational Experience:

2. Work Experience:

3. Relevant Skills and Abilities Developed:

4. Additional Education, Work Experience, Skills and Abilities Sought:

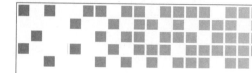

1. Job Search Research Conducted (skills and abilities required; industries that employ workers; geographic areas of employment; and potential employers):

2. Materials Development (resumes, cover letters, and letters of recommendation, introduction, and follow-up):

3. Interview Preparation (likely areas of discussion, content development, and rehearsal):

4. Job Search Experience (number of firms contacted, interviews received, and offers made):

5. Job Search Retrospective (given what your interviewee now knows, what might he or she do differently if that job search were to take place next month?):

PART B

Keys to Career Decisions

Guidance Keys to Career Decisions

Identification and description of four Guidance Keys

you should consider in selecting a career.

Overview

LEARNING OBJECTIVES

- Understand the need for and rationale of career decision-making Guidance Keys.
- Be able to articulate each Guidance Key and know how to measure individual characteristics, needs, and levels of competence against the criteria presented.
- Comprehend the distinctions of alternative socioeconomic lifestyles.
- Effectively relate Holland's personality types to career Interest Areas and the occupations they encompass.
- Understand the significance of Holland's Hexagon.
- Accurately relate your level of maturity to Super's five stages of career development.
- Be familiar with the *anticipation* and *accommodation* decision-making periods, and be able to articulate sound decision-making principles and a model ten-step career decision-making procedure.
- Utilize the *Employment Opportunity Database, Guide to Occupational Exploration* to select occupations that reflect your needs, interests, and capabilities.
- Understand and articulate family socioeconomic standing, and your social-economic expectations.
- Verify that occupations selected through use of the *Guide* are compatible with your personality.
- Identify the current stage of your career maturity, and forecast career status in each successive stage.

■ Apply the model ten-step career decision-making procedure to a relevant career issue or problem.

CHAPTER EXERCISES

Data-Speak: Follow the newly computerized and updated *Guide to Occupational Exploration* to select career possibilities that fit your Guidance Keys.

Career Inquiry: Investigate your social expectations, personality, stage of career development, and use of decision-making steps relative to occupations of interest.

Setting the Stage
UNDERSTANDING CAREER DECISION KEYS

Selecting a career is a complex challenge. To be completely satisfied with the work that we do, one would hope that it meets our socioeconomic standards, suits our personality, stimulates our interests, conforms to our values, provides a reasonable test of our aptitudes and abilities, and meets our criteria for financial well being. Complicating this choice is the fact that selection of a career is invariably tied to our own self-concept and self-esteem. Choosing a career is tantamount to telling the world who we think we are. This is why counselors will tell you that persistent delay in making serious career decisions may be a sign that the individual is simply unclear as to his or her identity, and therefore is unable to select a career that fits.

Study of the career selection process yields a number of "keys" that can be used to increase chances of meeting realistic career goals. To take advantage of these criteria, *Employment Opportunity* utilizes two broad categories of decision keys that impact the degree of fulfillment employment is likely to provide, Guidance Keys and Economic Keys. Understanding these indicators of future career satisfaction and applying them to your own situation will allow you to pursue *your* career selection process with more assurance.

Guidance Keys deal with characteristics of the individual. To a large extent, they are based upon the concepts discussed in Chapter 1, "The Human Side of Careers." For example, one career decision-making key is to ensure that the career chosen matches the personality of the individual. Utilizing the work of J. L. Holland, one can weigh an individual's personality type against jobs that most often suit that temperament.*

Economic Keys deal with characteristics of the economic environment in which the individual's career choice must fit. These keys are extensions of the concepts studied in Chapter 2, "The Economic Side of Careers." For example, one economic key is whether the demand for a particular occupation is adequate to ensure that a qualified applicant may find a good job. Utilizing Bureau of Labor Statistics' forecasts of the strength of demand for individual oc-

Holland, J. L., *Making Vocational Choices: A Theory Of Careers,* Prentice-Hall, Upper Saddle River, N.J., 1973.

cupations, one can gauge the likelihood of an open job being available when an applicant is due to complete the required education and training.

This chapter focuses on four Guidance Keys. After they are fully explained, you will utilize the newly automated and updated *Guide to Occupational Exploration,* within the *Employment Opportunity Database,* to begin selecting your career.

The *Guide* will help you to see yourself realistically with regard to your ability to meet job requirements. It provides information about the interests, aptitudes, adaptabilities, and other requisites of occupational groups. The *Guide* allows you to progress through its career selection process by making decisions, based upon what *you* know of yourself and your own preferences and desires.

Guidance Keys

THE SOCIAL EXPECTATIONS KEY

The first Guidance Key to be considered concerns the socioeconomic standards you wish to maintain. The *Social Expectations Key* refers to the social environment in which one hopes to live. Factors that shape social expectations include: the occupation and income of parents, education of parents, sex, race, ethnic group, religion, place and type of residence, family stability, size of family, birth order, values of peers, school environment, and community.

High socioeconomic status often is positively correlated with those who own their own business or manage a private concern. They stress educational achievement for their children and the use of contacts to maintain or promote family status. High incomes, investments over and above what's needed for a comfortable retirement, very long hours at the office, large homes, luxury cars, children in private schools/universities, expensive leisure activities, such as vacations in the islands and membership at country clubs, and enjoyment of the arts are characteristic of these lifestyles.

Those of middle socioeconomic status usually are in white-collar occupations. They stress maneuvering others to gain advantages for the family, and hard work in well-paying office jobs. Higher than average incomes, secure retirement funds, 40-hour workweeks, nice homes, medium-priced cars, children in public schools/universities, recreation on family trips, at public golf courses, and enjoyment of wide-screen TV and movies in theaters are typical of these lifestyles.

Low socioeconomic standing is characterized by blue collar jobs, manual labor, and an indifferent view of upward mobility. As a result, parental advice emphasizes income to meet basic needs and enjoyment of what life has to offer. Average or below average incomes, modest or nonexistent savings, hours of work directly dependent upon demand for goods or services provided, modest homes or apartments, lower-priced cars, children in public schools who are not likely to progress beyond 12th grade, and recreation through group activities (bowling and softball leagues, etc.) and TV sports and movies may be typical.*

FOR THE DOGS

Karen Miller is a high school senior finalizing her choices for college application. While she hasn't made a definitive career decision, she has decided that a tentative choice at this juncture would help her select a college that can best support her career aspirations. Karen's mother and father are both partners in a local law firm. Her older brother is in medical school. The Millers live in a posh suburb of Chicago. Karen has always loved animals and has been very strong in math and science courses. Consequently, she decided that a career in veterinary medicine is a promising possibility. Her tentative career choice and applications to college reflect her values, and will facilitate her eventual entrance into one of the nation's relatively few veterinary schools.

THE FIRST GRAD

Al James grew up in downtown Atlanta. The fifth child of Daniel and Kathleen James, Al decided at a young age that he would be the first in his family to graduate from college and work in a profession. Although he could play basketball with anyone on the block, his real loves were chess and mathematics. By 10th grade, he was a local chess champion, and was taking college advanced-placement courses. After considering his goals and interests, Al decided that he would become a college mathematics professor. His career choice was not traditional for his childhood environment, but reflected his own social aspirations.

THE PERSONALITY KEY

The *Personality Key* is based on the ability of careers to satisfy certain needs, reduce anxiety, and correspond with interests formed during early childhood development. Unless a worker's employment environment is an agreeable site for the individual's personality traits, frustration is likely to result. On the other hand, compatible personalities and work environments encourage job satisfaction, lower turnover (movement from job to job), and higher productivity.

The Interest Checklist completed for the Data-Speak Chapter 1 activity may be considered a "personality checklist," since it is based upon psychological and sociological factors. The likes and dislikes expressed, and the Interest Areas reflected in the responses given, reveal much about the personality of the individual completing it. In fact, the 12 Interest Areas embodied in the Checklist are the kicking-off point for the Guide that will be utilized for this chapter's Data-Speak activity.

*These group profiles are intended to provide a general image of how socioeconomic standing often translates into lifestyles. The reader should clearly recognize that diversity in these matters is common, as people express their individuality in spite of usual group preferences.

Holland's six personality types and the work environments compatible with each may be used to demonstrate how personality and career fit together, and how the *Guide* will help you to select occupations that are compatible with your temperament, as well as your skills, aptitudes, and abilities. The six types of personality are:

1. Realistic. This type of personality prefers to deal with work environments that call for objective, concrete, and physically manipulative processes. These individuals avoid goals and tasks that are subjective, intellectual, or artistic in nature, or are dominated by the exercise of social abilities. Interest Areas compatible with this personality type include Plants and Animals, Protective, and Mechanical and Industrial. Examples of career fields that are compatible with such individuals are engineering, skilled trades, agriculture, and technical jobs.

2. Investigative. These personalities prefer to utilize their intelligence, and the manipulation of ideas, words, and symbols on the job. They avoid social situations and view themselves as unsociable, masculine, persistent, scholarly, and introverted. The Scientific Interest Area corresponds to this personality type. Jobs that fit this type of personality include those in the sciences, such as chemists, meteorologists, and physicists.

3. Artistic. Personalities that prefer the arts favor work environments that require the creation of artforms and products. These individuals rely on subjective impressions, fantasies, and originality. They consider themselves to be unsociable, feminine, submissive, introspective, sensitive, impulsive, and flexible. The Artistic Interest Area matches this personality type. These individuals prefer careers in music, dance, literature, visual arts, and the dramatic fields.

4. Social. This personality type favors work environments in which handling and dealing with people is prominent. Individuals in this group utilize social skills, need social interaction, and see themselves as sociable, nurturing, cheerful, conservative, responsible, achieving, and self-accepting. Interest Areas that correspond with this personality type include Accommodating, Humanitarian, Leading-Influencing, and Physical Performing. Examples of careers in which this personality type thrives include education, therapy, religion, government, community services, and computer systems.

5. Enterprising. A personality that is enterprising prefers to express qualities that are adventurous, dominant, enthusiastic, and impulsive. They are persuasive, verbal, extroverted, self-accepting, self-confident, aggressive, and exhibitionistic. The Selling Interest Area corresponds with this personality group. Career preferences include sales, business management, and law/political vocations.

6. Conventional. This personality type seeks environments involving goals and activities that are socially accepted. Their approach to work tends to be stereotyped, correct, and unoriginal. They are sociable, neat, and conservative. The

Business Detail Interest Area represents them. Compatible occupations include those involving clerical and computational tasks, often found in business and economic fields.

Holland's research revealed that individuals are most comfortable with, enjoy being around, and are most like one, two, or three of the personality types described above. At the same time, workers tend to shy away from, and get annoyed by one, two, or three types. For example, actors and painters (artistic) associate freely with religious (social) and scientific (investigative) personalities, but rarely get close to clerical (conventional), craft (realistic), or sales (enterprising) workers.

Holland's Hexagon, shown in Figure 4.1, demonstrates how the six personality types are related. The closer the personality types are to one another, the more compatible they are. For example, Social and Artistic personalities tend to be compatible, while Social and Realistic types do not.

People search for environments that will allow them to exercise their skills and abilities, express their attitudes and values, and assume roles they enjoy. People also seek to be near similar individuals, and create environments that reflect their personality types. Behavior often is determined by the interaction between personality characteristics and the characteristics of the job environment.

FIGURE 4.1 Holland's Hexagon.

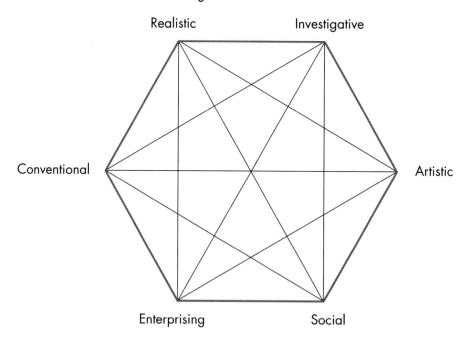

Note: The longer the connecting line, the more dissimilar the personality types, and vice-versa.

Example
BOOKKEEPING A PAIN

Richard Posner is a free spirit. Growing up outside Knoxville, he loved to play his guitar, and took weekend art lessons to help him paint some of the lovely country scenes along the Tennessee River. When it came to a career choice, Richard did not follow his personality. Instead, relatives convinced him that a safe career as a bookkeeper made the most sense. Richard completed a one-year course at a community college nearby. Within a week of graduation, he landed a job with one of the area's most successful real estate development firms. After two years on the job, and many unexplained migraines, Richard quit bookkeeping and is now working on set designs for the University of Tennessee Theater Company.

Example
SOCIAL ENGINEERING

Don Espisito's dad always wanted his son to be an engineer. A carpenter himself, Don's father worked long hours to save enough to send Don to the university. Although engineering never really appealed to him, Don felt he owed it to his dad to take advantage of the opportunity. Completing the rigorous engineering curriculum with good grades, Don located a job with a local engineering firm. The problem was that his work simply didn't offer him enough interaction with fellow employees and customers. After two rough years on the job, Don decided to apply his expertise to training foreign engineering students through the Peace Corps. Now in a more social environment, Don found fulfillment in his career.

THE STAGE OF DEVELOPMENT KEY

Stage of Development is another important key, influencing the extent to which serious decisions may be made.* Individuals often move through five distinct career stages. In Stage 1, *growth*, individuals develop their self-concept, as they grow both physically and psychologically, from birth to early teenage years. During this stage, individuals form interests and attitudes, and gain knowledge of their environment, including the world of careers.

Stage 2, from early teens to mid-twenties, is marked by *exploration,* including initial serious contacts with work. During this phase, individuals begin in fantasy, grasping at occupations that provide adventure and public acclaim, such as test pilot. Next, they move to a tentative phase, recognizing that their physical and mental capabilities, and the limited availability of dream jobs bring fantasies down to earth. Finally, a realistic phase narrows occupational selection to those occupations that are more accessible.

In Stage 3, from the mid-twenties to the mid-forties, careers are stabilized in an *establishment* stage. During this interval, decisions made during the exploratory

*D.E. Super, "Vocational Adjustment: Implementing a Self-Concept," *Occupations*, Vol. 30, No. 1, September 1951, pp. 1–5.

stage are tested. Trial and error results in the settling of the individual on an occupation in which investments are made. Eventually, the individual identifies with the occupation and a particular job.

Stage 4, *maintenance*, from the mid-forties to the mid-fifties or sixties, reflects advancement within the chosen field. Individuals work to enhance their occupational status, concentrating on aspects of their careers in which they are most interested and accomplished.

Stage 5, from the mid-fifties or sixties, marks career *decline*, with reduced career activity. Individuals begin this stage seeking to meet occupational standards and retain employment. Eventually, withdrawal from work is marked by retirement.

Of course, individuals are capable of moving at various speeds, and may return to an earlier stage because of specific circumstances. For example, a middle-aged tobacco company manager, laid off permanently because of falling domestic cigarette sales, shifts from Stage 4 to Stage 2, once again exploring career options. As mature individuals move through these development stages, they are able to formulate ideas about work, target their career direction, complete required education and training, begin employment, and advance and stabilize within their career field.

Example
GARBO

Harriet Singer is in the 10th grade and is positive she will be a famous actress. She has already starred in two school plays and is the envy of all her friends. In the initial meeting with her high school counselor, Harriet has informed Mrs. Gilchrist that upon graduation from high school, she will enter Carnegie Mellon University's drama curriculum. In the meantime, Harriet has requested as many drama-related courses as possible. While Mrs. Gilchrist admires Harriet's talent and drive, she urges her not to skip the unique opportunities for career exploration (Super's Stage 2) that are available in high school.

While trying not to discourage Harriet, Mrs. Gilchrist provides statistics concerning the small number of professional acting jobs relative to the number of applicants. After having her complete a battery of tests, Mrs. Gilchrist also points out that Harriet has a variety of talents and interests that could qualify her for other career fields. Harriet reluctantly agrees to seek an alternative career path, just in case her desire for acting subsides. Using after-school and summer jobs for exploration, and after accompanying several adults to work for first-hand exposure to different careers, Harriet has become very interested in speech therapy. She hasn't abandoned her acting goals, but if things don't work out, she has developed a realistic alternative employment opportunity.

Example
A GREAT COMMUNICATOR

Nikki Bumpus was beginning her senior year at Ohio University. She loved OU and the many friends she has made through her involvement in class council and her sorority. With a 3.3 grade point average, Nikki has surprised even herself. Hard work, interesting professors, and an interpersonal communications curriculum in which she was fascinated were a winning combination.

But now, as graduation approaches, Nikki knows she must get serious about a job. The downside of her communications curriculum is that it provides no automatic career opportunities. Medical students become doctors, law students become lawyers, and architecture students become architects. But communications majors often have to develop opportunities that take advantage of their substantial, but not always obvious, capabilities.

Nikki reasoned that she should try to identify the hottest career field and then apply her abilities in that area. With information technology booming, and many computer firms recruiting graduates from OU, Nikki sought a job in that industry. Given the tight labor market for computer scientists, her excellent communications skills, and her almost natural ability to get along with other students, her target position was entry-level recruiter. Within a month, she had five job offers. She plans to accept one and work her way up, eventually exploring other opportunities in the company, and establishing her career in training, marketing, or consulting.

THE LEVEL OF DECISION-MAKING SKILLS KEY

The *Level of Decision-Making Skills* is a key that has an important bearing on the effectiveness of career moves. While career development is a continuous process, there are critical points at which individuals must choose their own direction. When you complete high school, do you enter the job market or go on to college? When you graduate from college, do you enter the job market or go to graduate school? After three years with a large chemical firm, do you stay or do you move to a smaller firm, hoping to have more responsibility and freedom? The quality of such decisions is based upon your understanding of the choices, the extent to which you know yourself, your grasp of the economic environment, level of maturity, and ability to acquire knowledge.

The decision-making process can be broken into an *anticipation* period and an *accommodation* period. In the former, the individual begins by recognizing that there is a problem: a decision must be made, but information on which to base the decision is lacking. Therefore, alternatives are identified, costs and benefits quantified, and goals and values assessed. Development and analysis of such information allows one to narrow choices and reduce anxiety. In the final stages of the anticipation period, the individual sees a clear view of the future, doubts are removed, and decisions are made.

In the accommodation period, the individual makes contact with the chosen environment and begins to identify with that setting. Next, the individual begins to assert his or her views, becomes accepted by the work group, and builds a stronger self-image. Finally, the individual unites with the group and seeks to share a successful image.

Good decisions often are made when sound decision-making principles are observed: individuals understand themselves, accurately recognize current circumstances (don't live in the past), plan, initiate positive action before negative circumstances take effect, trust in their own judgment, are sensitive to others, are willing to change, and are honest when assessing their situation.

A model ten step decision-making procedure includes: (1) identifying the issue that requires a decision, (2) listing alternatives that are open, (3) obtaining information on each alternative, (4) examining each alternative in terms of one's values, interests, feelings, self-concept, and goals, (5) assessing the potential for success, risks, and failure, (6) reducing the number of alternatives to those that offer the best chances of success, (7) selecting the most desirable alternative, (8) planning to initiate the decision made, (9) taking action to implement the plan, and (10) evaluating the decision and the process utilized.

Example DECISIONS, DECISIONS, DECISIONS

The word on Bruce Troll is that he is incapable of making a decision. In fact, in high school he had been known to stand in front of a candy machine for 20 minutes, then walk away, change in hand, simply unable to decide between a Hershey Bar and a Milky Way. Today, however, Bruce has more significant decisions before him. His high school counselor has given him two weeks to complete his college applications and provide drafts for her review. The problem is that Bruce isn't sure he wants to go to college, and hasn't developed a list of prospective universities, let alone obtained applications.

In a panic, Bruce sits down with his best friend's mother, who happens to be a private career consultant. After a difficult hour of what seemed to him were an endless string of embarrassing questions, Mrs. Pearl says she's ready with some tentative ideas:

1. Bruce's reluctance to make decisions stems from the fear of making a mistake. By simply withdrawing from the decision-making process, he fails to gain any of the information on which a decision may be based.

2. The problem with Bruce's subconscious strategy is that by not making a decision, often the circumstances dictate the decision for him. For example, if he doesn't get college applications in on time, he is prohibited from entering college, regardless of his own preference. His failure to decide has effectively made an involuntary decision for him.

3. Bruce is told that he should understand that there is no such thing as a sure-fire decision. We all make mistakes, and he will too. The trick is to try to raise the odds of success through a comprehensive decision-making process. By not deciding, he lets the circumstances make decisions that may not be in his best interest.

4. Mrs. Pearl volunteered to call Bruce's counselor and request a two-week extension on college applications. In the meantime, Mrs. Pearl and Bruce reviewed and finalized a rational decision-making process to determine whether Bruce should decide to attend college, and if so, which colleges appear most appropriate for him.

After a second two-week extension, Bruce completed his decision-making process. He made the decision to attend college, but is still not certain of his career objective. He drafted four college applications, which have been provided to his school counselor.

Example THE EYE OF A PAINTER

Harry Kuptzin always dreamed of becoming a painter. Throughout grammar school, junior high school, and high school, he excelled in art class. Perhaps the ultimate satisfaction he received came during the week before Halloween, when he and six other art students spent three days downtown painting fall scenes on the insides of store display windows. Friends and relatives marveled at how Harry and the other art students transformed a rather plain few blocks into a charming fall village.

Once in college, it became clear to everyone but Harry that he was not going to become a successful painter. While he was very skilled at copying scenes out of a book, he just didn't have the imagination and eye necessary to make it. In spite of uniform criticism, Harry could not accept such responses to his work, and he rejected advice that he shift into a related field. After graduation, and three years of further rejection, Harry finally recognized that while he had certain artistic talent, he did not have the makings of a painter.

Once he understood his situation, it didn't take long for Harry to return to school, and complete coursework in computer-assisted commercial art. Harry now owns his own commercial art business, providing computer-generated artwork to retail and other satisfied customers.

Data-Speak SELECT CAREER PROSPECTS

Now, utilize the *Employment Opportunity DataBase* to select career possibilities that fit your Guidance Keys.

1. Return to Chapter 1's Data-Speak Worksheet 1.A, and review and record the Interest Areas represented by your Interest Checklist selections.
2. In the CD-ROM *Employment Opportunity Database*, select Chapter 4— *Guide to Occupational Exploration, Definitions of Interest Areas*. Review the other Interest Area definitions and note any others that seem appealing.
3. Select the *Work Groups and Subgroups* screen, and then select the *Interest Area* of greatest attraction to you on the *Interest Areas and Work Group's* screen above. For example, if you select *Artistic*, you will view that interest area and the work groups *Literary Arts, Visual Arts, Performing Arts: Drama, Music, Dance, Craft Arts, Elemental Arts, and Modeling.*
4. Review the more detailed description of Artistic within the *Guide Narrative and Occupations* screen below. Return to the top screen and select the *Work Group* (*Literary Arts,* for example) of most interest.

5. Review all of the narrative information for that work group which appears in the screen below. It describes the work that you would do, skills and abilities needed, how to know if you would like or could learn to do this work, how to prepare to do this work, and other facts to be considered.

6. At the end of the narrative information are the *Employment Opportunity* and *DOT* occupations —grouped by subgroup—that fall under the work group selected. Review and select the occupations that you may wish to pursue. Record your choices on Data-Speak Worksheet 4.A. Note that you will be provided with much additional information about these occupations (especially *Employment Opportunity* occupations) in later chapter Data-Speak exercises.

7. Return to the *Interest Areas and Work Groups* screen and select other work groups of interest. Review the corresponding information, as before, and make appropriate choices.

8. Repeat the above process for other Interest Areas you wish to consider, until you have exhausted all realistic possibilities. Then proceed to this chapter's Career Inquiry tasks.

Career Inquiry

OCCUPATIONS AND THE CAREER CHALLENGE

1. *Identifying your socioeconomic expectations.* Based upon this chapter's section on socioeconomic groups, and Chapter 1's Career Genogram, analyze your family's current status. How would you characterize your family's socioeconomic standing? What are *your* socioeconomic expectations? Provide this information on Career Inquiry Worksheet 4.A.

2. *Know your personality.* On Career Inquiry Worksheet 4.B, rank Holland's six personality types in terms of the extent to which each reflects your own temperament (1 = most descriptive; 6 = least descriptive). How do the occupations selected through your use of the Guide correspond with your personality? *Guide Interest Areas* correspond to Holland's Personality Types in the following manner:

   a. **Realistic:** Plants and Animals, Protective, Mechanical and Industrial
   b. **Investigative:** Scientific
   c. **Artistic:** Artistic
   d. **Social:** Accommodating, Humanitarian, Leading-Influencing, and Physical Performing
   e. **Enterprising:** Selling
   f. **Conventional:** Business Detail

If you believe any of the selected occupations conflict with your temperament, return to the *Guide* to develop additional choices. (Note that Accommodating includes a few occupations covered by Holland's Enterprising and

Realistic categories, in addition to those covered by the Social Category; also, Leading-Influencing, in addition to including those occupations in Holland's Social Category, covers business management and law/politics occupations in the Enterprising Category, and social science occupations covered by the Investigating Category.)

3. *Career stage status and goals.* In terms of careers, how would you characterize your current stage of development? How would you visualize your career status in each successive stage? Provide this information on Career Inquiry Worksheet 4.C.

4. *Using decision-making steps.* Identify a career decision you are currently contemplating. Utilize the ten decision-making steps presented in this chapter to analyze relevant issues and make a tentative decision. Provide the findings of each step on Career Inquiry Worksheet 4.D.

DATA-SPEAK WORKSHEET 4.A
OCCUPATIONS OF CHOICE

FIRST CHOICE:

    Interest Area:

    Work Group(s):

    Occupation(s):

SECOND CHOICE:

    Interest Area:

    Work Group(s):

    Occupation(s):

THIRD CHOICE:

    Interest Area:

    Work Group(s):

    Occupation(s):

CAREER INQUIRY WORKSHEET 4.A
YOUR SOCIOECONOMIC STANDING

Analysis of Family's Current Standing:

Statement of Your Social Expectations:

CAREER INQUIRY WORKSHEET 4.B
KNOW YOUR PERSONALITY

PERSONALITY	TYPE RATING	EXPLANATION OF RATING
Realistic		
Investigative		
Artistic		
Social		
Enterprising		
Conventional		

CAREER INQUIRY WORKSHEET 4.C
CAREER STAGE STATUS AND GOALS

STAGE OF DEVELOPMENT	CAREER STATUS—GOALS
Growth	
Exploration	
Establishment	
Maintenance	
Decline	

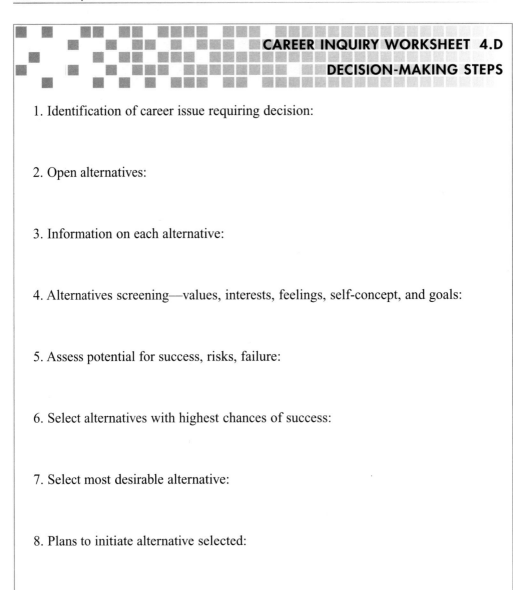

CAREER INQUIRY WORKSHEET 4.D
DECISION-MAKING STEPS

1. Identification of career issue requiring decision:

2. Open alternatives:

3. Information on each alternative:

4. Alternatives screening—values, interests, feelings, self-concept, and goals:

5. Assess potential for success, risks, failure:

6. Select alternatives with highest chances of success:

7. Select most desirable alternative:

8. Plans to initiate alternative selected:

9. Initial action to initiate plan:

10. Decision process evaluation:

Economic Keys to Career Decisions

*Identification and description of four Economic Keys
you should consider in selecting a career.*

Overview

LEARNING OBJECTIVES

- Understand the need for and rationale of career decision-making Economic Keys.
- Understand why the use of economic data may facilitate informed career decisions.
- Be able to articulate each Economic Key and know how to utilize corresponding data in career decision making and job search.
- Know the forces that determine an occupation's level of salary and benefits.
- Be able to describe the concept of derived demand and why it is important.
- Know how to articulate the relationship between changes in the level of wages and the supply and demand for labor.
- Be able to explain the formation of internal labor markets and define their characteristics.
- Understand the concepts of labor productivity and entrepreneurial loss.
- Be familiar with factors that contribute to productivity of the worker and how various environments treat productivity differently.
- Utilize the *Employment Opportunity Database* to retrieve Economic Profiles for all occupations of interest, providing occupational measures of compensation, supply–demand, internalization, and productivity.
- Analyze Economic Profile data for selected occupations in order to rank them based upon their Economic Keys.

CHAPTER EXERCISES

Data-Speak: Construct Economic Profiles of careers in which you are interested.

Career Inquiry: Based upon your own values, rank the Economic Profiles you have developed, and explain your preferences.

Setting the Stage
THE RELEVANCE OF ECONOMIC DATA

There are those who contend that economic data have no place in career decisions. These observers claim that data on wages, job openings, and projected trends in employment simply change too often to warrant much attention. At the same time, they say that if an individual wants to pursue a given career, one should not let workforce statistics get in the way.

This has been the philosophy that has held sway with many career professionals and job-seekers. In fact, even when there has been a desire to consult relevant labor statistics, many interested parties have not been knowledgeable enough to locate and properly interpret the information available. Contributing to this problem has been the fact that statistical and related job information has not always been presented in user-friendly formats.

All too often, failure to consult appropriate economic intelligence handicaps career decision-making and job-search activities. In fact, economic information is an essential tool to understand the labor market setting in which a career is practiced. Economic conditions often play an important role in determining such variables as chances of employment in a given occupation or industry, wage rates, and promotional prospects. Therefore, it is unwise to ignore such information, especially when it is accurate and easy to obtain, such as data provided in the *Employment Opportunity Database*.

This is not to say that economic information should necessarily drive career decisions. For example, a high school senior learns that a surplus is projected for a certain type of physician. He has always dreamed of being that type of doctor, and has exhibited the skills and abilities that should serve him well in college and medical school. If he is willing to weather the likelihood of an unfavorable supply–demand situation, there is no reason for him to change course. On the other hand, once he becomes aware of this contingency, he has the option of trying to insulate himself by acquiring special skills that are likely to be in demand, therefore enhancing his chances.

The *Employment Opportunity* approach raises your awareness of the Economic Keys likely to influence the course of your career. Then, for each specific occupation, data are provided to characterize the status of that occupation for that particular key. For example, level of compensation is established as an Economic Key. For each specific occupation, the *Employment Opportunity Database* provides information on the amount of income generally provided and the corresponding lifestyle/standard of living for that income. Taken together, the *Economic Keys* form a labor market profile for each specific occupation.

Economic Keys

Four Economic Keys should be considered when making career decisions. Jointly, they paint a picture of the economic environment of a chosen career.

THE COMPENSATION KEY

The *Compensation Key* refers to the salary and benefits likely to be provided to individuals working in that occupation. Factors influencing the level of compensation include: the strength of demand relative to the supply of workers in that occupation; the sensitivity of demand to a change in the wage (e.g., a top box-office draw in the movies doubles his revenue requirements, with no apparent decrease in the demand for his services); the extent of education and training required to perform the tasks involved (i.e., level of investment in human capital); the ease with which workers in that occupation may be substituted for by other workers or equipment (e.g., automated teller machines); and the extent to which workers in that occupation contribute to employer revenues/profits.

In recent years, with rapid advancement in technology and rising competition from workers in other nations, the ease with which tasks performed by U.S. workers may be replicated by low-wage foreign labor or new equipment has become an important determinant of income levels. If your work can be accomplished by an efficient piece of equipment or a low wage worker from a developing country, any leverage you may have to demand higher wages is drastically reduced, if not eliminated.

Example **LEGAL INCOME COMPUTES**

Monica Reid has expensive tastes. She has always liked the finer things in life. In making a career choice, she decided to be a systems analyst, because computers held the promise of high income. She had read about the millions of dollars made by computer moguls and wanted a piece of that pie. She spent five years at Northeastern University, majoring in computer science and participating in a co-op program with one of the nation's larger software companies. Upon graduation, Monica accepted a position with her co-op company. But after two years, Monica realized that while computer programmers and systems analysts make "good" money, very few make the kind of income she desired. Monica quit her job, entered law school, specialized in intellectual property, and is now a partner in one of the Washington area's larger patent-law firms. Combining her computer background with a law degree was the ticket to the higher income she sought.

THE SUPPLY–DEMAND KEY

The *Supply–Demand Key* refers to the strength of demand for workers in a specific occupation, relative to the supply of such workers. As noted in Chapter 2, the demand for labor is a derived demand, i.e., it is created by a demand for some product or service. All else remaining the same, the stronger the demand for the product or service that workers produce, the higher the demand for the associated workers. In general, when the price of labor rises, demand falls (unless you're a top movie star), as employers seek less expensive means of meeting their production goals. On the other hand, if wages decline, demand for workers tends to increase. At the same time, a higher wage attracts a larger supply of workers, while a reduced wage usually results in fewer employment candidates.

The degree to which suitable substitutes for products, services, or workers are available also has a strong bearing on the relative level of demand. The more unique a product, service, or worker, the stronger the demand and the more resistant that demand is to the negative effects of rising prices/wages.

Example

DOWN PLEASE

It is 1952 and Josh Levine has just received a promotion. For three years he was a stock boy for Donnelly's clothing store in Madison, Wisconsin. Last week the store's elevator operator retired and Josh, who has been training for the anticipated opening, now holds this key position. He transports passengers easily between floors of the men's department store, manipulates the control levers to smoothly start and stop the elevator, opens and closes the safety gate and elevator door, and provides customers with information regarding which departments are on which floors. Because of a strong demand for elevator operators and a limited supply of those with the necessary skills, Josh is looking forward to a long and relatively prosperous career. In fact, these jobs pay as much as most clothing sales jobs, offer good vacation time, and even provide a pension for long-term workers.

But circumstances would not be kind to Josh. Just one year after he became an elevator operator, the Otis Elevator Company introduced a push button elevator, requiring no operator. The strong demand for operators virtually disappeared in just a few years, and Josh joined thousands of former operators on the unemployment lines. The advance of technology reversed a favorable supply–demand situation.

THE INTERNALIZATION KEY

The *Internalization Key* refers to the extent to which a specific labor market has been removed from the perils of the free market. Employers form "internal" markets because they seek to retain workers in whom they have invested. After spending thousands of dollars and hundreds of hours training a new employee, that worker's departure nullifies the investment made. In order to protect such investments, employers internalize their markets by:

- Restricting entry to the firm to jobs with low levels of responsibility.
- Favoring promotion from within.
- Establishing career ladders through which employees routinely progress.
- Providing formal, in-service training, including training specific to the individual employer.
- Maintaining superior salary schedules that are developed through formal job grading and evaluation schemes.
- Encouraging customary practices that promote equity in the workplace.
- Restraining reaction to changed economic conditions, such as retraining rather than laying off surplus workers.

Those employers who place a premium on the development and retention of a skilled and stable labor force, such as government civil service systems, and those employers whose workers are represented by unions tend to be the sites of strong internal labor markets that offer employees incentives to stay. On the other hand, employers who traditionally do not attempt to lower labor turnover, such as agricultural employers and restaurateurs, generally accept very high rates of separation, while minimizing internal market incentives.

Example

NO SALE

Don Kravitz is ready to quit his job and go back to school. Three years after high school graduation, he began working as a salesman for a large liquor company. Don was attracted to the idea of not being in an office, driving about the picturesque suburbs of Seattle, and dealing one-on-one with owners of bars and liquor stores. Don knew a lot about the business from working in his dad's bar and restaurant after school and on weekends. But things weren't working out. He had been promised a large territory and high commissions. He put many extra hours into developing new customers for the company. But then he learned that his territory had become so lucrative that it was being subdivided and parceled to two new salesmen. Although he felt that his success deserved a promotion, there was no higher-level job to which he might be promoted.

While Don was selling liquor around Seattle, his older brother, Seymour, who had graduated as a business administration major from Marquette, was beginning his third year with a large pharmaceutical company. Entering with the title of Budget Analyst I, he had already received two promotions—to Budget Analyst II and III—and was scheduled for a third, in six months. His health insurance and pension benefits provided him with a sense of security that Don never had, and likely never would have, as a liquor salesman. Seymour enjoyed the teamwork of his large, structured company, and gained satisfaction providing services to those advancing the development of various medicines.

THE PRODUCTIVITY KEY

The *Productivity Key* deals with the relationship between the value of what an individual worker produces and the cost that the worker represents to the firm. Economic research reveals that as more and more workers (labor) are hired, assuming that the other factors of production (land, capital, and business ability) are held constant, output per worker eventually declines. This is because the increasing number of workers is sharing smaller and smaller portions of the other factors of production. Sooner or later, as the employer continues to hire new workers, the value of the product of the last worker hired will just equal what that worker costs the firm, in wages and benefits. If the firm hires more workers, beyond the break-even point, those additional employees would actually cost the firm more in compensation than their output would be worth. Such workers would represent what economists call an "entrepreneurial loss."

It stands to reason, then, that the higher your productivity—the higher the value of your output is relative to your compensation—the more attractive you are to your current and prospective employers. These days, ensuring that you offer employers maximum productivity means that you are proficient in your occupation's most advanced skills, are able to utilize the latest technology available, and are a competent communicator and collaborator. At the same time, given the speed with which technology is advancing, one needs to demonstrate a willingness and ability to learn new skills and adapt effectively to innovation.

Two words of caution when it comes to being appropriately recognized for *your* productive contributions. First, certain environments lend themselves to high productivity, while others do not. For example, business consulting firms in highly competitive environments milk every ounce of technological advantage from the latest innovations, such as providing employees with laptop computers for use at home and on trips. On the other hand, state and local government employees rarely have the productive benefits of tools such as laptops.

Second, certain employers tend to relate productivity to the workforce as a whole, while others tend to scrutinize the individual. Managers of a large auto assembly line may be forced to evaluate *average* productivity per worker, while law firms typically track the billing hours of *each* individual attorney. Therefore, the most efficient, fulfilled employment may be encouraged through identification of high-productivity employers who seek to recognize superior producers for their individual contributions.

Example
NETWORKING SUCCESS

Steve Hunter didn't like school. Right from the start, he was a weak reader and a poor student. Somehow, though, he got through grammar, junior high, and high school, and spent a year at a community college that specializes in getting its students up to speed for four-year colleges and universities. Through sheer desire and hard work, Steve caught up, transferred to a traditional university, and graduated with a major in economics.

Acting on information provided by a friend in Boston, Steve found out that the Boston Regional Office of the Environmental Protection Agency was hiring. Before long, he was a GS-5 (entry-level) federal employee, working in the Office of Human Resources.

Although Steve intended to transfer to an economic research job when one became available, after six months time he learned of an opening in the Automation Branch, a job that was sure to lead to a promotion. He transferred into that job and after just a few weeks was amazed to realize that he had somehow found his niche. Fascinated with everything about computers, he began working 12- to 15-hour days. After a couple of months, he seemed to know more than almost everyone else in the Branch. He became a favorite of staff that relied on him to set up and repair computer systems.

But after a year, Steve became frustrated. Much of the staff resented his extra-hours work. Also, in spite of the vast gains in productivity for which he felt he was personally responsible, it would be years before he could move into a job that reflected his new expertise. Seeking a more equitable, less structured, and faster track, Steve left the federal government and joined one of the nation's largest business consulting firms. Today, he is that organization's top LAN (Local Area Network) expert, enjoying the routine and substantial recognition provided for his high productivity.

Selected References

America's Career InfoNet, U. S. Department of Labor, Employment and Training Administration (http://www.acinet.org).

Employment Outlook: 1996–2006, U. S. Department of Labor, Bureau of Labor Statistics, BLS Bulletin 2502.

Occupational Projections and Training Data, 1998 Ed., U. S. Department of Labor, Bureau of Labor Statistics, BLS Bulletin 2501.

Data-Speak
ECONOMIC PROFILES

Now, utilize the *Employment Opportunity Database Warehouse* to obtain Economic Profiles for the occupations you identified as most interesting after using the Chapter 4 Data-Speak Guide. Select *Chapter 5, Occupational Economic Profile.* Select the first occupation of interest. The *Employment Opportunity Database* will display:

1. *Compensation key.* Average annual salary and the occupation's rank, relative to six standard of living levels. (See Appendix E for criteria.)

2. *Supply–demand key.* National employment for the selected occupation for 1996 and projected to 2006, the expected change, annual openings resulting from growth and replacement, and their rank. (See Appendix E.)

3. *Internalization key.* Total replacement rate and rank, reflecting internal market strength. (See Appendix E.)

4. *Productivity key.* Occupational unemployment rate, likely reflecting the strength of the occupation's productivity. (See Appendix E.)

Obtain this information for any other occupation of interest, and record your findings on Data-Speak Worksheet 5.A.

Career Inquiry
RANKING ECONOMIC PROFILES

Carefully review the Economic Profiles you recorded on Data-Speak Worksheet 5.A. Contrast the strengths and weaknesses for each occupation. Based upon your own values, rank the Economic Profiles of these occupations in order of preference. Use Career Inquiry Worksheet 5.A for this information.

DATA-SPEAK WORKSHEET 5.A
ECONOMIC PROFILES FOR OCCUPATIONS OF INTEREST

OCCUPATION TITLE: _____

Compensation Key:

    Annual Salary: _____

    Rank: _____

Supply–Demand Key:

    Employment Change 1996–2006

        Number/Rank: _____

        Percent/Rank: _____

    New Entrants Needed per Year

        Number/Rank: _____

Internalization Key:

    Total Replacement Rate: _____

    Internal Market Strength: _____

Productivity Key:

    Occupational Unemployment Rate: _____

    Productivity Strength: _____

CAREER INQUIRY WORKSHEET 5.A

RANKING ECONOMIC PROFILES

For each element of the Economic Profile, fill in an abbreviation for the occupation that fits the appropriate rank. For example, if you are considering four occupations, and you believe the compensation of one of the four ranks fourth—lowest among the four—write an abbreviation for that occupation in the Compensation column, fourth row.

	Compensation	Supply–Demand	Internalization	Productivity	Overall
1.					
2.					
3.					
4.					
5.					
6.					
7.					

PART C

Career Income and Investments

Career Income

Statement of ten principles by which you may maximize

your income.

Overview

LEARNING OBJECTIVES

- Explain the significance of income data to career decision making and job search.
- Understand the challenge of relating current salary and benefit levels to standard of living, costs, and future requirements.
- Be able to articulate career income principles and explain their significance for career selection, job search, and employment decisions.
- Be familiar with constraints on occupational income based upon technology, productivity, and the market.
- Define *wage differentials* and provide examples in which they do and do not apply.
- Define and explain the significance of "directed" education and training.
- Distinguish the significance of advanced education relative to government policy versus job applicant credentials.
- Define *asymmetry of information* and explain how it applies to jobseekers and employers.
- Be familiar with the three-step process to minimize applicant information deficits concerning employer operations.
- Be aware of employee reliance on support from the organization in circumstances in which pay is driven by performance as opposed to time.
- Define and explain the significance of *moral hazard.*
- Understand the need to take advantage of career opportunities when they appear.

- Know the many forms in which compensation may be provided.
- Understand the significance of High Density Career Areas (HDCAs), and provide several examples.
- Recognize the role that company superstars play in grooming future achievers.
- Demonstrate the ability to use the *Employment Opportunity Database* to determine whether occupations of interest are likely to support desired living standards/lifestyles.
- Explore previous, current, and future application of the Career Income Principles.

CHAPTER EXERCISES

Data-Speak: Use the *Employment Opportunity Database* to identify those occupations whose incomes usually support your desired standard of living.
Career Inquiry: Explore how to apply the chapter's ten principles of income maximization.

Setting the Stage
THE CRITICAL NATURE OF INCOME DECISIONS

As explained in Chapter 1, career choice involves more than money. However, for the great majority of individuals who rely on their careers for income and necessary benefits, such as health insurance, it is critical to understand the monetary implications of career decisions. Most people spend the bulk of their waking hours going to, at, or coming from work. Often, the energy expended to do one's job leaves little for other endeavors. At the very least, therefore, you should understand what you're getting out of it.

Of course, you also need to understand the potential for rewards other than money, such as status, the friendship of fellow employees, and the satisfaction one receives by seeing the results of a job well done. These considerations, if most important to you, may override material matters. However, there is no getting away from the cold, hard fact that the income you receive for working, and possibly that of your spouse, will determine your standard of living. College students who report that their primary reason for attending college is to prepare for a career that will offer them a comfortable lifestyle recognize this.

It may be fun and exciting to imagine that a lottery win or inheritance will bail you out of depending on a job. Unfortunately, we all know that such occurrences are *very* remote. What you earn from work usually determines your standard of living. Therefore, one would think that before selecting a career, the decision-maker would have comprehensive information about the type of compensation workers typically earn in that occupation, and what that income can buy.

The reality, unfortunately, is that very few individuals understand the full dollar (living standard) implications of their career decisions. In fact, many people make such decisions while they are still in school and don't have the experience to put money matters in their proper perspective. For example, to a student who has been just getting by, and hasn't seen more than a few hundred dollars at a time, a salary of $25,000 a year sounds great. But does this student really understand what $25,000 means in terms of living standards in a given geographic area? What will that $25,000 buy in terms of housing, transportation, and entertainment? Also, if one begins with a starting salary of $25,000, what can be expected five, ten, or twenty years later?

A salary meant to support a single, recent graduate might not be what is needed a few years later to place a family in a good neighborhood with excellent schools, build a house in which the family can grow, send the children to college, and contribute to a "nest egg" for a comfortable retirement. If you are a teen or in your twenties, it may seem premature to consider such factors now. However, the decisions you make over the next several years may put you on a track that dictates how you will live the rest of your life.

Employment Opportunity provides two types of information that offer insight into the monetary rewards of careers. First, the text offers ten principles to understanding career incomes. These principles help you to guard against decisions that are not in your interest. Second, the *Employment Opportunity Database* provides information on average annual salaries by occupation, and groups each by the living standard category in which it falls (Appendix E). The lifestyles made possible by each standard of living group may be based on the expenditures data presented in Appendix F. Salary information may be adjusted for cost of living through use of the indexes in Appendix G.

Career Income Principles

PRINCIPLE NO. 1 There Is Little Correlation Between Devotion and Dollars

Many people believe that their devotion to a job is proportional to the income they will receive. Certainly, level of effort may influence income levels within an occupational range, and may even lead to a more lucrative job. But the range of income within an occupation is generally set by technology, productivity, and the market situation of the job, all of which are mostly beyond the influence of an individual worker. Thus, no matter how devoted Registered Nurse Grogen is on the job, her salary will never approximate that of Dr. Mamana. Her skill, hard work, and dedication may boost her annual salary from $45,000 to $55,000, but she will never make the $225,000 of the physician.

Conclusion: Don't select an occupation that pays below your targeted living standard. No matter how hard you work, your income is likely to be limited within an occupational range, and this is beyond your control.

PRINCIPLE NO. 2: Within an Occupation, Disagreeable Jobs Require No Less Effort and Pay No More

It seems logical to conclude—as many economic theorists do—that jobs that are more disagreeable pay a premium ("wage differential") to attract candidates willing to subject themselves to the difficulties of a subpar employment situation. For example, jobs that are exceptionally dangerous reward employees for risk taking. But within an occupation, wage differentials rarely are associated with inferior jobs. In fact, the opposite generally is true. The well-organized, most efficient firm often pays the highest salaries in order to attract and retain the most productive employees. On the other hand, poorly organized, inefficient companies tend to be less particular when it comes to staff quality, pay less, but are likely to require no less effort than that required by top-of-the-line employers. In fact, because a firm is not as organized or well managed and is less productive, existence within that environment is likely to generate more aggravation for employees for fewer dollars. Therefore, it is not surprising that when Howard Leone lost his job as a buyer for a desperate and now bankrupt department store chain, and luckily landed a comparable job with the most successful sporting goods chain in the country, his job satisfaction shot up along with his salary.

Conclusion: Seek employment with "top of the line" companies. The best organizations generally provide the best work environments and the highest wages, and require no more effort than do less efficient firms.

PRINCIPLE NO. 3: There Is a Strong Correlation Between Directed Education and Training and High-Income Jobs

Study after study concludes that the more advanced and directed your education and training, the more pay you are likely to receive for your work. The term "directed" is used here to indicate that the subject education and training recieved are part of a coordinated effort to prepare you for a specific career area.

Economists often question whether added education is responsible for graduate success, or whether the bright, motivated individuals would succeed whether or not they enrolled in advanced curriculums. Such questions may be meaningful to help set government policy on the support of higher education and training. However, as long as employers treat the completion of relevant coursework as a necessary *credential* for higher paying jobs, directed educational investments deserve serious consideration by career candidates.

Candidates should weigh the costs of advanced education and training, such as tuition, fees and books, and lost time before beginning or continuing a career. In addition, you must consider the psychic price paid while giving up entertainment and relaxation for sometimes boring lectures, intensive study, and the pressure of exams. A career candidate must view such expenditures relative to eventual gains in income, standard of living, status, and job satisfaction that would result from the additional preparation. While each case may be unique, research has concluded that additional investments in education and training usually pay for themselves many times over. (Note that Chapter 7 provides a process to help you weigh additional expenditures in education and training against their likely benefit.)

Conclusion: Invest wisely in education and training. Employers generally reserve the highest paying jobs for those with extensive education and training credentials.

PRINCIPLE NO. 4: Asymmetry of Information Requires Effective Communications and Perceptive Investigation

You know more about yourself than any prospective employer. To take advantage of this inequality of knowledge, you must effectively communicate your strengths. Let the employer know that you can more than justify the salary and benefits that the firm typically offers to the best job applicants. You can design and compose the resume, select those who provide recommendations, and give solid and honest answers to the interviewer's questions.

On the other hand, there is also an asymmetry of information when it comes to knowledge about the firm. Which firms actually pay top-dollar salaries and benefits? Which firms really try to promote from within? Which provide a pleasant work environment and are likely to prosper? While government agencies routinely collect and publish data on the average wages of specific occupations, obtaining information on the salary levels of individual employers is much more difficult. In fact, this is a fairly complex matter, since "pay" may not include just salary, but benefits, such as health insurance and retirement funding. The firm knows what it pays and probably has a good idea of how it ranks among its competitors, but you don't. Therefore, there is an inequality of information concerning how much you and the employer know about compensation practices.

There is no easy way to erase this information deficit. Most employers consider their salary information so vital that they keep it from competitors and provide it only for confidential government surveys. However, you may attempt to narrow the information gap in the following manner:

■ *First,* utilize the *Employment Opportunity Database* information developed at the end of Chapter 5—national average information on salary levels for your occupation. Remember that pay rates and the cost of living vary by area, and also tend to cancel each other out. New lawyers in New York City, for example, may make $100,000 per year, but they also must pay $1,500 a month in rent for a nice studio apartment in Manhattan! (To find out how to adjust the salary for an occupation against the cost of living in a specific Economic Area, refer to Appendix G.)

■ *Second,* seek interviews first from high status, large, well-established employers. These tend to pay the highest salaries. Their reputations (and sometimes higher prices they charge) depend on their attracting and keeping accomplished staff. They can afford higher salaries by spreading their costs across large sales and revenue dollars. Furthermore, they have had enough experience to know what it takes to provide employees with desirable benefit programs (health insurance, retirement plans, etc.). Set your salary expectations against the offers of these employers. For example, if this employer generally offers a starting salary of $35,000 a year to attractive candidates in your occupation, set that amount as your high-end target.

■ *Third,* seek interviews from other employers that are less well established, but may be desirable for other reasons. Remember that starting salaries and benefits do not necessarily represent the best indicator of long-run compensation. A smaller but fast-growing firm may pay less to start, yet offer superior opportunities for advancement.

Conclusion: Take advantage of your self-knowledge and thoroughly investigate employer salaries, benefits, and promotional potential to help identify your ideal position. Use information about you to win attractive employment offers; analyze offers from several firms before determining which one provides the best overall compensation package.

PRINCIPLE NO. 5: Pay for Performance vs. Time Requires Trust in Company Quality and Initiative

For the most part, workers are paid by time. Employers expect a good eight-hour day, and assume that most employees' productivity approximates the average. In such circumstances, supervisors are hired to weed out the poor producers, and to identify for promotion those with potential.

However, many of today's better jobs pay based upon performance, more than time. The TV entertainer, investment banker, or corporate administrator is expected to show results. It is assumed that they will work many hours past the usual 40-hour week; however, their monetary rewards are not based on hours worked, but on ratings achieved, profitable deals cut, or upward movement in corporate profits and stock values.

Remember, if you enter such jobs, your performance and pay will be greatly influenced by the support provided by your organization. Whether it is the TV series time slot, the ease of access to vital financial information, or the quality of middle-level managers on whom you must rely, the results you obtain, and your corresponding rewards, will be impacted.

Conclusion: Before accepting a "pay-for-performance" opportunity, carefully scrutinize the support likely to be provided by the organization. If such support appears inadequate, either obtain commitments for upgrade, or seek another opening.

PRINCIPLE NO. 6: Moral Hazard Jeopardizes Your Pay and Security

In the employment relationship, moral hazard refers to the risk employers take by trusting employees to perform at or near an average level of productivity. Jeopardy from those who systematically shirk their responsibilities is the result of several factors: hourly pay, failure to properly screen and motivate employees, ineffective supervision, and failure to hold workers accountable for their output. Of course, every organization will have a relatively small number of freeloaders. However, know that when moral hazard runs rampant, company profits and continued viability of firms are threatened. Such problems may eventually undermine your compensation and security.

Conclusion: Verify a company's ability to motivate employees, to spot and promote exceptional producers, and to release those who fail to produce adequately. Without accountability, those exploiting moral hazard will share in your successes, and endanger your rewards.

PRINCIPLE NO. 7: Never Allow Circumstances or Folly to Interrupt Your Momentum to Higher-Paying Positions

Your quest for fulfilled employment can be much like a poker game. There will be times when you have a run of good luck and numerous opportunities for upward mobility. Also, there will be times when you can't buy a move up, no matter how hard you try or what you accomplish. Therefore, when opportunities present themselves, it is sheer foolishness to turn away and not attempt to take advantage.

An often unwise example is the recent college graduate who shrinks from the challenge of job search to "take some time off" for a six-month European vacation, just having fun or working at jobs that require no educational prerequisites. These students often believe that family contacts will be available to get them a job when they are ready. But the truth is that they will never be more ready than they are at graduation. Coursework is familiar, professor references are easy to obtain, and the university guidance and placement network is available. Although family resources and friends may bail them out (and there is nothing wrong with using them), there is no substitute for winning that first job because of what you have accomplished or have demonstrated you can bring to the position on your own. Few of these students starve, but too many of them spend months or years attempting to get back on track.

Another usually counterproductive decision is the employee who rejects a promotional opportunity because of an honest belief that he or she needs more preparation before the higher level job can be successfully tackled. The truth is that we are rarely, if ever, completely ready to take on the added responsibilities of a new job. Of course, basic knowledge and experience are required; but most of us learn the job on the job. You can toil away for less pay at a lower level job and never regain the career thrust of the promotional opportunity bypassed. Remember, as you are sticking it out in your lower level job, someone else is working at the higher level position, progressing toward a job with even higher pay, benefits, and esthetic rewards. You can stretch yourself and learn that higher level job, or you can shrink from the challenge and give the extra status and salary to someone else.

Finally, it is not uncommon for employees to reject a promotional opportunity because it requires movement to another firm. Unfortunately, some firms bypass deserving current employees with the attitude that they are already on board, working for them. Promoting them would just create another vacancy, which would have to be filled. If you face management with this mindset, your job has become dead-ended, and you *must* move to advance.

Conclusion: Take full advantage of opportunities for first jobs and promotions. Never slow or interrupt your momentum toward higher paying jobs because you think you may not be ready, or out of loyalty, or desire for a break. If you have the fundamental qualifications, and are willing to put out extra effort for a while, you can learn the new job on the job. Your loyalty to the old job may be appreciated by your current supervisor, but will not be appreciated by the higher level staff intending to promote you.

PRINCIPLE NO. 8: Fair Compensation May Take Many Forms

Most of us have a sense of what represents an equitable level of compensation. We reach such conclusions based upon the salary and benefits of others in positions with which we are familiar. We also may have direct knowledge of our worth from specific accomplishments for which we were responsible. For example, a litigator wins a case that brings the firm $1 million.

The problem is that firms often resist the payment of larger sums that would normally go to those in higher level positions. For example, based on company policy, management may feel that it would have to promote you to pay you the higher salary, and it may feel that you haven't been in the job long enough to merit promotion. In such circumstances, remember that there are many ways open to the firm to appropriately recognize you. Just a few such means include bonuses, stock options, low-interest loans, and company cars. If the firm wants to do the right thing, a way can be found.

Conclusion: If you believe your compensation falls short of what is deserved, suggest alternative ways in which the firm can supplement your pay. Lengthy periods of being undercompensated (and therefore underappreciated) are a sign that you should be shopping for another firm.

PRINCIPLE NO. 9: Income Opportunities Are Maximized in High Density Career Areas (HDCAs)

Throughout the United States, there are certain concentrations of economic activity that offer unusually favorable environments for workers in certain careers. Such HDCAs include computer chip manufacturers in Silicon Valley; lobbying firms in Washington, D.C.; movie production companies in Hollywood; and advertising firms in New York City. The networks, communications, and sophisticated production processes established over many years of growth and experience in these HDCAs provide fertile ground for rapid career advancement. Meet or beat the competition of others in your field and the sky's the limit.

Conclusion: If you have the skills and the drive to effectively compete, seek job opportunities in HDCAs. There are significant financial rewards to succeeding where standards are the highest.

PRINCIPLE NO. 10: Ride a Star to the Top

Organizations have recognized "stars" who outperform their competition and usually rise to the top of responsibility, authority, and compensation gauges. Since these employees are always looking for workers to support and contribute to their efforts, dividends may be earned by proving yourself to these super achievers. Stars generally reward those who assist them with perks and opportunities to move up.

Conclusion: Seek the earned recognition and friendship (if socially acceptable) of company stars. Your trip to a target position may be greatly facilitated by high achievers who believe in your capabilities.

Data-Speak

PRICE OCCUPATIONAL LIVING STANDARDS

Utilize the *Employment Opportunity Database* to determine whether occupations in which you are interested are likely to support your desired standard of living. Go to the *Employment Opportunity Database Warehouse, Chapter 6, Occupational Living Standards.* Select *Annual Salary by Rank.* Find the living standard rank and salary for each occupation of interest, and record that information on Data-Speak Worksheet 6.A.

Next, turn to Appendix F, Annual Average Expenditures by Living Standard Group. For the living standard groups represented on Data-Speak Worksheet 6.B, record the average annual expenditures for major expenditure categories, such as food, housing, apparel, transportation, health care, entertainment, education, and personal insurance and pensions. Also, provide expenditure information for other items that correspond to your desired lifestyle, such as mortgage interest and charges, if you are planning on owning a home. Record this information on Data-Speak Worksheet 6.B.

Now adjust the Worksheet 6.B expenditure data to account for the cost of living in the area in which you are currently residing. Turn to Appendix G, Cost of Living Indexes. Find an area that corresponds to the one in which you are currently located. Adjust the Data-Speak 6.B Worksheet totals based upon the cost of living index entries. For example, if you are in Binghamton, NY, and your occupation of interest is in living standard 2 ($50,000 – $69,999), you would adjust the average annual housing expenditure—$14,454—by multiplying it by 0.973, and entering the product—$14,064—on Data-Speak Worksheet 6.C. (The transportation entry for Binghamton would be multiplied by 1.028.) If you are unable to locate index data for your area, simply repeat the national averages from Worksheet 6.B.

Career Inquiry

DEFINING LIVING STANDARDS AND APPLYING INCOME PRINCIPLES

For each expenditure amount on Data-Speak Worksheet 6.C, describe what may be purchased in your current area of residence. For example, a real estate agent in Binghamton could be consulted to determine the type of housing that might be available for $19,014 per year. Summarize this information on Career Inquiry Worksheet 6.A.

After you have constructed descriptions of the goods and services that may be obtained by each living standard group represented, determine whether the occupations of interest are likely to provide you with a satisfactory lifestyle. If one or more of the occupations appear to provide adequate income, circle them on Data-Speak Worksheet 6.A.

If no occupation is likely to provide your desired lifestyle, return to the *Employment Opportunity Database, Chapter 6.* Explore the three available screens to identify occupations with higher-level living standards. Be sure that alternative occupations selected conform to the other career selection criteria utilized thus far. Then repeat the process just used to examine the adequacy of the living standards represented by the higher-level group(s). Examine these lifestyles as before, and proceed.

On Career Inquiry Worksheet 6.B, briefly describe any experience you have had in the application of each Career Income Principle. Then indicate how you might apply each principle along your current and anticipated career path.

DATA-SPEAK WORKSHEET 6.A
OCCUPATIONAL LIVING STANDARDS

	OCCUPATIONAL TITLE	LIVING STANDARD CATEGORY	AVERAGE ANNUAL SALARY
1.			
2.			
3.			
4.			
5.			
6.			
7.			

DATA-SPEAK WORKSHEET 6.B
EXPENDITURES BY LIVING STANDARD GROUP

NATIONAL

Average Annual Expenditure by Group

Expenditure Category	1	2	3	4	5	6
Food						
Housing						
Apparel						
Transportation						
Health care						
Entertainment						
Education						
Insurance/ Pensions						
Other						

DATA-SPEAK WORKSHEET 6.C
EXPENDITURES BY LIVING STANDARD GROUP

AREA OF RESIDENCE

Average Annual Expenditure by Group

Expenditure Category	1	2	3	4	5	6
Food						
Housing						
Apparel						
Transportation						
Health care						
Entertainment						
Education						
Insurance/ Pensions						
Other						

CAREER INQUIRY WORKSHEET 6.A
GOODS AND SERVICES BY LIVING STANDARD GROUP

Expenditure Category	AREA OF RESIDENCE Description of Goods and Services for Living Standard Category
Food	
Housing	
Apparel	
Transportation	
Health care	
Entertainment	
Education	
Insurance/ Pensions	
Other	

CAREER INQUIRY WORKSHEET 6.B
APPLICATION OF CAREER INCOME PRINCIPLES

1. Little correlation between devotion and dollars.

2. Disagreeable jobs require no less effort and pay no more.

3. Strong correlation between directed education and training, and income.

4. Asymmetry of information requires effective communications and perceptive investigation.

5. Pay for performance requires trust in your company.

6. Moral hazard jeopardizes your pay and security.

7. Don't interrupt your momentum to higher-paying positions.

8. Fair compensation may take many forms.

9. Income opportunities are maximized in High Density Career Areas.

10. Ride a star to the top.

Investing in Your Own Stock

Seven Investment Keys to maximize your value

to employers.

Overview

LEARNING OBJECTIVES

- Understand the implications of advanced skills in providing an enhanced worklife.
- Be able to articulate each General Investment Skill and explain the rationale and benefits of each.
- Explain how globalization of the U. S. economy came about, and what it means for U. S. firms and employees.
- Explain how the pace of technological advance has established a need for continuous learning.
- Articulate how the need for accelerating productivity has impacted the shape of corporate organizations and the nature of communications.
- Be aware of the origin and role of increased collaboration in a global economy.
- Comprehend the advantages of utilizing the latest in technological advances to improve personal productivity and project a positive image.
- Know the components of becoming a force for positive change.
- Understand the concept of system thinking.
- Explain the enhanced role for evaluation in our global economy and provide examples of modern evaluation tools.
- Be able to articulate the major tenants of quality management.
- Identify common techniques utilized by firms to achieve productivity gains in our global environment.

- Utilize the *Employment Opportunity Database* to retrieve information on the educational, training, and aptitude requirements of occupations of interest.
- For occupations of interest, measure your levels of accomplishment against education, training, and aptitude requirements. Articulate how all criteria might be met in the future.
- Describe your accomplishments in General Investment Skills, and indicate how capabilities might be raised to meet desired levels.

CHAPTER EXERCISES

Data-Speak: Use the *Employment Opportunity Database* to identify the education and training requirements of the occupations in which you are interested.

Career Inquiry: Plan how you might obtain the education, training, and general investment skills necessary to succeed in selected occupations.

Setting the Stage

ADVANCED SKILLS AND THE CHALLENGE OF GLOBALIZATION

The more specialized and advanced your skills become, the higher your rank in a given occupation. The doctor specializing in brain surgery, the designer who is expert in sports cars, and the professor who paints statistical portraits of economic history have all invested heavily in personal stock. The payoff, in addition to the great joy of practicing a profession at the top, is expressed by the respect of peers and monetary dividends. Employers and clients extend the greatest rewards to those who practice at the highest levels of occupational sophistication.

Workers possessing the most advanced skills fear less from competition, either in the form of labor-saving equipment or other workers. Their capabilities are just too difficult to replace. At the same time, employers fear the loss of such personnel, dreading the task of recruiting qualified replacements. As a result, premiums are paid to attract and keep such human "assets" happy and available.

How much should you invest in *your* stock, i.e., your knowledge and skills? The answer to that question depends upon what you believe your potential may be, and the degree to which investments in education and training may allow you to reach your career goals. Of course, you can make investments in your human capital over a period of many years. However, investments made directly after high school often build the foundation on which your future career path will depend.

Employment Opportunity provides two types of information to assist you with your investment portfolio. First, this chapter provides information on "general investment skills" that are essential to career success, regardless of your occupation. Whether your career is in the arts, business, science, or sales, mastering these general investment skills will help to keep your career moving forward. Once these general skills have been explored, the *Employment Opportunity Database* offers a process to determine the education and training in which you must invest to qualify for those occupations in which you are interested. Referral to comparative wage data helps to reveal the monetary payoff of one occupation's investments against another.

Globalization of the U. S. economy has elevated the importance of these skills. In fact, globalization of the U. S. economy has become so important that a brief explanation is required.

From the end of World War II until the mid-1970s, large American corporations were able to set prices with little consideration of competing firms of other nations. With very modest outside competition, innovations could be phased in deliberately; standard operating procedures could be documented, learned, and practiced by most employees; quality could be sacrificed for profits; and large structured bureaucracies could be easily maintained, with communications following vertical lines. Employee wages—almost regardless of productivity and quality—could be raised regularly, and then offset by higher prices.

However, the mid-1970s saw the birth of highly efficient, quality-oriented foreign corporations. Seeking to capture world markets, especially those in the United States, these new players offered the American public higher quality products at lower prices.

To survive in this new environment, American firms were forced to change the way they do business. The search for productivity and quality-enhancing innovations was raised to a fever pitch; large, structured bureaucracies were downsized and re-tooled to accommodate the need for flexibility and creativity; and new emphasis was placed on employing workers who could learn and apply new techniques and adapt to a constantly changing workplace. Communications shifted from formal vertical lines to informal and horizontal patterns, based upon need and talent rather than position.

With prices now set through fierce competition, the search for profits has become synonymous with quality and productivity. To reach these goals, American firms have formed alliances with corporations around the world, establishing *global webs*. Wherever quality and efficiency are the highest, and sometimes wages the lowest, the global web can set up production facilities and gain an edge on the competition. While this new mode of operation has once again returned profits to American firms, workers may suffer reduced compensation and security. For example, "American" cars are being produced and assembled all over the world by workers who are not American citizens, while some U. S. workers face auto plant downsizing.

General Investment Skills

INVESTMENT SKILL NO. 1 Learn to Learn

We are living through a period of incredible growth in knowledge and technology. The Hubbell Telescope redefines our universe; gene technology reshapes the practice of medicine; cell phones expand communications exponentially; subwoofers bring the sounds of all too real dinosaurs into our family rooms; and computers change almost everything, from office operations to auto assembly lines.

Perhaps the most unique feature of such developments is not the extent to which our lives are being altered, but the constant barrage of change that we must absorb. A never-ending parade of new, higher quality, more efficient innovations marches into our environments with little fanfare. Just as we learn and get comfortable with WordPerfect 6.0, along comes Word for Windows 95, and Windows 98, each requiring us to start learning again.

Under these circumstances, those who are the most successful are those who have the will and confidence to learn and apply the latest concepts and technology. Since enhanced quality and efficiency are the tickets to company profits, firms will constantly look to recruit those who can bring innovations into their production processes.

Portfolio Recommendation: Make every conceivable effort to understand the latest concepts and learn how to utilize the newest technology that may be relevant to your current or future employment. Such knowledge may be the edge that you need to win the best job opportunities. Without such investments, you invite others to pass you by.

INVESTMENT SKILL NO. 2 Communicate and Collaborate

The days of triangular-shaped organizations (many production workers at the bottom, a number of middle managers, and a few high-level executives on top), with strict rules of vertical communications, appear to be numbered. With production workers stationed around the world, corporate headquarters often include top executives, highly motivated professionals, and skilled technicians, operating on a horizontal plane. As firms push productivity forward, ease of communications among those who have ideas for improvement takes priority over the niceties of corporate etiquette. This means that the comfort of standard operating procedures and routine processes is vulnerable to constant attack from today's innovators. In the 1950s, new ideas were not always met enthusiastically, especially if they were offered by those outside top management. Profits were being made, workers were satisfied, and there was little to fear from competitors. But today, living in the shadow of competitors who can drive firms from the playing field with little notice, new ideas are likely to be considered regardless of their source.

Generating new ideas is futile without the ability to communicate them in an effective manner. Success requires the knack to describe problems and potential solutions in a credible way. With a high premium placed on imaginative solutions, business organizations require the collaboration of divergent staff and divisions.

Often, it is collaboration among unfamiliar parties that leads to new ideas and success. Sharing knowledge already known to all accomplishes little. On the other hand, having engineers, scientists, production managers, and marketing experts work together to brainstorm alternative ways of solving a complex customer problem holds real promise. Therefore, communications skills must be extended to be the first step in collaboration, the art of working together with others to identify and solve problems.

Portfolio Recommendation: Invest in coursework and other activities that will teach you to communicate and collaborate. Extracurricular activities such as student government, debate club, and Model United Nations are particularly good examples.

INVESTMENT SKILL NO. 3 Capitalize and Computerize

Businesses acquire capital equipment in order to advance efficiency and quality. Traditionally, this has been most true in manufacturing. Re-tooling the assembly line, introducing robotics, or employing lasers results in greater output per worker and enhanced quality.

Today, the use of capital equipment in general, and computers in particular, transcends the nature of production. The technology associated with such innovative systems as automatic bank tellers, supermarket bar code readers, and instant gas station credit approvals boosts productivity across industries.

Just as businesses take advantage of capital equipment and computers to raise efficiency levels and quality, you too may extend your positive reach through use of the latest innovations. Personal computers enhance your ability to compose papers, control data, and transform worksheets into convincing exhibits. Cell phones allow you to become accessible for business communications almost any time during the day or night. Portable computer notebooks extend your time at work into commuter hours. Knowing how to acquire and utilize such technology is evidence of your own potential for bringing high productivity and quality to your employer.

Portfolio Recommendation: Take full advantage of every opportunity to become well versed in use of the latest capital equipment (technological advances), especially personal computers and those electronic devices that facilitate communications. The more you know, the more evidence you can present of your dedication to productivity, quality, and profits. Also, the more you know now, the easier it will be for you to adjust to the next generation of innovations.

INVESTMENT SKILL NO. 4 Imagine, Analyze, and Act

With today's operating processes always suspect, new ideas have an unprecedented opportunity for consideration and acceptance. To take advantage of this environment, you must be able to visualize new or improved processes that may boost efficiency and/or quality. However, the ability to form such ideas, determine what it would take to make the required changes, and obtain the policy approvals and resources necessary still constitute difficult and complex battles. Being an instrument of innovative change is not an innate ability, but is learned through experience and experimentation.

One advantage in developing proposals for change is to become a "system thinker," viewing the entire scope of a challenge, and devising a solution drawn from your universal perspective. For example, a narrow view of a commuting problem would recommend that more and better highways be constructed. On the other hand, a system solution might institute flexiplace or telecommuting (work from home), reducing the need for highways by allowing certain employees to work without leaving home. This is made possible through the use of personal computers, modems to access company databases, and fax machines to facilitate instant transmittal of needed documents.

Another plus is to gain experience, improving processes while you are still in school. Such experimentation will allow you to learn from your failures, build upon your successes, and hone your skills as one who can make a positive difference.

Portfolio Recommendation: While still in school, select an issue of change; e.g., volunteer to start a new club, rejuvenate school government, or streamline some outdated apparatus. Use this experience as a base upon which you can build to demonstrate your ability to visualize and institute improvements.

INVESTMENT SKILL NO. 5 Evaluate

If productivity and quality are paramount, then evaluation becomes an important prerequisite. How do you know the firm's current level of success, or the improvement provided by specific change, unless there is a capability to accurately track and measure output and customer service? Evaluation involves skills to measure costs relative to benefits, conduct customer satisfaction surveys, and form and learn from focus groups.

Portfolio Recommendation: Study and utilize techniques required for evaluative processes. Such procedures involve both human sensitivity to properly interpret customer information, and statistical skills to properly collect and analyze evaluation data.

INVESTMENT SKILL NO. 6 Push Quality

Since the emergence of global competition, management systems that advance the concept of quality have been in vogue. Quality circles, total quality management, and homegrown variations of such quality systems have been employed by U. S. firms to fight off foreign attempts to capture American markets. Although specific forms of quality enhancement processes may come and go, the notion of improving quality to protect firms from aggressive competitors is here to stay. Fundamental themes of quality management processes include: (1) not losing sight of the customer's needs (seeking to *delight* the customer), (2) fully utilizing employee teams, (3) problems generally traced to faulty processes, not individuals at fault, (4) continuing efforts to improve work processes, and (5) communicating freely.

Portfolio Recommendation: Become familiar with the basic tenants of quality management. Utilize such techniques to gain experience in their application.

INVESTMENT SKILL NO. 7 Push Efficiency

Industrialization made it clear to business managers that increasing output per unit of labor was the path to greater productivity and profits. Since globalization, productivity gains have become a matter of survival. Those firms which have been able to reorganize into global webs; restructure operations into tightly managed and downsized organizations; introduce the latest technological innovations; jettison unprofitable units; and retrain and motivate their workforce, have been able to survive, and often prosper. Firms that failed to address the fundamental issues of efficiency have disappeared. Managers who are well versed in the basic ingredients of productivity enhancement, and have had experience boosting output, become leaders entrusted with the future of the firm.

Portfolio Recommendation: Fully understand the concepts underlying gains in productivity. Utilize such concepts to obtain experience in their application.

Data-Speak ASSESS EDUCATION AND TRAINING REQUIREMENTS

Utilize the *Employment Opportunity Database* to learn the educational and training requirements of occupations in which you may have an interest. Note that aptitude information and training time relate only to *detailed* occupations, which are grouped under each general occupation. These occupational titles are from the *Dictionary of Occupational Titles* (*DOT*), a U. S. Department of Labor publication that includes titles and definitions for 12,000 occupations.

Select the *Chapter 7 Data-Speak* section, *Education and Training Requirements.* Further select *Education and Training.* Then click on an occupation of interest. The *Employment Opportunity Database* provides the usual education and/or training requirement, and a percent distribution of the educational level of employees in that occupation. Record educational and training requirements on Data-Speak Worksheet 7.A.

Next, select *DOT Characteristics.* Click on an occupation of interest to view its *DOT* code, *Guide Subgroup,* worker functions (data, people, things, aptitude levels), general educational development (reasoning, math, and language), and time to reach average performance level. (Detailed definitions of these terms and levels are presented in Appendix H.) Also record these findings on Data-Speak Worksheet 7.A.

Career Inquiry
PLANNING TO ACQUIRE YOUR HUMAN CAPITAL

On Career Inquiry Worksheet 7.A, for each occupation of interest, repeat the requirements data recorded on Data-Speak Worksheet 7.A. Then, briefly describe your level of accomplishment in the educational, training, and aptitude requirements of occupations in which you are interested. Also, indicate how you might raise those credentials to the levels required.

On Career Inquiry Worksheet 7.B, briefly describe your current level of accomplishment in the General Investment Skills described in this chapter. Then indicate how you might raise those skills to the levels required for your most likely career choices.

DATA-SPEAK WORKSHEET 7.A
OCCUPATIONAL EDUCATION AND TRAINING REQUIREMENTS

OCCUPATIONAL TITLE: _____

Education and Training Categories: _____

    DOT Occupation: _____

    Aptitudes:

        Data _____ People _____ Things _____

        Reasoning _____ Math _____ Language _____

        Training Time to Average Performance _____

OCCUPATIONAL TITLE: _____

Education and Training Categories: _____

    DOT Occupation: _____

    Aptitudes:

        Data _____ People _____ Things _____

        Reasoning _____ Math _____ Language _____

        Training Time to Average Performance _____

CAREER INQUIRY WORKSHEET 7.A
EDUCATION AND TRAINING ASSESSMENT AND ENHANCEMENT

OCCUPATIONAL TITLE: _____

    DOT Occupation: _____

	REQUIREMENT	CURRENT LEVEL*	ENHANCEMENT PLAN
Education	_____	_____	_____
Training	_____	_____	_____
Data	_____	_____	_____
People	_____	_____	_____
Things	_____	_____	_____
Reasoning	_____	_____	_____
Math	_____	_____	_____
Language	_____	_____	_____

Training Time _____

*See Appendix H for detailed descriptions of terms.

CAREER INQUIRY WORKSHEET 7.B
APPLICATION OF GENERAL INVESTMENT SKILLS

1. Learn to learn

   Current level of accomplishment:

   Ideas for enhancement:

2. Communicate and collaborate

   Current level of accomplishment:

   Ideas for enhancement:

3. Capitalize and computerize

   Current level of accomplishment:

   Ideas for enhancement:

4. Imagine, analyze, and act

   Current level of accomplishment:

   Ideas for enhancement:

(continued)

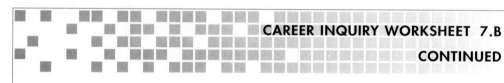

5. Evaluate

Current level of accomplishment:

Ideas for enhancement:

6. Push quality

Current level of accomplishment:

Ideas for enhancement:

7. Push efficiency

Current level of accomplishment:

Ideas for enhancement:

PART D

Unlocking the Doors to Fulfilled Employment

Dealing with Employers

Points of contact, networking, written materials, and employment interviews.

Overview

LEARNING OBJECTIVES

- Understand the distinction between selling your labor and selling your possessions.
- Be able to articulate the problems of mismatched employment for employers and employees.
- Know the value of pre-employment, employment (work-study programs, internships, and summer jobs).
- Be familiar with use of friends, relatives, and the telephone in establishing contact with prospective employers.
- Be able to articulate the content and use of each Materials Building Block: Self-Inventory, Employer Requirements Assessment, and Accomplishment-Requirement Match.
- Be able to describe and understand written material used to contact employers: cover letter, resume, resume follow-up, thanks-for-the-opportunity transmittal, and employment acceptance.
- Know the three resume rules.
- List the three interview stages and explain the purpose of each.
- Understand the content and use of an interview "success" essay.
- Be prepared to deal with interview segments that include unfamiliar topics and/or open-ended questions.
- Be sensitive to the need for you to pose your own questions during interviews, and to thoroughly assess the employer's offer and employment environment.

131

- Utilize the *Employment Opportunity Database,* other tools (such as Internet job and employer listings), and other sources of information to identify prospective employers who are likely to hire workers in relevant occupations, industries, and areas.
- For selected employers, develop your written materials building blocks.
- Utilize the above building blocks and other information in this chapter to develop your cover letter, resume, follow-up letter, thanks-for-the-opportunity transmittal, and employment acceptance letter.
- Prepare your interview success essay to correspond to the above job search materials.

CHAPTER EXERCISES

Data-Speak: Utilize the *Employment Opportunity Database*, the Internet (e.g., America's Career Infonet), and/or library research to generate a listing of employers likely to hire workers in occupations and geographic areas of interest. Supplement that listing with additional sources of information on vacancies in those occupations and areas.

Career Inquiry: Apply the techniques described to develop written materials and prepare for job interviews so you may find a rewarding job in your chosen career field.

Setting the Stage
PRESENTING WHO YOU ARE AND WHAT YOU KNOW

Now that you have come a long way toward selecting your career—and charting your course to fulfilled employment—it's time to prepare for contact with prospective employers. Many view the process of persuading those in charge to offer you employment as a "sales job." Put your best foot forward; appeal to the employer's culture; write those things that will cause the reviewer of your resume to request an interview; and convince the interviewer(s) that you are just what the firm is looking for.

Of course, you want to do all those things. But if you know the industry, if you know the occupation, if you know you are suited for this work, and if you know that you are thoroughly prepared to tackle the challenge of this job, then a sales job is not really necessary or appropriate. You don't need to *sell* yourself; you just need to present who you are and what you know.

Remember that selling your labor is *not* comparable to selling your house or car. Once you sell a product you own, your relationship with the purchaser ends. You may get an irate call or two about the leaky basement or a transmission gone bad. But for the most part, once you transfer ownership and receive payment, the relationship between buyer and seller ends.

On the other hand, once an employer offers you a job and you accept it, your employment relationship has only begun. Therefore, if you have *sold* the employer by promising that which you cannot deliver, or pretending to be what you are not, awkward and unpleasant experiences are likely to follow. Moreover, if you have focused exclusively on selling yourself and not assessing the employer and the work environment it offers, you could end up with a job you really don't want.

Successfully approaching employers rests on completing your homework. You must prepare thoroughly; effectively communicate your skills, abilities, and experiences; and perceptively assess the job and the employer environment.

Points of Contact

PRE-EMPLOYMENT EMPLOYMENT

The most assured point of contact is one that has been firmly established prior to your job search. Today's employers go to great lengths to avoid making hiring mistakes. Investing in recruitment, orientation, and training only to find that the wrong individual has been hired wastes valuable resources and denies management required staff.

From the employee's viewpoint, mismatched employment presents similar problems: wasted time and effort going through the application and interview process, orientation and training for a job that is inappropriate and probably short-lived, trying to adjust to an environment that just doesn't fit you, and future explanations required for a brief-tenured job on the resume.

The most effective way of avoiding such problems is to have already worked in a similar job within the work environment in which you are interested. Through formal or informal work-study programs, internships, and summer jobs, employers and potential employees may get to know one another and accurately assess what each has to offer. **Providing an employer with objective evidence of your current worth is the best indicator of your potential**.

The intern who works long and hard, learns quickly, and is a team player is likely to possess the same qualities in permanent employment. Likewise, employers who provide interns with a stimulating and challenging environment, furnish valuable training, and pay top dollar are not likely to treat permanent employees differently. Evidence of a "split employment personality" could be easily uncovered during temporary employment.

TO THE GLOBE

Amber was a junior at Boston College majoring in journalism when her advisor called her in. She suggested that Amber interview with a suburban weekly newspaper for an internship that it makes available each year. Amber reasoned that the downside was the added workload that could potentially be a burden on grades; the potential upside was the terrific experience, and contacts she could make.

Accepting the position, Amber worked directly under a retired reporter from the *Boston Globe*. She claims she learned more in her internship than in any journalism class. The result was a second-year internship, and upon graduation, a permanent job with the same paper. In addition, Amber feels she may be able to jump to the *Globe* after a year or two.

TELEPHONE

Establishing personal and positive contact with a potential supervisor or any respected employee of a firm in which you are interested can greatly boost your chances of employment. The best way in, if you don't already know staff personally, is to network, i.e., know someone who knows someone. Combining this with clever use of the telephone can mean a job.

COUSIN-AID

Jennifer found out that her cousin Marty has a neighbor who is a high-ranking executive at a management-consulting firm. She mentioned to Marty that this firm is the exact type of company for which she is hoping to work. It has a young and bright staff, and the company has a reputation for treating its employees well. At a cookout, planned weeks before, Marty told his neighbor about Jennifer: "I've known her all her life. She's a great kid. She's bright and enthusiastic, hard working, and graduated with honors just a few weeks ago." After hearing this, the neighbor suggested that Jennifer call him at the office.

After sketching out the points she wanted to make, Jennifer phoned Marty's neighbor. She emphasized that she was a psychology major with a minor in business studies and that she received great private sector experience through the University's work-study program. She told him how she worked her way up from being a University Tour Guide to Tour Guide Coordinator, how she was elected to the Student Senate, and that she was appointed to the Search Committee as the student representative to help select the next Dean of the Psychology Department. She also discussed how her senior research project on marketing quality helped to develop her marketing skills.

After a ten minute conversation, the neighbor asked Jennifer if she might be interested in an entry-level marketing position vacancy of which he was aware. Two weeks and two interviews later, Jennifer had the job. Six months later, the neighbor received a $1,500 bonus from the company for successfully recruiting her.

WRITTEN MATERIALS

Regardless of your initial method of contact, you need to create written materials that accurately and effectively present who you are, what you know, what you have accomplished, and where you hope to go. Writing your way into a job requires careful research, development, and editing skills. Even if your written package doesn't initiate contact, before long, your prospective employer will request it. Development of written materials may be facilitated through the use of three *materials building blocks*:

1. Self-inventory. Begin by taking stock of what you have accomplished. At this point, don't limit yourself to what you think might be most relevant to particular employers. Give yourself a few days to list and describe progress you have made at school, in activities, and in employment. Be sure to include all instances in which you have been recognized for excellence or for specific achievements. (A sample self-inventory is provided in Figure 8.1 at the end of this chapter.)

2. Employer Requirements Assessment. In Step 2, you must determine the education, skills, abilities, experience, and worker characteristics sought by the employers in which you are interested. Talk with those working in the type of job and work environment you are trying to enter. Review information in the *Guide to Occupational Exploration* (Chapter 4 Data-Speak) to identify those characteristics that correspond to the occupations you desire. Call associations that represent these employers. The idea is to develop a profile of the perfect candidate for the occupation in which you are interested. (See the sample employer requirements assessment in Figure 8.2.)

3. Accomplishment–Requirement Match. Step 3 calls on your analytical and creativity skills. You must match the specific high priority needs of employers with what you offer. Review your self-inventory and employer requirements assessment, select those abilities and accomplishments that are relevant to employer needs, and then add to your self-inventory relevant skills and accomplishments that match employer needs but didn't occur to you initially. Of course, some of this will be easy. For example, if employers require candidates to have a specified academic degree, and you have that degree or its equivalent, you have a match. On the other hand, you may have learned that the top employers look for candidates to have potential ability to devise unique solutions to complex problems. Convincing employers that you have such potential could be a difficult challenge. (See Figure 8.3, sample accomplishment–requirement match.)

Now that you know what employers are looking for, and which of your accomplishments meet employer criteria, it's time to develop those written materials that will effectively present your credentials. For the entire job search process, it's best to have your cover letter, resume, and other needed letters (discussed below) drafted and ready to go, with little need for additional work.

Cover Letter

This is a brief letter of introduction that informs the recipient, preferably the appropriate department head, but often the human resources chief, that you are interested in working for that firm. If you are responding to a specific vacancy announcement, be sure to specify the opening for which you wish to be considered. If there is no known vacancy, but your research concludes that this employer may have an opening in your career field, simply describe the type of position in which you are interested. Develop detailed information about the industry and firm, and include it. Also, be sure to include a brief description of one or two of your most impressive skills or accomplishments. This is likely to be your first substantive contact with the firm and, therefore, your first opportunity to show recruiters what you have to offer. A well-written and promising letter of introduction can get you to the next step in the hiring process. (See sample cover letter in Figure 8.4.)

Resume

Since getting a professional job usually requires a resume (normally enclosed with your cover letter or posted on an Internet website), there are countless books about resume development and format. You should refer to such resource materials to view the variety of acceptable formats and to fashion your own version.

The key to a successful resume is presentation of information that shows the reviewer that you have the skills, abilities, and characteristics the company wants. No matter how cleverly you format your resume, you have slim chances of scheduling an interview and landing a job if you don't meet employers' basic requirements. Overall, the resume should describe who you are, what you know (that matches employer needs), and what your career goals are. You should also include brief information about your recreational interests or hobbies. How you communicate this information within your resume is up to you (see sample resume in Figure 8.5). But, regardless of the format and content you choose, it is vital that you follow these three resume rules:

Resume Rule No. 1: Make no spelling mistakes or errors in grammar. Be *sure* your resume is free of any content inaccuracies. Effective use of spellchecker, resume review by appropriate friends or relatives, and/or use of a professional resume preparation service should help to ensure perfection. Remember, however, that an error-free resume is *your* responsibility.

Example
THE WRONG DRAFT

Steve Jones graduated from one of the nation's top graduate schools, with a Ph.D. in American Literature. Somehow, the professional service he had hired to print his resumes used an earlier draft that contained several spelling and grammatical errors. Assuming that the printer would get it right, Steve didn't double-check the resumes before sending them out. As a result, Steve received no interviews from the resume mailing, and his career never really recovered from this mistake.

Resume Rule No. 2: Never promise what you cannot deliver or include statements that are in any way deceptive. Misleading employers may win you a job in the short-run, but could ultimately cost you a career.

Example

FORGET THE ODDS

Linda Friedman graduated from college with a specialization in information systems software and showed real promise as an accomplished computer programmer. Although she never learned COBOL, she included it in a listing of computer languages she had mastered. Her idea was that knowledge of COBOL would help present her as a well-rounded programmer, while the odds of actually having to use this generally antiquated language were quite remote. After landing a job with her "dream" employer, her very first assignment involved analysis and solution of a "Year 2000" problem on a government contract, a task requiring full knowledge of COBOL. Linda is no longer with that employer, and when word spread through the industry of her deception, she had serious difficulty landing another job.

Resume Rule No. 3: Keep your resume brief, precise, and Internet-friendly.
The idea is to give reviewers a picture of who you are, what you've accomplished, and what you offer. There should be no need for reviewers to dig through narrative in order to get the point. Lengthy explanations that provide depth may be appropriate during an interview, but not in a resume. Therefore, you must continually edit resume content until it is as "tight" as you can make it. Lengthy sentences and explanations should give way to action verbs and brief statements. Given the current trend towards electronic recruiting and job search, the odds are that your resume will be scanned and stored in a computer. To increase the likelihood that your resume will be selected in response to expected search criteria, include key words (e.g., Ph.D., COBOL, etc.) that describe your attributes that are most in demand by targeted employers. Also, use white paper; avoid abbreviations not in common use; use a non-decorative, 12-point font; reserve bold-facing for major headings; and use a standard layout.

Letters at the Ready

Once you have initiated contact with employers, you will need a set of "ready letters" drafted to respond in certain situations. Since response time may be vital, it is best to have transmittals prepared in advance, with some space left to accommodate specific details:

Resume Follow-Up. You've sent your resume to a number of employers that are high on your list of desirable places to work. After several weeks, you have yet to receive any response from three of your top choices. The resume follow-up letter reminds the employer of your availability and your worth. Since your cover letter and resume failed to generate a response so far, include new positive information, or restate some of your strong points in a different way. (See Figure 8.6 for a sample resume follow-up letter.)

Thanks for the Opportunity. If you receive notice that the firm will not be pursuing you further, be sure to thank the employer for the consideration given to your qualifications. You never know if that employer may decide to reconsider your candidacy at some point in the future. Also, you may have dealings with that firm in the future, and your last contact could form the basis of a positive relationship. (See Figure 8.7 for an example of a thanks-for-the-opportunity letter.)

Employment Acceptance. If the employer has offered you a position and you decide to accept it, document your acceptance in writing. Your future employer may or may not have communicated details of the offer in writing. This is *your* opportunity to convey exactly what has been promised. If the firm has not effectively communicated details of the offer, you may uncover misunderstandings that need to be resolved before you begin work. It's better to get the details straight now, rather than after you have started work and turned away other potential employers. (See Figure 8.8 for an example of an acceptance letter.)

Interviews

Jobs are won with interviews. The employer has reviewed your written materials and determined that you are worth consideration. Meanwhile, you are still considering different employers and have now agreed to invest more time and effort in winning an offer from a particular firm.

Most successful interviews proceed in three stages: dance, substance, and decision. You should be ready to do your part to promote useful exchanges through each stage.

THE "DANCE" STAGE

The "dance" stage of the interview has the interviewer and candidate search for common ground. This stage may be skipped, if, for example, the interview is actually a pre-screening campus session designed to make sure you are worth a serious look. However, typical interviews, in which the employer is trying to make up the company's mind about a possible job offer, usually begin with this informal feeling-out to see who you are.

The conversation could be based upon the activities section of your resume, about sports, the weather, the latest clothing styles, where you are from, or what you experienced in London on your semester abroad. The objectives of this stage are to highlight your personality, and to see how well you make conversation under pressure. While it may seem inconsequential at first glance, this is a vital phase because it lays the foundation for what follows. If you can strike a common chord, your comfort level and effectiveness should be enhanced.

THE SUBSTANCE STAGE

This stage is your opportunity to articulate what you know, what your potential is, how you are likely to assist this firm, and why you should be selected before other competing candidates. While the interviewer may ask some specific questions, he or she will generally give you opportunity to chronicle your academic and work experience and to highlight your accomplishments. Think of this recitation as a carefully crafted essay (success essay), covering those topics that open doors to accounts of your successes.

If you are expected to meet certain basic requirements (i.e., receive a bachelor's degree), don't make a big deal about meeting such criteria. On the other hand, have one or two associated areas of accomplishment ready to deliver:

> While I was completing my bachelor's degree, I worked at the university's computer lab. This gave me hands-on experience in understanding customer software problems and in dealing one-on-one with struggling students. For example, I helped students to learn updated versions of university software.

While you don't want to simply repeat your resume, do emphasize those accomplishments that match important employer requirements. Having examples ready to deliver is a key part of this process. Don't just say, "I'm a people person." Instead, say, " I really enjoy working with people. When I sold clothes at a local men's shop over the summer, I won the employee-of-the-month award for more than satisfying most of my customers."

A good interviewer should allow you the freedom to cover *your* topics, but will also probe into other areas important to the firm, but not covered by your resume:

> When you were working at the University's computer lab, what type of hardware and computer languages were involved?
>
> Although I'm sure you would eventually get around to it, let's spend a little time now to talk about your coursework in statistical methods.

If the interview shifts to a topic that is unfamiliar or difficult to explore, try to stay relaxed. The interviewer may simply be assessing your ability to stay cool under pressure. Provide honest information, and don't hesitate to offer to review the area of inquiry and provide supplemental information after the interview:

> I really enjoyed the two semesters of statistics, but it's been over two years since I completed this requirement. I'd be glad to review the course outlines and my notes to provide you with a more comprehensive list of topics covered.

Be prepared for one or more open-ended questions during the substance phase of the interview. Common inquiries include: Tell me about yourself. What do you look for in a supervisor? Why are you interested in our company? What can you do for our company? What motivates you? What are your weaknesses? How would you define success on the job? What is your "ideal" job?

THE DECISION STAGE

This stage usually begins with the interviewer asking for questions *you* may have. It is very important that you have two or three questions ready to go. Of course, the questions you have will depend upon what has already been addressed in the interview. But your ability to clarify issues or raise relevant areas that have not yet been covered reflects well on your abilities. For instance, you might investigate the job's travel requirements: "I know this position involves some travel. Can you tell me how many weeks during the year that I would be in travel status?"

This final interview stage should provide you with some idea of your status as a job candidate. If the interviewer has the authority, and is convinced that you are right for the job, he may make an offer. Before you decide to accept or reject the offer, get all the relevant details:

- What are the tasks involved?
- For whom would you be working?
- What are the job's salary and benefits? (Make sure that you don't provide the interviewer with *your* salary expectations *before* you are informed of the usual salary range. If the job normally pays $35,000 to $38,000 per year, and you indicate that your expectations are $35,000, you have probably lost $3,000 by providing that information.)
- What are the promotional opportunities?
- What kind of support staff will be made available?
- What equipment will be made available?
- What are the usual hours worked per week?
- What vacation time is provided?
- What office accommodations will be provided?
- What other perks (e.g., stock options, etc.) are made available?

Find out how long you have to consider the offer. Don't be in a hurry to accept—wait until you have thought through all the implications.

If the interviewer indicates that you will be contacted soon regarding a possible second interview, stay optimistic. Tell the interviewer that as long as you are still considering alternative opportunities, you would be glad to participate in a second session.

As the company is weighing your qualifications, you should be assessing that firm. Are the people you have met the type of people with whom you would like to work? Do the offices reflect a sound structure that is organized and well managed? Is the employment offer being discussed consistent with your capabilities and target living standard?

If you become convinced that the firm is not for you under any circumstances, don't waste your time and energy with future contact. Simply revise your "thanks-for-the-opportunity" letter to thank the firm for its interest, and indicate that you are pursuing other opportunities.

If the interviewer indicates that you will not be considered further, maintain your demeanor and provide sincere thanks for their interest in you. If you have established a good rapport with the interviewer, you may inquire as to any skills or qualifications lacking which would have improved your chances. However, since you rarely know for sure why you are not selected, weigh such information carefully before you take any remedial action.

Sample self-inventory (accomplishments). **FIGURE 8.1**

University Tour Guide, 1997–98

Tour Guide Coordinator, 1998–99

Due to graduate Cum Laude, May 1999

Elected to Student Senate, 1998–99

Appointed Student Representative on Search Committee for New Dean of the Psychology Department, 1999

Dean's List, 1998—99

Women's Intramural Golf, 1996

Major: Psychology; Minor: Business Studies

Work-Study Program, Telephone Co. Marketing Dept., 1997–99

Senior Research Project: Psychological Aspects of Marketing Quality

Member: Pi Beta Phi, 1996–99; Social Chair, 1997–98

Semester Abroad, London, Spring 1998

Employer requirements assessment. **FIGURE 8.2**

Target: Entry Level Marketing Position

Bachelor of Science degree with business major or minor

Easily learn and apply new computer systems

Skilled in written and oral communications

Experience within a business environment

Adaptable to change, travel, long hours

Mathematical, statistical, and analytical skills

Interpret technical information

Potential to generate innovative sales ideas

Loyalty to the organization

Sample accomplishment–requirement match. **FIGURE 8.3**

REQUIREMENT	ACCOMPLISHMENT
BS, Business	BS, Business Minor
Computer Applications	Word; GBSTAT
Oral Communications	Tour Guide; Student Senate
Written Communications	Quality Research Report
Business Familiarity	Work-Study program
Adaptability	London; Pi Beta Phi
Analysis, Statistics	Research project
Innovation	Tour Guide Scheduling
Loyalty	Dean, Search Committee

FIGURE 8.4 Sample cover letter.

28 Lawrenceville Road
Lawrenceville, NJ 08618
(609) 555-6868
jensenior@bol.com

April 3, 1999

Mr. James Hart
Director of Marketing
National Management Systems
85 Prince Street
Philadelphia, PA 07612

Dear Mr. Hart:

My education in psychology and business studies and my work-study experience prepared me well for a National Management Systems (NMS) entry-level marketing position.

Development of my Senior Research Project, "The Psychological Aspects of Marketing Quality," and skills developed through my work-study marketing position should allow me to contribute to NMS' plans for expanded marketing campaigns. For example, I utilized GBSTAT software to analyze trends in telephone marketing.

My strong interest and experience studying and working in business marketing have provided me with a realistic perspective of today's marketing environment. I hope to apply what I have learned within an innovative firm such as NMS.

Please review the enclosed resume and call to schedule an interview for me. I may be reached during the morning hours at (609) 555-6868, or you may contact me through my e-mail address, jensenior@bol.com. Thank you for your consideration.

Sincerely,

Jennifer Simms

Enc. resume

JENNIFER SIMMS

School Address:
28 Lawrenceville Road
Lawrenceville, NJ 08618
(609) 555-6868
jensenior@bol.com

Permanent Address:
33 Elwood Drive
Yardly, PA 23064
(205) 555-4491
jensenior@bol.com

Professional Objective

An entry-level marketing position that fully utilizes my education and experience.

Education

Bachelor of Science, Rider University, May 1999.
GPA: 3.4. Will Graduate Cum Laude. Deans List: 1998–99.
Major: Psychology; Minor: Business Studies.
   * Appointed student representative to Dean of Psychology Search Committee.
   * Senior Research Project: "Psychological Aspects of Marketing Quality."
   * Gained analytical skills through statistical methods and software use.

Work Experience

AT&C, University Work-Study Program, Marketing Aide, 1997–99.
   * Utilized GBSTAT to analyze local trends in telephone marketing.

University Tour Guide, 1997–98; Tour Guide Coordinator, 1998–99.
   * Based tour guide scheduling on analysis of attendance over 3-year period.

Yardly YMCA Summer Camp Counselor and Lifeguard, 1996–98.

Activities

Student Senate, 1998–99.
   *   Chaired Public Relations Committee. Led campaign to increase student community involvement.

Semester Abroad, London, 1998.
   *   Prepared research paper on European marketing practices in the 1980s.

Pi Beta Phi Social Chair, 1997–98; Member 1996–99.
   *   Led Social Committee to plan and organize annual social events.

Women's Intramural Golf, 1996.

FIGURE 8.6 Sample resume follow-up letter.

28 Lawrenceville Road
Lawrenceville, NJ 08618
(609) 555-6868
jensenior@bol.com

April 24, 1999

Mr. James Hart
Director of Marketing
National Management Systems
85 Prince Street
Philadelphia, PA 07612

Dear Mr. Hart:

The experience I've gained through Rider University's work-study program, my senior project on marketing quality, participation in the Student Senate, and as the University's Tour Guide Coordinator demonstrates an ability to work hard and get results. I believe I possess significant potential to make meaningful contributions to an innovative marketing staff, such as the NMS marketing team.

I would appreciate the opportunity to discuss my qualifications further through a personal interview. Please call (609) 555-6868, or contact me through my e-mail address, jensenior@bol.com, to schedule an interview.

Thank you for your consideration.

Sincerely,

Jennifer Simms

Enc. resume

28 Lawrenceville Road
Lawrenceville, NJ 08618
(609) 555-6868
jensenior@bol.com

May 10, 1999

Mr. James Hart
Director of Marketing
National Management Systems
85 Prince Street
Philadelphia, PA 07612

Dear Mr. Hart:

Thank you for the interview opportunity. I really enjoyed meeting you and Marketing Team Supervisor Flynn, and learning about National Management Systems' marketing practices and plans. I appreciated the chance to describe my quaiifications and career goals.

   Although you indicated that NMS would not now be interested in employing me in an entry-level position, I remain optimistic that I will locate the right position soon.

   Thanks again for your consideration.

Sincerely,

Jennifer Simms

FIGURE 8.8 Sample employment acceptance letter.

28 Lawrenceville Road
Lawrenceville, NJ 08618
(609) 555-6868
jensenior@bol.com

May 23, 1999

Mr. James Hart
Director of Marketing
National Management Systems
85 Prince Street
Philadelphia, PA 07612

Dear Mr. Hart:

I was surprised and gratified to learn that NMS has now decided to offer me the entry-level position of Marketing Assistant. I am pleased to accept your offer.

Based upon our telephone conversation yesterday, my starting salary will be $31,000, plus the full NMS benefit package, and two weeks vacation leave for the first year. My start date will be July 17. I understand that written confirmation of this offer, as well as information on salary and benefit details, will be mailed to me in a few days.

Thank you again for providing me with this opportunity. I look forward to joining the NMS Marketing Team.

Sincerely,

Jennifer Simms

Data-Speak

TARGETING PROSPECTIVE EMPLOYERS

Use the *Employment Opportunity Database* to determine which industries and areas employ large numbers of workers in an occupation of interest. Then use *America's Career InfoNet* to identify specific employers.

This Data-Speak exercise focuses on obtaining the names, addresses, and telephone numbers of employers to target for job search activities. The purpose is to expand the universe of employers beyond those with advertised job openings. Most jobs are never advertised, but are filled through word of mouth.

Information from two *Employment Opportunity* screens helps you link your chosen occupation with employers who hire workers in that occupation in selected areas. You may identify relevant employers by linking an occupation to associated industries and areas via the *Employment Opportunity Database.*

After you have chosen an occupation, use the first screen in the *Employment Opportunity Database,* Chapter 8 (Chapter 3's *Employment by Area and Industry*) to select industries that include significant employment in that occupation. Under *Economic Areas,* select *Region & Economic Area* (the top heading on the left screen). Next, select the occupation of interest from the top right screen. Displayed in the bottom right screen is the U. S. total employment for the selected occupation by industry, 1996 and projected to 2006. Now, select industries of interest that include significant employment in the subject occupation. To obtain estimates of employment for particular geographic areas of interest for that occupation and industry, select these areas from the left screen of this display.

The Chapter 8 second screen (Chapter 2's *Employment by Industry*) provides information on industry employment by area. Select the industry of interest from the top screen. Then, select those areas below that reflect significant employment totals.

Record the industries and areas selected for the subject occupation on Data-Speak Worksheet 8.A.

Using the industries and areas selected above, enter the WWW site for America's Career InfoNet (http://www.acinet.org/acinet/). Select *Employers* and then *Industry and Local Area Search.* Follow these directions to narrow your search criteria to the specific industries and areas of interest:

1. Select the general industry that applies (e.g., *Services* for Business Services) and click on *Search.* (You may want to consult Appendix B or the *Employment Opportunity Database,* Chapter 2, Industry Titles, for assistance.)
2. Select the applicable state (*New York* for Binghamton) and *Search.*
3. Select a more specific industry *(Business Services)* and the area of interest within the state *(Binghamton),* and *Search.*
4. Select the city of most interest within the area (e.g., *Endicott*) and *Search.*
5. Select the specific industry *(Computer Programming Services)* and *Search.*
6. Select employer names of interest to obtain the applicable street address, telephone number, business description, and related information. Additional

information about these employers may be obtained from Job Service One-Stop Centers and through library research of employer databases, such as Dunn and Bradstreet reports.

Supplement this information with employer job listings for the subject occupation. Be sure to utilize Internet websites devoted to job search, such as Careerpath.com, Monster.com, and America's Job Bank (http://www.ajb.org/). Once you have identified additional employers, enter this information on (or attach it to) Data-Speak Worksheet 8.A. **At the same time, be sure to take advantage of opportunities to list your resume on appropriate sites.**

Career Inquiry
DEVELOPING MATERIALS FOR YOUR JOB SEARCH

1. For selected employers identified in this chapter's Data-Speak task, develop your three building blocks to employer contact: self-inventory, employer requirements assessment, and accomplishments–requirements match. Record the information developed on Career Inquiry Worksheets 8.A, 8.B, and 8.C. (If you are close or ready to initiate your job search, record actual information in your self-inventory and accomplishments–requirements match. However, if you are more than a year from this point, enter information that reflects anticipated accomplishments.)

2. For the job search described in No. 1, prepare your cover letter, resume, resume follow-up letter, thanks-for-the-opportunity transmittal, and employment acceptance letter. These written materials should be recorded in Career Inquiry Worksheets 8.D–8.H.

3. Prepare your interview essay, corresponding to the above job search, and record the essay on Career Inquiry Worksheet 8.I.

DATA-SPEAK WORKSHEET 8.A

TARGET EMPLOYERS

Selected Occupation: _____

Industries with Significant Employment:

Selected Industry: _____

Economic Areas with Significant Employment:

Selected Economic Area: _____

Employers within Industry and Area:

Employers listing corresponding job vacancies:

Accomplishments

School and Activities

Skills and Abilities

Work Experience

Worker Characteristics

Other

CAREER INQUIRY WORKSHEET 8.B
BUILDING BLOCK: EMPLOYER REQUIREMENTS ASSESSMENT

Education

Skills and Abilities

Work Experience

Worker Characteristics

Other

CAREER INQUIRY WORKSHEET 8.C
BUILDING BLOCK: ACCOMPLISHMENTS–REQUIREMENTS MATCH

SELECTED REQUIREMENTS   SELECTED ACCOMPLISHMENTS

Education and Activities

Skills and Abilities

Work Experience

Worker Characteristics

Other

CAREER INQUIRY WORKSHEET 8.D
JOB SEARCH TOOL: COVER LETTER

CAREER INQUIRY   WORKSHEET 8.E
JOB SEARCH TOOL: RESUME

CAREER INQUIRY WORKSHEET 8.F
JOB SEARCH TOOL: RESUME FOLLOW-UP LETTER

CAREER INQUIRY WORKSHEET 8.G
JOB SEARCH TOOL: OPPORTUNITY LETTER

CAREER INQUIRY WORKSHEET 8.H

JOB SEARCH TOOL: EMPLOYMENT ACCEPTANCE LETTER

CAREER INQUIRY WORKSHEET 8.1
JOB SEARCH TOOL: JOB INTERVIEW ESSAY

Planning for Fulfilled Employment

Ten steps to develop a comprehensive career/job search plan.

Overview

LEARNING OBJECTIVES

- Review and consider knowledge and competencies gained through the *Employment Opportunity System.*
- Identify and understand the composition of each step of the *Employment Opportunity* planning process.
- Verify your occupational choice.
- Screen your selected occupations against the Guidance Keys.
- Identify and evaluate relevant industries and areas.
- Screen your selected occupations against the Economic Keys.
- Assess education and training requirements, aptitudes, and General Investment Opportunities.
- Assess the rewards of occupations selected.
- Make your occupational choice.
- Make investments in your human capital.
- Develop job search materials and interview techniques.
- Identify target employers.
- Initiate job search activities.
- Stay current regarding forces that may impact your career.

EMPLOYMENT OPPORTUNITY PLANNING

Review and update information you generated through *Employment Opportunity* Data-Speak and Career Inquiry tasks to construct a comprehensive

159

career/job search plan. Utilize your new knowledge and competencies to find fulfilled employment.

Setting the Stage
REVIEWING AND APPLYING KNOWLEDGE YOU HAVE GAINED

Completing *Employment Opportunity* Chapters 1–8, you have learned much about the forces that shape success and failure in the world of careers. In Chapters 1 and 2, you explored the two sides of careers. In Chapter 1, you delved into the emotional side of careers, uncovering the forces of personality, values, interests and attitudes, aptitudes and abilities, and stage of development. In addition, you surveyed the influence of genetics, gender, and childhood environment, and considered the impact of self-concept and motivation. You then utilized the Interest Checklist to begin identifying your career interests, and constructed a Career Genogram to weigh the impact of your family's educational and occupational profile.

In Chapter 2, you took a crash course in the economics of careers, and you explored the *Employment Opportunity Database* to learn about industries important to the nation and of interest to you. You conducted research to learn about the impact of technology, labor markets, and the business cycle.

Chapter 3 focused on labor markets, the site where human feelings and economic reality meet. You reviewed the four stages of market operations: development of labor, job search, employment, and disemployment, and reviewed the specialization of labor in occupations. In this chapter's Data-Speak exercises, you utilized the *Employment Opportunity Database Warehouse* to study the labor market for occupations of interest, including trends by area, industry, and for the nation. You then began building a bank of occupational information relevant to your needs, surveyed your human capital, and explored job search experiences.

In Chapters 4 and 5, you became aware of guidance and economic keys that match people and occupational opportunities by understanding the importance of individual characteristics and the economic environment. In that connection, you used the *Employment Opportunity Database, Guide for Occupational Exploration* to see which occupations appear to meet your individual needs, and obtained economic profiles for these occupations.

Your Career Inquiry research provided you the opportunity to explore your socioeconomic standing and desires. You also contrasted your personality type with the personalities usually compatible with your occupations of interest, and you examined your stage of career development and utilized career decision-making steps. In addition, you ranked the economic profiles you obtained for your occupations of interest.

Chapters 6 and 7 provided you with principles to maximize your income and your value to employers (human capital). The *Employment Opportunity Database* furnished you with information on the living standard category and salary of selected occupations, and the average annual expenditures of each living standard group for the necessities of life. You then adjusted those expenditures for the cost of living in your current area of residence, and for Career Inquiry research, found out what you can buy for such expenditures. Career Inquiry exercises also called on you to explore application of Chapter 6's Career Income Principles. Chapter 7's Data-Speak focused on investments in education and training you must make in order to qualify for careers in which you are interested. Career Inquiry tasks applied principles of income maximization and designed plans to acquire education, training, and general investment skills associated with various occupations.

In Chapter 8, you focused on dealing with employers, how they may be contacted, processes to develop job search materials, and the conduct of positive employment interviews. You used the *Employment Opportunity Database* and the Internet's *America's Career Infonet* to identify employers likely to have openings in selected occupations, industries, and areas. Career Inquiry provided an opportunity to apply techniques described to develop written job search and interview materials.

Having all this new knowledge greatly enhances your understanding of careers and what you need to do to reach fulfilled employment. Now, *Employment Opportunity* provides you with a comprehensive framework to directly apply what you have learned. Follow the steps listed below, and enter the resulting information in the Planning Worksheets provided at the end of this chapter. For the most part, you will be utilizing or updating information already developed for the Data-Speak and Career Inquiry tasks of previous chapters.

Ten Steps To Fulfilled Employment

STEP 1: Verify Your Occupational Choice

Return to the *Guide for Occupational Exploration* (Chapter 4). Knowing what you now know about yourself and the world of careers, once again travel through the Data-Speak and Career Inquiry tasks to update your choice of occupations that appear to meet your needs and reflect your abilities. Compile a list of Interest Areas, Work Groups, and Occupations on Planning Worksheet 9.A.

STEP 2: Screen Your Selected Occupations Against the Guidance Keys

Review the Data-Speak and Career Inquiry Worksheets from Chapter 4. Screen each selected occupation and your own abilities against the Guidance Keys discussed in Chapter 4. How do the occupations you selected measure up relative to your social aspirations, personality, stage of development, and decision-making process? If any of the occupations selected are not a good fit, you may want to reconsider those occupations. Assess your own stage of development and level of decision-making skills. Keep an open mind in evaluating your own situation. When in doubt, seek objective information and advice from a qualified career counselor or other appropriate professional and then rework your analysis. Record the results on Planning Worksheet 9.B.

STEP 3: Identify and Evaluate Relevant Industries and Areas

Review Data-Speak and Career Inquiry Worksheets from Chapters 2 and 3. Determine the industries and geographic areas that account for the greatest share of employment in the occupations of interest. (Chapter 3's *Employment Opportunity Database* section provides easy procedures to develop this information.) If there are selected industries or economic areas that compose a relatively high proportion of total employment, you need to learn more about them.

Do firms that compose the industries in question (e.g., business services/computer programmers) appear to provide the types of environments in which you would be comfortable? (Detailed industries may be found within the *Employment Opportunity Database*, as described at the end of Chapter 2.) Review Chapter 2 References, visit some of these firms, talk to employees in the occupations of interest, and form an objective opinion. If you are still in school, try to get summer employment in an industry of interest.

Do geographic areas that contain high concentrations of occupational employment (e.g., New York City's Broadway for live stage shows) appeal to you? Don't dismiss an area based on what you have heard from others. Visit the area yourself. Spend some time there and see if the lifestyle lived by those in occupations being considered appeals to you.

Of course, you may be able to find employment in an industry or area other than those that represent large proportions of workers in the occupation in question. If this is your preference, you need to take specific measures to target your occupational preparation and job search. After you have concluded this investigation, record your target industries and areas on Planning Worksheet 9.C.

STEP 4: Screen Your Selected Occupations Against the Economic Keys

Assemble new or updated (where possible) Economic Profiles for the occupations you selected (Chapter 5). (Note that the *Employment Opportunity Database* is updated annually.) What are the corresponding levels of compensation, the strength of demand, the degree of internalization, and the likely level of productivity workers bring to the job? Are there any government policies, global developments, or technological advances that will affect the attractiveness of any of the occupations you have selected? Are the industries or geographic areas that represent large proportions of occupational employment experiencing economic trends that might impact your employment?

Analyze these trends and developments, and where appropriate, devise strategies to maximize your employment prospects. For example, if the data uncover an Economic Area experiencing sharp growth in your selected occupation, you may decide to direct much of your job search activities to employers in that area. On the other hand, if you found out that the occupation you selected is expected to experience severe employment loss, you may want to acquire certain skills that help to insulate you from the downturn and improve your chances of employment, or you may decide to explore alternative occupations.

After gathering the relevant information, record your findings, the required action, and strategies on the two parts of Planning Worksheet 9.D.

STEP 5: Assess Education and Training Requirements, Aptitudes, and General Investment Opportunities

Review Chapter 7 Data-Speak and Career Inquiry Worksheets. For new occupations selected, obtain information on the education, training, and aptitude requirements of each. You may find such information in Chapter 7's Data-Speak section, Assess Education and Training Requirements. Specifically, it indicates the occupational level of education (i.e., high school diploma; some college, but no degree; associate degree; bachelor's degree; master's degree; doctoral degree; and professional degree) and training (i.e., work experience in a related occupation; short-term on-the-job training (OJT); moderate term OJT; and long-term OJT. Also provided are aptitude information concerning data, people, and things; reasoning, math, and language; and training time required to reach journeyworker status. This information corresponds to the more detailed *DOT* occupations. Record your findings on Planning Worksheet 9.E(1).

Before you settle on an occupation, be sure that you can meet these requirements. If you are well below the specified levels, believe that you will have difficulty measuring up, or feel that the time required would be excessive, don't force the issue. . . select an alternative occupation. Of course, there may be one or two requirements that may call for extra effort on your part. If you are willing to take additional courses and work longer than usual hours and the occupation in question is that important to you, don't be dissuaded. But, as a general rule, if you don't have the natural aptitudes to do well enough in more than one of these areas, you will probably be happier and more successful in an occupation for which you are better suited.

Gather information on the content and cost of the curriculums covered by the required occupational preparation. Consider the cost of tuition, room and board (above what you would be spending anyway), books, and related expenses, as well as the lost income as you remain in school or in training. Then compute the extra income you are likely to earn that would be derived from the education/training you are considering (the difference between your likely annual income with and without the program you are considering, times your number of years working).

After you have had a chance to obtain and review relevant materials, make an appointment to visit with staff who offer quality programs in the curriculums of interest. Discuss curriculum content and requirements. Sit in a few classes, and ask yourself how enthusiastic you would be spending years of your life dedicated to such study. Talk with the students and determine if they represent compatible classmates. If you have serious concerns that the education or training requirements are not right for you, drop the questionable occupation, scrutinize another of your selections, or go back to Step 1 to generate another choice. Record your findings and plans on Planning Worksheet 9.E(2).

For each of the selected occupations, generate ideas to meet the seven General Investment Keys defined in Chapter 7: learn to learn; communicate and collaborate; capitalize and computerize; imagine, analyze, and act; evaluate; push quality; and push efficiency. These ideas should also be recorded on Planning Worksheet 9.E(3).

STEP 6: Assess the Rewards of Occupations Selected

Review Chapter 6 Data-Speak and Career Inquiry Worksheets and the procedures used to produce them. Return to *Employment Opportunity Database—Occupational Living Standards*—and Appendices F and G, and once again consider the standard of living that meets your needs. Of course, we would all like to be millionaires. However, the point of this planning section is to identify the income level that will satisfy you . . . make you feel that your investments in human capital have paid off. Now, see if the income usually provided by your selected occupations will support an acceptable standard of living. While it's not feasible to quantify, also describe and consider the non-monetary rewards you deem likely from practice in a chosen occupation. What is the depth of satisfaction that you will feel from performing the mission of that job? If the rewards don't measure up, once again, drop the questionable occupation and replace it with a better fit. Document this process on Planning Worksheet 9.F(1–5).

With your selected occupations in mind, return to Chapter 6 and review the Career Income Principles relative to your occupational choices. Also, consider these principles and how they may impact your path to fulfilled employment. Record your ideas on the appropriate section of Planning Worksheet 9.F(6).

STEP 7: Make Your Occupational Choice

Review all of the above information and make your final occupational choice. If you are still in school, you may have the luxury of a broader scope of occupations, which you can eventually narrow. If you are currently employed (or unemployed), or near graduation, closing in on one occupation makes more sense. However, regardless of your current status, this step requires that you narrow your choice to one occupation.

Record the general occupational title selected, a brief description, and any related *DOT* title of choice on Planning Worksheet 9.G.

STEP 8: Make Investments in Your Human Capital

Now that you have selected and successfully screened occupations that are likely to form the basis of your career, it's time to draw a path from your current position to an appropriate job. This begins with investing in your stock, i.e., obtaining the education and training that will make you attractive to productivity-conscious employers. You have already identified the investments required and investigated alternatives. Therefore, selecting the educational or training facilities and/or program of study you will enter is the next major task.

Be sure that the appropriate preparation is offered. If it isn't, investigate alternative programs that might be available to you, or other ways to supplement your education. This may be achieved by taking courses from other institutions, through extracurricular activities, or through school-to-work opportunities.

The choice of the right program can be vital to your effort to reach fulfilled employment. For some career fields, graduating from a well-respected program means affluent summer internships, signing bonuses, and very high starting salaries and benefits. On the other hand, graduating from a mediocre program can mean unemployment and frustration. Be sure that you know the implications of alternative choices. When investigating, obtain information on the employment success rate of graduates in your field.

Regardless of curriculum requirements, be sure that the right investments are made. For example, if the school does not require calculus, but you know that most employers in the selected field would prefer that you complete the basic course in calculus, take the coursework that employers prefer.

The best way to develop sensitivity to employer likes and dislikes is to work. Make extra efforts to enter either formal or informal co-op programs. They greatly enhance your employability, and often result in permanent job offers from the firms with which you are "temporarily" employed.

Record your program choices, including final general investment plans, on Planning Worksheet 9.H(1–2).

STEP 9: Develop Job Search
Materials and Interview Techniques

A couple of months before you are ready to begin your job search, begin developing materials and honing your interview skills to convince prospective employers of your worth. Your main objective is to show employers that if they invest in you, there is a high probability that such investments will pay off. Remember, you know more about you than anyone else. Take advantage of this information inequality by presenting your characteristics and accomplishments in an honest and effective manner. Enlist those professors, employers, and others who know you well and would be willing to write excellent recommendations. Develop a networking strategy, identifying individuals who may be able to assist your job search. Let them know of your availability, goals, and qualifications. Team up with fellow students and jobseekers, review draft materials, and role play simulated interviews. Finalize your job search building blocks and materials (Chapter 8), and record them on Planning Worksheet 9.I(1–8).

STEP 10: Identify Target Employers and Initiate Job Search Using America's Career InfoNet

When you are ready to initiate your job search, return to *Employment Opportunity Database* (Chapter 8 Data-Speak), to obtain a listing of those industries and areas that employ workers in the occupation for which you are seeking employment. Now, generate a listing of employers (names, addresses, and phone numbers) in those industries, in the geographic areas that are of interest to you. Record this list on Employment Opportunity Planning Worksheet 9.J.

Once you have assembled a comprehensive employer listing, begin your job search initiative on several fronts: (a) Initiate your networking strategy, contacting all those who may advance your job search; (b) enter your resume in all suitable automated talent banks (for example, America's Talent Bank, at http://atb.mesc.state.mi.us/atb/); (c) mail cover letters and resumes to all promising employers; (d) a few weeks after resume transmittal, call and/or write selected company contacts or human resource staff and seek interviews; (e) make extensive efforts (over and above your networking plan) to connect with respected employees of the listed firms, or friends or business acquaintances of staff (don't hesitate to develop connections through your friends and/or relatives; note that at some firms, those who make referrals that result in new hires are rewarded with significant bonuses); and (f) respond directly to appropriate job openings listed in want ads, computer directories on the Internet, and other sources, such as those prospects provided through college job fairs.

Because most employers consider seriously the significant expenditures they have to make to bring new hires on board and up to speed, it is routine for interested firms to require two or three interviews of those candidates in the running. Stay patient and optimistic as the process proceeds.

Be sure to thoroughly investigate those employers that may make you an offer. Just as you have an information advantage concerning your qualifications, the firm knows much more than you do about its financial health and working conditions. Seek to minimize this advantage by reviewing annual financial reports and relevant trade literature, and by speaking to current employees.

When the offers begin coming in, consider them carefully, relative to the minimum standard of living you have expressed. Scrutinize the work for which you will be initially responsible, and try to determine the career path and likely timing of your progress within the firm.

When you accept the best offer, you are on your way to fulfilled employment. However, keep in mind that most workers have over a dozen jobs in their employment lifetime. So . . . keep *Employment Opportunity* close by. More current information may be obtained from annually updated versions of the *Employment Opportunity Database* and by utilizing the *Employment Opportunity Website* News Service at http://www.prenhall.com/success/Moss.

STEP 1
EMPLOYMENT OPPORTUNITY PLANNING WORKSHEET 9.A

Selected Interest Areas, Work Groups, & Occupations

Interest Area:

Work Group:

Occupation:

General:

Detailed:

Interest Area:

Work Group:

Occupation:

General:

Detailed:

Interest Area:

Work Group:

Occupation:

General:

Detailed:

STEP 2

EMPLOYMENT OPPORTUNITY PLANNING WORKSHEET 9.B

Guidance Key Screening

Occupation _____

	Adequate	Not Adequate
Social Aspirations		
Personality		
Stage of Development		
Level of Decision-Making Skills		

Occupation: _____

	Adequate	Not Adequate
Social Aspirations		
Personality		
Stage of Development		
Level of Decision-Making Skills		

Occupation: _____

	Adequate	Not Adequate
Social Aspirations		
Personality		
Stage of Development		
Level of Decision-Making Skills		

STEP 3
EMPLOYMENT OPPORTUNITY PLANNING WORKSHEET 9.C

Target Industries and Areas

Occupation _____

Environment

	Adequate	Not Adequate

Industry Concentrations

_____

_____

_____

_____

Area Concentrations

_____

_____

_____

_____

Other Industries or Areas

_____

_____

_____

_____

STEP 4

EMPLOYMENT OPPORTUNITY PLANNING WORKSHEET 9.D(1)

Economic Profiles

Occupation Title and Code: _____

Compensation Key

    Annual Salary _____

    Rank _____

Supply–Demand Key

    Employment Change 1996–2006

        Number/Rank _____

        Percent/Rank _____

    New Entrants Needed per Year

        Number/Rank _____

Internalization Key

    Total Replacement Rate _____

    Internal Market Strength _____

Productivity Key

    Occupational Unemployment Rate _____

    Productivity Strength _____

Required Action:

(continued)

WORKSHEET 9.D(2)
CONTINUED

	ANTICIPATED DEVELOPMENTS	STRATEGY TO PURSUE
Government		
Policies		
Global		
Technological		
Industry		
Area		

STEP 5

EMPLOYMENT OPPORTUNITY PLANNING WORKSHEET 9.E(1)

Education, Training, and Aptitude Requirements,
General Investment Opportunities, and Related Plans

Occupational Title and Code: _____

Education and Training Categories: _____

    DOT Occupation: _____

    Aptitudes:

        Data _____ People _____ Things _____

        Reasoning _____ Math _____ Language _____

        Training Time to Average Performance _____

Occupational Title and Code: _____

Education and Training Categories: _____

    DOT Occupation: _____

    Aptitudes:

        Data _____ People _____ Things _____

        Reasoning _____ Math _____ Language _____

        Training Time to Average Performance _____

Occupational Title and Code: _____

Education and Training Categories: _____

    DOT Occupation: _____

    Aptitudes:

        Data _____ People _____ Things _____

        Reasoning _____ Math _____ Language _____

        Training Time to Average Performance _____

(continued)

WORKSHEET 9.E(2)
CONTINUED

Curriculum Program Review

Description of content:

Time to complete:

Cost:

    Tuition:

    Room and board:

    Books:

    Other expenses:

    Income loss while in school:

Extra income derived from program completion:

On-site program evaluation:

    Curriculum content/requirements:

    Staff:

    Students:

(continued)

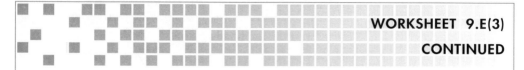

Application of General Investment Skills

1. Learn to learn:

   Current level of accomplishment:

   Ideas for enhancement:

2. Communicate and collaborate:

   Current level of accomplishment:

   Ideas for enhancement:

3. Capitalize and computerize:

   Current level of accomplishment:

   Ideas for enhancement:

4. Imagine, analyze, and act:

   Current level of accomplishment:

   Ideas for enhancement:

5. Evaluate:

   Current level of accomplishment:

   Ideas for enhancement:

6. Push quality:

   Current level of accomplishment:

   Ideas for enhancement:

7. Push efficiency:

   Current level of accomplishment:

   Ideas for enhancement:

STEP 6
EMPLOYMENT OPPORTUNITY PLANNING WORKSHEET 9.F(1)

Career Rewards

Occupational Living Standards

OCCUPATIONAL TITLE	LIVING STANDARD CATEGORY	AVERAGE ANNUAL CATEGORY
1.		
2.		
3.		
4.		
5.		
6.		
7.		

(continued)

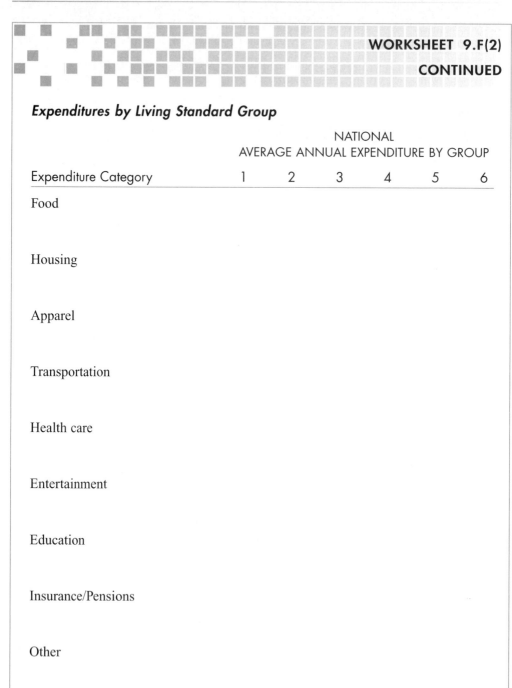

(continued)

WORKSHEET 9.F(3)
CONTINUED

Expenditures by Living Standard Group

AREA OF RESIDENCE
AVERAGE ANNUAL EXPENDITURE BY GROUP

Expenditure Category	1	2	3	4	5	6
Food						
Housing						
Apparel						
Transportation						
Health care						
Entertainment						
Education						
Insurance/Pensions						
Other						

(continued)

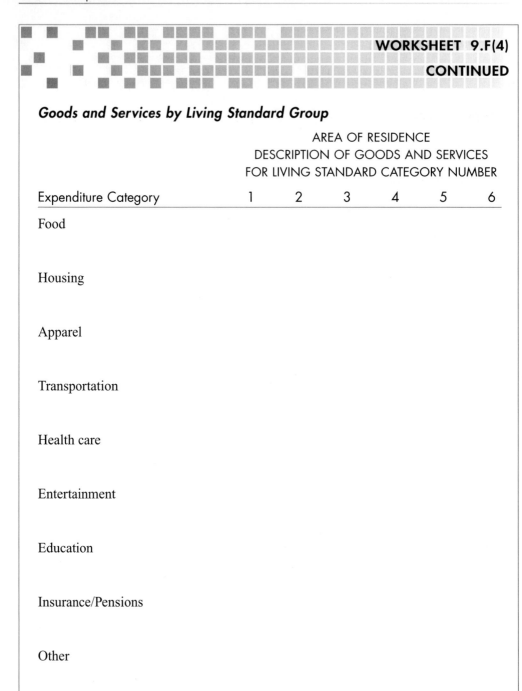

WORKSHEET 9.F(4)
CONTINUED

Goods and Services by Living Standard Group

AREA OF RESIDENCE
DESCRIPTION OF GOODS AND SERVICES
FOR LIVING STANDARD CATEGORY NUMBER

Expenditure Category	1	2	3	4	5	6
Food						
Housing						
Apparel						
Transportation						
Health care						
Entertainment						
Education						
Insurance/Pensions						
Other						

(continued)

WORKSHEET 9.F(5)
CONTINUED

Personal Satisfaction

Work Environment:

Work Mission:

Staff:

Clients:

Other:

(continued)

Application of Career Income Principles

1. Little correlation between devotion and dollars.

2. Disagreeable jobs require no less effort and pay no more.

3. Strong correlation between directed education and training, and income.

4. Asymmetry of information requires effective communications and perceptive investigation.

5. Pay for performance requires trust in your company.

6. Moral hazard jeopardizes your pay and security.

7. Don't interrupt your momentum to higher-paying positions.

8. Fair compensation may take many forms.

9. Income opportunities are maximized in High Density Career Areas.

10. Ride a star to the top.

STEP 7
EMPLOYMENT OPPORTUNITY PLANNING WORKSHEET 9.G

Selected Occupation

Occupation Title:

    General: _____

    DOT: _____

Occupation Description:

STEP 8
EMPLOYMENT OPPORTUNITY PLANNING WORKSHEET 9.H(1)

Education–Training Program Selection

Institution Selected:

Program Title and Description:

Work Experience Plans:

    Employer:

    Job Content:

(continued)

Application of General Investment Skills

1. Learn to learn:

2. Communicate and collaborate:

3. Capitalize and computerize:

4. Imagine, analyze, and act:

5. Evaluate:

6. Push quality:

7. Push efficiency:

STEP 9
EMPLOYMENT OPPORTUNITY PLANNING WORKSHEET 9.1(1)

Building Block: Self-Inventory

ACCOMPLISHMENTS

School and Activities:

Skills and Abilities:

Work Experience:

Worker Characteristics:

Other:

Building Block: Employer Requirements Assessment

Education:

Skills and Abilities:

Work Experience:

Worker Characteristics:

Other:

(continued)

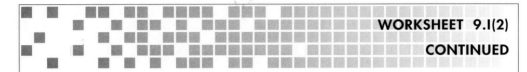

Building Block: Accomplishments–Requirements Match

EMPLOYER REQUIREMENTS   SELECTED ACCOMPLISHMENTS

Education and Activities

Skills and Abilities

Work Experience

Worker Characteristics

Other

(continued)

WORKSHEET 9.1(3)
CONTINUED

Job Search Tool: Cover Letter

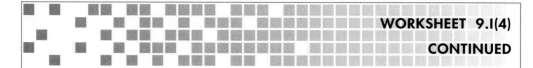

Job Search Tool: Resume

WORKSHEET 9.1(5)

CONTINUED

Job Search Tool: Resume Follow-up Letter

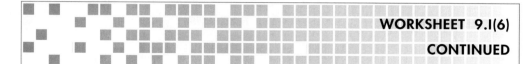

Job Search Tool: Opportunity Letter

WORKSHEET 9.1(7)

CONTINUED

Job Search Tool: Employment Acceptance Letter

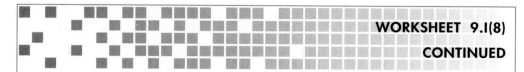

Job Search Tool: Job Interview Essay

STEP 10

EMPLOYMENT OPPORTUNITY PLANNING WORKSHEET 9.J

Target Employers

Selected Occupation: _____

Industries with Significant Employment:

Selected Industry: _____

Economic Areas with Significant Employment:

Selected Economic Area: _____

Employers within Industry and Area:

Employers listing corresponding job vacancies:

The Nation's 172 Economic Areas

Region & Economic Area

NEW ENGLAND

Bangor, ME
Boston Metro
Burlington, VT-NY
Portland, ME

MIDEAST

Albany-Schenect-Troy
Buffalo Metro
Harrisburg Metro
New York Metro
Philadelphia Metro
Rochester, NY-PA
Salisbury, MD-DE-VA
State College, PA
Syracuse, NY-PA
Washington Metro

SOUTHEAST

Albany, GA
Asheville, NC
Atlanta, GA-AL-NC
Augusta-Aiken, GA-SC
Charleston Metro, SC
Charleston, WV-KY-OH
Charlotte Metro
Chattanooga, TN-GA
Columbia, SC
Columbus, GA-AL
Dothan, AL-FL-GA
Fayetteville, NC
Fort Myer-Cape Coral
Greensboro Metro
Greenville Metro
Greenville, NC
Hickory-Morganton

Jacksonville, FL-GA
Johnson City Metro
Knoxville, TN
Lexington Metro, KY
Macon, GA
Miami-Ft Laudr,Metro
Norfolk Metro,VA-NC
Orlando, FL
Raleigh-Durham, NC
Richmond-Peter, VA
Roanoke, VA-NC-WV
Sarasota-Bradenton
Savannah, GA-SC
Staunton, VA-WV
Tallahassee, FL-GA
Tampa-St. Petersburg
Wilmington, NC-SC

GREAT LAKES

Appleton-Oshkosh-Nee
Champaign-Urbana, IL
Chicago Metro
Cincinnati-Hamilton
Cleveland Metro
Columbus, OH
Dayton-Springfield
Detroit Metro
Elkhart-Goshen, IN-M
Erie, PA
Evansville-Henderson
Fort Wayne, IN
Grand Rapid Metro,mi
Green Bay, WI-MI
Indianapolis, IN-IL
Louisville, KY-IN
Milwaukee-Racine, WI
Nashville, TN-KY
Northern Michigan

Paducah, KY-IL
Pittsburgh, PA-WV
Toledo, OH
Traverse City, MI
Wheeling, WV-OH

PLAINS

Aberdeen, SD
Baton Rouge, LA-MS
Beaumont-Port Arthur
Biloxi-Gulfport-Pasc
Birmingham, AL
Bismarck, ND-MT-SD
Cedar Rapids, IA
Columbia, MO
Davenport Metro
Des Moines, IA-IL-MO
Duluth-Superior, MN
Fargo-Moorhead, ND
Fayetteville Metro
Fort Smith, AR-OK
Grand Forks, ND-MN
Grand Island, NE
Greenville, MS
Huntsville, AL-TN
Jackson, MS-AL-LA
Jonesboro, AR-MO
Joplin, MO-KS-OK
Kansas City, MO-KS
La Crosse, WI-MN
Lafayette, LA
Lake Charles, LA
Lincoln, NE
Little Rock Metro,AR
Madison, WI-IL-IA
Memphis, TN-AR-MS-KY
Minneapolis-St. Paul
Minot, ND

Mobile, AL
Monroe, LA
Montgomery, AL
New Orleans, LA-MS
North Platte, NE-CO
Omaha, NE-IA-MO
Pensacola, FL
Peoria-Pekin, IL
Rapid City, SD-MT-NE
Rochester, MN-IA-WI
Shreveport-Bossier
Sioux City, IA-NE-SD
Sioux Falls Metro,SD
Springfield, IL-MO
Springfield, MO
St. Louis, MO-IL
Topeka, KS
Tupelo, MS-AL-TN
Wausau, WI
Wichita, KS-OK

SOUTHWEST

Abilene, TX
Amarillo, TX-NM
Austin-San Marcos,TX
Corpus Christi, TX
Dallas-Fort Worth,TX
Hobbs, NM-TX
Houston-Galveston
Lubbock, TX
McAllen-Edin-Miss,TX
Odessa-Midland, TX
Oklahoma City, OK
San Angelo, TX
San Antonio, TX
Santa Fe, NM
Tulsa, OK-KS
Western Oklahoma, OK

ROCKY MOUNTAIN

Billings, MT-WY
Boise City, ID-OR
Casper, WY-ID-UT
Denver Metro
Great Falls, MT
Idaho Falls, ID-WY
Missoula, MT
Pueblo, CO-NM
Scottsbluff, NE-WY
Spokane, WA-ID
Twin Falls, ID

FAR WEST

Albuquerque, NM-AZ
Anchorage, AK
El Paso, TX-NM
Eugene-Springf,OR-CA
Farmington, NM-CO
Flagstaff, AZ-UT
Fresno, CA
Honolulu, HI
Las Vegas, NV-AZ-UT
Los Angeles Metro
Pendleton, OR-WA
Phoenix-Mesa, AZ-NM
Portland-Salem,OR-WA
Redding, CA-OR
Reno, NV-CA
Richland Metro, WA
Sacramento-Yolo, CA
Salt Lake City-Ogden
San Diego, CA
San Francisco Metro
Seattle Metro
Tucson, AZ

The Nation's 309 Industries

AGRICULTURE, FORESTRY, AND FISHING

Agricultural services
All other agriculture, forestry, and fishing

MINING

Metal mining
Coal mining
Oil and gas extraction
    Crude petroleum, natural gas, and gas liquids
    Oil and gas field services
Nonmetallic minerals, except fuels

CONSTRUCTION

General building contractors
    Operative builders
Heavy construction, except building
    Highway and street construction
    Heavy construction, except highway and street
Special trade contractors
    Plumbing, heating, and air-conditioning

Painting and paper hanging
Electrical work
Masonry, stonework, and plastering
Carpentering and floor work
Roofing, siding, and sheet metal work
Concrete work
All other special trade contractors

MANUFACTURING

Durable goods manufacturing
    Lumber and wood products
        Logging
        Sawmills and planing mills
        Millwork, plywood, and structural members
        Wood containers and misc wood products
        Wood buildings and mobile homes
Furniture and fixtures
    Household furniture
    Office and misc furniture and fixtures
    Partitions and fixtures
Stone, clay, and glass products
    Flat glass and products of purchased glass
    Glass and glassware, pressed or blown
    Concrete, gypsum, and plaster products
    All other stone, clay, & misc mining product
Primary metal industries
    Blast furnaces and basic steel products
    Iron and steel foundries
    Nonferrous rolling and drawing
    Nonferrous foundries (castings)
    All other primary metals
Fabricated metal products
    Metal cans and shipping containers
    Cutlery, handtools, and hardware
    Plumbing and heating, except electric
    Fabricated structural metal products
    Screw machine products, bolts, etc.
    Metal forgings and stampings
    Ordnance and accessories, nec
    Miscellaneous fabricated metal products

Industrial machinery and equipment
    Engines and turbines
    Farm and garden machinery
    Construction and related machinery
    Metalworking machinery
    Special industry machinery
    General industrial machinery
    Computer and office equipment
    Refrigeration and service machinery
    Industrial machinery, nec
Electronic and other electrical equipment
    Electric distributing equipment
    Electrical industrial apparatus
    Household appliances
    Electric lighting and wiring equipment
    Household audio and video equipment
    Communications equipment
    Electronic components and accessories
    Misc electrical equipment and supplies
Transportation equipment
Motor vehicles and equipment
    Aircraft and parts
    Ship and boat building and repairing
    Guided missiles, space vehicles, and parts
    All other transportation equipment
Instruments and related products
    Search and navigation equipment
    Measuring and controlling devices
    Medical instruments and supplies
    Photographic equipment and supplies
    All other prof and scientific instruments
Miscellaneous manufacturing industries
    Jewelry, silverware, and plated ware
    Manufactured products, nec
    Toys and sporting goods
Food and kindred products
    Meat products
    Dairy products
    Preserved fruits and vegetables
    Grain mill products and fats and oils
    Bakery products

Sugar and confectionery products
Beverages
Miscellaneous foods and kindred products
Tobacco products
Textile mill products
Weaving, finishing, yarn and thread mills
Knitting mills
Carpets and rugs
Miscellaneous textile goods
Apparel and other textile products
Apparel
Miscellaneous fabricated textile products
Paper and allied products
Pulp, paper, and paperboard mills
Paperboard containers and boxes
Miscellaneous converted paper products
Printing and publishing
Newspapers
Periodicals
Books
Miscellaneous publishing
Commercial printing and business forms
Blankbooks and bookbinding
All other printing trade services
Chemicals and allied products
Industrial inorganic chemicals
Plastics materials and synthetics
Drugs
Soap, cleaners, and toilet goods
Paints and allied products
Industrial organic chemicals
Agricultural chemicals
Miscellaneous chemical products
Petroleum and coal products
Petroleum refining
Miscellaneous petroleum and coal products
Rubber and miscellaneous plastics products
Tires and inner tubes
Rubber products & plastic hose and footwear
Miscellaneous plastics products

Leather and leather products
    Luggage, handbags, & leather products, nec
    Footwear, except rubber and plastic

TRANSPORTATION AND PUBLIC UTILITIES

Local and interurban passenger transit
    Local and suburban transportation
    School buses
    All other local and interurban transportatio
Trucking and warehousing
    Local & long distance trucking & terminals
    Public warehousing and storage
Water transportation
Transportation by air
    Air carriers
    Airports, flying fields, and services
Pipelines, except natural gas
Transportation services
    Passenger transportation arrangement
    Freight transportation arrangement
    Transporation services, nec
Communications
    Telephone communications
    Telegraph and communication services, nec
    Radio and television broadcasting
    Cable and other pay TV services
Electric, gas, and sanitary services
    Electric services
    Gas production and distribution
    Combination utility services
    Water supply and sanitary services

WHOLESALE AND RETAIL TRADE

Wholesale trade
    Motor vehicles, parts, and supplies
    Machinery, equipment, and supplies
    Groceries and related products
    etroleum and petroleum products
    Wholesale trade, other
Retail trade

Building materials and garden supplies
Lumber and other building materials
Paint, glass, and wallpaper stores
Hardware stores
Retail nurseries and garden stores
General merchandise stores
Department stores
General merchandise stores, nec
Food stores
Grocery stores
Meat and fish markets
Food stores, nec
Retail bakeries
Automotive dealers and service stations
Motor vehicle dealers
Auto and home supply stores
Gasoline service stations
Boat and miscellaneous vehicle dealers
Apparel and accessory stores
Clothing and accesories stores
Shoe stores
Miscellaneous apparel and accessory stores
Furniture and homefurnishings stores
Furniture and homefurnishings stores
Appliance, radio, TV, and music stores
Eating and drinking places
Miscellaneous retail stores
Drug stores and proprietary stores
Liquor stores
Used merchandise and retail stores, nec
Miscellaneous shopping goods stores
Nonstore retailers
Fuel dealers

FINANCE, INSURANCE, AND REAL ESTATE

Depository institutions
Banking and closely related functions, nec
Comm banks, savings institut & credit unions
Nondepository institutions
Federal and business credit institutions

Personal credit institutions
Mortgage bankers and brokers
Security and commodity brokers
Security and commodity brokers and dealers
Security and commodity exchanges and services
Insurance carriers
Life insurance
Medical service and health insurance
Fire, marine, and casualty insurance
Pension funds and insurance, nec
Insurance agents, brokers, and service
Real estate
Real estate operators and lessors
Real estate agents and managers
All other real estate
Holding and other investment offices

SERVICES

Hotels and other lodging places
Personal services
Laundry, cleaning, and garment services
Photographic studios, portrait
Beauty shops
Funeral service and crematories
All other personal services
Business services
Advertising
Credit reporting and collection
Mailing, reproduction, & stenographic services
Services to buildings
Miscellaneous equipment rental and leasing
Personnel supply services
Computer and data processing services
Miscellaneous business services
Auto repair, services, and parking
Automotive rentals, no drivers
Automobile parking
Automotive repair shops
Automotive services, except repair
Miscellaneous repair services

Electrical repair shops
All other repair shops and related services
Motion pictures
Motion picture production and distribution
Motion picture theaters
Video tape rental
Amusement and recreation services
Producers, orchestras, and entertainers
Bowling centers
Commercial sports
All other amusement and recreation services
Health services
Offices of physicians including osteopaths
Offices and clinics of dentists
Offices of other health practitioners
Nursing and personal care facilities
Hospitals, public and private
Medical and dental laboratories
Home health care services
Health and allied services, nec
Legal services
Education, public and private
Social services
Individual and miscellaneous social services
Job training and related services
Child day care services
Residential care
Museums and botanical and zoological gardens
Business and professional organizations
Labor organizations
Civic and social associations
Membership organizations
Religious organizations
Engineering and management services
Engineering and architectural services
Accounting, auditing, and bookkeeping
Research and testing services
Management and public relations
Services, nec

GOVERNMENT

APPENDIX

Interest
Checklist

Read each of the items below and indicate how you feel about the activity by placing a ✓ under:

L = LIKE   **?** = UNCERTAIN   **D** = DISLIKE

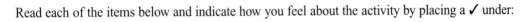

			L	?	D

ARTISTIC

01.01 Write short stories or articles
Edit work of writers
Write review of books or plays

01.02 Teach classes in oil painting
Carve figures of people or animals
Design artwork for magazines

01.03 Direct plays
Perform magic tricks in a theater
Announce radio or television programs

01.04 Conduct a symphony orchestra
Compose or arrange music
Play a musical instrument

01.05 Create routines for professional dancers
Dance in a variety show
Teach modern dance

01.06 Restore damaged works of art
Carve designs in wooden blocks for printing greeting cards
Design, cartooning, or animation

01.07 Analyze handwriting and appraise personality
Introduce acts in a circus
Guess weight of people at a carnival

01.08 Model clothing for customers
Pose for a fashion photographer
Be a stand-in for a television star

02.01 Develop chemical processes to solve technical problems
Analyze data on weather conditions
Develop methods to control air or water pollution

SCIENTIFIC

02.02 Study causes of animal diseases
Develop methods for growing better crops
Develop new techniques to process foods

02.03 Examine teeth and treat dental problems
Diagnose and treat sick animals
Give medical treatment to people

(continued)

205

	L	?	D
02.04 Prepare medicines according to prescription	—	—	—
Study blood samples using a microscope	—	—	—
Test ore samples for gold or silver content	—	—	—

PLANTS/ANIMALS

	L	?	D
03.01 Manage a beef or dairy ranch	—	—	—
Operate a commercial fish farm	—	—	—
Manage the use and development of forest lands	—	—	—
03.02 Supervise farm workers	—	—	—
Supervise a logging crew	—	—	—
Supervise a park maintenance crew	—	—	—
03.03 Train horses for racing	—	—	—
Feed and care for animals in a zoo	—	—	—
Bathe and groom dogs	—	—	—
03.04 Pick vegetables on a farm	—	—	—
Catch fish as a member of a fishing crew	—	—	—
Trim branches and limbs from trees	—	—	—

PROTECTIVE

	L	?	D
04.01 Direct police activities	—	—	—
Issue tickets to speeding motorists	—	—	—
Enforce fish and game laws	—	—	—
04.02 Guard inmates in a prison	—	—	—
Guard money in an armored car	—	—	—
Fight fires to protect life and property	—	—	—

MECHANICAL

	L	?	D
05.01 Plan and design roads and bridges	—	—	—
Design electrical equipment	—	—	—
Plan construction of a water treatment plant	—	—	—
05.02 Direct operations of a power plant	—	—	—
Direct construction of buildings	—	—	—
Supervise operations of a coal mine	—	—	—
05.03 Survey land to determine boundaries	—	—	—
Make drawings of equipment for technical manuals	—	—	—
Operate a radio transmitter	—	—	—
Design and draft master drawings of automobiles	—	—	—
Direct air traffic from an airport control tower	—	—	—
Conduct water pollution tests	—	—	—

	L	?	D
05.04 Pilot a commercial aircraft	—	—	—
Operate a ferry boat	—	—	—
Captain an oil tanker	—	—	—
05.05 Build frame houses	—	—	—
Make and repair dentures	—	—	—
Prepare and cook food in a restaurant	—	—	—
Plan, install, and repair electrical wiring	—	—	—
Repair and overhaul automobiles	—	—	—
Set up and operate printing equipment	—	—	—
05.06 Operate generators at an electric plant	—	—	—
Operate boilers to heat a building	—	—	—
Operate water purification equipment	—	—	—
05.07 Inspect fire-fighting equipment	—	—	—
Inspect aircraft for mechanical safety	—	—	—
Inspect cruise control in automobiles	—	—	—
Grade logs for size and quality	—	—	—
05.08 Drive a tractor-trailer truck	—	—	—
Operate a train	—	—	—
Operate a motorboat to carry passengers	—	—	—
05.09 Prepare items for shipment and keep records	—	—	—
Receive, store, and issue merchandise	—	—	—
Record amount and kind of cargo on ships	—	—	—
05.10 Develop film to produce negatives or prints	—	—	—
Repair small electrical appliances	—	—	—
Paint houses	—	—	—
05.11 Operate a bulldozer	—	—	—
Operate a crane	—	—	—
Operate an oil drilling rig	—	—	—
05.12 Recap truck tires	—	—	—
Operate a duplicating or copying machine	—	—	—
Clean and maintain office buildings	—	—	—

INDUSTRIAL

	L	?	D
06.01 Set up and operate a lathe to cut and form metal	—	—	—
Drill tiny holes in industrial diamonds	—	—	—
Hand polish optical lenses	—	—	—

(continued)

	L	?	D

06.02
- Operate a drill press
- Operate a power saw in a woodworking factory
- Assemble refrigerators and stoves in a factory
- Operate a power sewing machine to make clothing
- Operate a dough-mixing machine for making bread
- Assemble electronic components

06.03
- Inspect bottles for defects
- Sort fruit according to size
- Test electronic parts before shipment

06.04
- Work on a factory assembly line
- Operate a machine that fills containers
- Hand package materials and products
- Assemble parts to make computer components
- Drive a forklift truck to move materials in a factory

BUSINESS DETAIL

07.01
- Use word-processing equipment, handle business details
- Search records to verify land ownership
- Maintain records on real estate sales

07.02
- Maintain spread sheets
- Keep time card records
- Compute average weekly production from automated record systems

07.03
- Receive and pay out money in a bank
- Sell tickets at places of entertainment
- Operate a cash register in a grocery store

07.04
- Answer questions at an information counter
- Interview persons opening checking accounts

07.05
- Check typewritten material for errors
- Compile and maintain employee records
- Deliver mail to homes and businesses

07.06
- Input letters and reports
- Operate a personal computer to prepare, send, or receive information
- Operate a billing system to prepare customer bills

07.07
- File office correspondence
- Locate and replace library books on shelves
- Hand stamp return addresses on envelopes

SELLING

08.01
- Sell telephone and other communications equipment
- Sell newspaper ad space
- Select and buy fruits and vegetables for resale

08.02
- Sell automobiles
- Demonstrate products at a trade exhibit
- Sell articles at auction to highest bidder

08.03
- Sell merchandise from door to door
- Sell candy and popcorn at sports events
- Sell products through infomercials

ACCOMMODATING

09.01
- Supervise activities of children at vacation camp
- Greet and seat customers in a restaurant
- Serve meals and beverages to airline passengers

09.02
- Give haircuts
- Style, color, and treat hair
- Give scalp-conditioning treatments

09.03
- Drive a bus
- Drive a taxicab
- Teach automobile driving skills

09.04
- Wait on tables in a restaurant
- Park automobiles
- Cash checks and give information to customers

09.05
- Check passenger baggage
- Help hotel guests get taxicabs
- Operate a carnival ride

(continued)

HUMANITARIAN

10.01
Plan and carry out religious
   activities   ___ ___ ___
Work with juveniles on
   probation   ___ ___ ___
Help people with personal or
   emotional problems   ___ ___ ___

10.02
Provide nursing care to hospital
   patients   ___ ___ ___
Plan and give physical therapy
   treatment to patients   ___ ___ ___
Teach the blind to read Braille   ___ ___ ___

10.03
Give hearing tests   ___ ___ ___
Care for children in an
   institution   ___ ___ ___
Prepare patients for examination
   by a physician   ___ ___ ___

LENDING/INFLUENCING

11.01
Plan and write computer
   programs to help solve
   scientific problems   ___ ___ ___
Plan collection and analysis of
   statistical data   ___ ___ ___
Apply knowledge of statistics to
   set insurance rates   ___ ___ ___

11.02
Teach courses in high school   ___ ___ ___
Teach vocational education
   courses   ___ ___ ___
Manage the library program for
   a community   ___ ___ ___

11.03
Conduct research to develop
   new teaching methods   ___ ___ ___
Conduct research to understand
   social problems   ___ ___ ___
Review and analyze economic
   data   ___ ___ ___

11.04
Serve as a court judge   ___ ___ ___
Advise clients on legal matters   ___ ___ ___
Settle wage disputes between
   labor and management   ___ ___ ___

11.05
Manage a department of a large
   company   ___ ___ ___
Plan and direct work of a
   government office   ___ ___ ___
Purchase supplies and
   equipment for a large firm   ___ ___ ___

11.06
Examine financial records to
   determine tax owed   ___ ___ ___
Approve or disapprove requests
   for bank loans   ___ ___ ___
Buy and sell stocks and bonds
   for clients   ___ ___ ___

11.07
Direct administration of a large
   hospital   ___ ___ ___
Serve as principal of a school   ___ ___ ___
Direct operations of a museum   ___ ___ ___

11.08
Write news stories for
   publication or broadcast   ___ ___ ___
Broadcast news over radio or
   television   ___ ___ ___
Direct operations of a
   newspaper   ___ ___ ___

11.09
Plan advertising programs for
   an organization   ___ ___ ___
Direct fund-raising for a
   nonprofit organization   ___ ___ ___
Lobby for or against proposed
   legislation   ___ ___ ___

11.10
Direct investigations to enforce
   banking laws   ___ ___ ___
Inspect work areas to detect
   unsafe working conditions   ___ ___ ___
Inspect cargo to enforce customs
   laws   ___ ___ ___

11.11
Manage a hotel or motel   ___ ___ ___
Direct activities of a branch
   office of an insurance company   ___ ___ ___
Manage a grocery, clothing, or
   other retail store   ___ ___ ___

11.12
Investigate and settle insurance
   claims   ___ ___ ___
Obtain leases for outdoor
   advertising sites   ___ ___ ___
Sign entertainers to theater or
   concert contracts   ___ ___ ___

PHYSICAL PERFORMING

12.01
Manage a professional baseball
   team   ___ ___ ___
Referee sporting events   ___ ___ ___
Drive in automobile races   ___ ___ ___

12.02
Perform as a trapeze artist in a
   circus   ___ ___ ___
Perform stunts for movie or
   television scenes   ___ ___ ___
Perform juggling feats   ___ ___ ___

*Now go back and doublecheck at least five
activities that you would most like to do.*

APPENDIX D

The Nation's 600-plus Occupations

Occupation Titles

EXECUTIVE, ADMINISTRATIVE, AND MANAGERIAL OCCUPATIONS

Managerial and administrative occupations
Administrative services managers
Communication, transportation, and utilities
Construction managers
Education administrators
Engineering, mathematical, and natural science
Financial managers
Food service and lodging managers
Funeral directors and morticians
General managers and top executives
Government chief executives and legislators
Industrial production managers
Marketing, advertising, and public relations
Personnel, training, and labor relations
Property and real estate managers
Purchasing managers
All other managers and administrators

Management support occupations
Accountants and auditors
Budget analysts
Claims examiners, property and casualty insurance
Construction and building inspectors
Cost estimators
Credit analysts
Employment interviewers, private or public
Inspectors and compliance officers (not construction)
Loan officers and counselors
Management analysts
Personnel, training, and labor relations spec
Purchasing agents, not whole, retail and farm
Tax examiners, collectors, and revenue agents
Underwriters
Wholesale and retail buyers, except farm prods
All other management support workers

PROFESSIONAL SPECIALTY OCCUPATIONS

Engineers
Aeronautical and astronautical engineers
Chemical engineers
Civil engineers, including traffic engineers
Electrical and electronics engineers
Industrial engineers, except safety engineer
Mechanical engineers
Metallurgs and metallurg, ceramic, and matl engs
Mining engineers, includ mine safety engs
Nuclear engineers
Petroleum engineers
All other engineers
Architects and surveyors
Architects, except landscape and marine
Landscape architects
Surveyors
Life scientists
Agricultural and food scientists
Biological scientists

Foresters and conservation scientists
Medical scientists
All other life scientists
Computer, mathematical, and operations research
Actuaries
Systems analysts, engineers, and scientists
Computer engineers and scientists
Computer engineers
All other computer scientists
Systems analysts
Statisticians
Mathematician and all other math scientists
Operations research analysts
Physical scientists
Chemists
Geologists, geophysicists, and oceanographers
Meteorologists
Physicists and astronomers
All other physical scientists
Social scientists
Economists
Psychologists
Urban and regional planners
All other social scientists
Social, recreational, and religious workers
Clergy
Directors, religious and education
Human services workers
Recreation workers
Residential counselors
Social workers
Lawyers and judicial workers
Judges, magistrates, and other judicial worker
Lawyers
Teachers, librarians, and counselors
Teachers, preschool and kindergarten
Teachers, elementary
Teachers, secondary school
Teachers, special education

College and university faculty
Other teachers and instructors
Farm and home management advisors
Instructors and coaches
Adult and vocational education teachers
Instructors, adult (nonvocational)
Teachers and instructors, vocational educ
All other teachers and instructors
Librarians, archivists and curators
Curators, archivists and museum technicians
Librarians, professional
Counselors
Health diagnosing occupations
Chiropractors
Dentists
Optometrists
Physicians
Podiatrists
Veterinarians and veterinary inspectors
Health assessment and treating occupations
Dietitians and nutritionists
Pharmacists
Physician assistants
Registered nurses
Therapists
Occupational therapists
Physical therapists
Recreational therapists
Respiratory therapists
Speech pathologists and audiologists
All other therapists
Writers, artists, and entertainers
Artists and commercial artists
Athletes, coaches and umpires
Dancers and choreographers
Designers
Designers, except interior designers
Interior designers
Musicians

Photographers and camera operators
Camera operators, TV, movies and video
Photographers
Producers, directors and actors
PR specialists and publicity writers
Radio and TV announcers and newscasters
Reporters and correspondents
Writers and editors, technical writers
All other professional workers

TECHNICIANS AND RELATED SUPPORT OCCUPATIONS

Health technicians and technologists
Cardiology technologists
Clinical lab technologist and technicians
Dental hygienists
Electroneurodiagnostic technologists
EKG technicians
Emergency medical technicians
Licensed practical nurses
Medical records technicians
Nuclear medicine technologists
Opticians, dispensing and measuring
Pharmacy technicians
Psychiatric technicians
Radiologic technologists
Surgical technologists
Veterinary technicians and tehnologists
Other health professionals and paraprofession
Engineering and science technicians and technologt
Engineering technicians
Electrical and electronic technicians
All other engineering technicians
Drafters
Science and mathematics technicians
Techs, not health, engineering and science
Aircraft pilots and flight engineers
Air traffic controllers and dispatchers
Broadcast technicians

Computer programmers
Legal asst andnd technicians, not clerical
Paralegals
Title examiners and searchers
Other legal assts, including law clerks
Programmers, numerical, tool, etc
Technical assistants, library
All other technicians

MARKETING AND SALES OCCUPATIONS

Cashiers
Counter and rental clerks
Insurance sales workers
Marketing and sales worker supervisors
Real estate agents, brokers, and appraisers
Brokers, real estate
Real estate appraisers
Sales agents, real estate
Salespersons, retail
Securities and financial services sales workers
Travel agents
All other sales and related workers

ADM SUPPORT OCCUPATIONS, INCLUDING CLERICAL

Adjusters, investigators, and collectors
Adjustment clerks
Bill and account collectors
Insurance claims and policy processing
Insurance adjusters, examiners, etc
Insurance claims clerks
Insurance policy processing clerks
Welfare eligibility workers and interviewers
All other adjusters and investigators
Communications equipment operators
Telephone operators
Central office operators
Directory assistance operators
Switchboard operators

Other communications equipment operators
Computer operators and peripheral equipment
Computer operators, except peripheral equip
Peripheral EDP equipment operators
Information clerks
Hotel desk clerks
Interviewing clerks, except personnel and so
New accounts clerks, banking
Receptionists and information clerks
Reservation and transportation ticket agents
Mail clerks and messengers
Mail clerks, not machine and postal
Messengers
Postal clerks and mail carriers
Postal mail carriers
Postal service clerks
Material records, scheduling, dispatching
Dispatchers
Dispatchers, not police/fire/ ambulance
Dispatchers/police/fire/ambulance
Meter readers, utilities
Order fillers, wholesale and retail sales
Procurement clerks
Production, planning, and expediting clerks
Stock clerks
Traffic, shipping, and receiving clerks
Weighers, measurers, checkers, etc
Other material recording, scheduling, etc
Records processing occupations
Advertising clerks
Brokerage clerks
Correspondence clerks
File clerks
Financial records processing occupations
Billing, cost, and rate clerks
Calculating machine operators
Bookkeeping and accounting clerks
Payroll and timekeeping clerks
Library assistants and bookmobile drivers

Order clerks, materials, merchandise, and svc
Personnel clerks, not payroll and timekepping
Statement clerks
Secretaries, stenographers, and typists
Secretaries
Legal secretaries
Medical secretaries
Secretaries, except legal and medical
Stenographers
Typists and word processors
Other clerical and adm support workers
Bank tellers
Clerical supervisors and managers
Court clerks
Credit authorizers, checkers, etc
Credit authorizers
Credit checkers
Loan and credit clerks
Loan interviewers
Customer service representatives
Data entry keyers, except composing
Data entry keyers, composing
Office machine operators
General office clerks
Municipal clerks
Proofreaders and copy markers
Real estate clerks
Statistical clerks
Teacher aides and educational assistants
All other clerical and adm support workers

SERVICE OCCUPATIONS

Cleaning and bldg service occps not private
Institutional cleaning supervisors
Janitors and cleaners
Pest controllers and assistants
All other cleaning and building service worker
Food preparation and service occupations

Chefs, cooks, and other kitchen workers
Cooks, except short order
Bakers, bread and pastry
Cooks, institution or cafeteria
Cooks, restaurant
Cooks, short order and fast food
Food preparation workers
Food and beverage service occupations
Bartenders
Dining room and cafeteria attend helpers
Food counter workers
Hosts and hostesses
Waiters and waitresses
All other food preparation workers
Health service occupations
Ambul drivers/attendants, not EMTs
Dental assistants
Medical assistants
Nursing aides and psychiatric aides
Nursing aides, orderlies, and attendants
Psychiatric aides
Occupational therapy assistants and aides
Pharmacy assistants
Physical/corrective therapy assistants
All other health service workers
Personal service occupations
Amusement and recreation attendants
Baggage porters and bellhops
Barbers
Child care workers
Cosmetologists and related workers
Hairdressers, hairstylists, and cosmetologst
Manicurists
Shampooers
Flight attendants
Homemaker-home health aides
Home health aides
Personal and home care aides
Ushers, lobby attendants, and ticket takers

Private household workers
Child care workers, private household
Cleaners and servants, private household
Cooks, private household
Housekeepers and butlers
Protective service occupations
Firefighting occupations
Fire fighters
Fire fighting and prevention supervisors
Fire inspection occupations
Law enforcement occupations
Correction officers
Police and detectives
Police and detective supervisors
Police detectives and investigators
Police patrol officers
Sheriffs and deputy sheriffs
Other law enforcement occupations
Other protective service workers
Detectives, except public
Guards
Crossing guards
All other protective service workers
All other service workers

AGRICULTURE, FORESTRY, FISHING OCCUPATIONS

Animal breeders and trainers
Animal caretakers, except farm
Farm workers
Gardening, nursery, and greenhouse and lawn svc
Gardeners and groundskeepers, except farm
Lawn maintenance workers
Lawn service managers
Nursery and greenhouse managers
Nursery workers
Pruners
Sprayers/applicators
Farm operators and managers

Farmers
Farm managers
Fishers, hunters, and trappers
Captains and other officers, fishing vessels
Fishers, hunters, and trappers
Forestry and logging occupations
Forest and conservation workers
Timber cutting and logging occupations
Fallers and buckers
Logging tractor operators
Log handling equipment operators
All other loggings ocupations
Supervisors, farming and forestry
Veterinary assistants
All other agricultural workers

PRECISION PRODUCTION, CRAFT, AND REPAIR

Blue collar worker supervisors
Construction trades
Bricklayers and stone masons
Carpenters
Carpet installers
Ceiling tile installers
Concrete and terrazzo finishers
Drywall installers and finishers
Electricians
Glaziers
Hard tile setters
Highway maintenance workers
Insulation workers
Painters and paperhangers
Paving equipment operators
Pipelayers and pipelaying fitters
Plasterers
Plumbers, pipefitters, and steamfitters
Roofers
Structural and reinforcing metal workers
All other construction trades workers

Extractive and related workers
Oil and gas extraction occupations
Roustabouts
All other oil and gas extraction occps
Mining, quarrying, and tunneling occupations
All other extraction and related workers
Mechanics, installers, and repairers
Communications equipment mechanics
Central office and PBX installers and repair
Radio mechanics
All other communications equipment
Electrical/electronic equipment mechanics
Data processing equipment repairers
Electrical powerline installer and repairer
Electronic home entertainment equip repair
Electronics repair
Station installers telephone
Telephone/cable TV line, install and repair
Other electrical and electronic
Machinery and related mechanics
Industrial machinery mechanics
Maintenance repairers, general utility
Millwrights
Vehicle and mobile equipment
Aircraft mechanics
Aircraft engine specialists
Aircraft mechanics
Automotive body and related repairers
Automotive mechanics
Bus and truck mechanics and diesel engine
Farm equipment mechanics
Mobile heavy equipment mechanics
Motorcycle and boat mechanics
Motorcycle repairers
Small engine specialists
Other mechanics, installers, and repairers
Bicycle repairers
Camera and photographic equipment
Coin and vending machine

Electric meter installers and repairers
Electromedical and biomedical
Elevator installers and repairers
Heat, air conditioning, and refrigeration
Home appliance and power tool repairers
Locksmiths and safe repairers
Musical instrument repairers and tuners
Office machine and cash register servicers
Precision instrument repairers
Riggers
Tire repairers and changers
Watchmakers
Other mechanics, installers, and repairers
Production occupations, precision
Assemblers, precision
Aircraft assemblers, precision
Electrical/electronic equipment assemblers
Electromechanical equipment
Fitters, structural metal, precision
Machine builders
Other precision assemblers
Food workers, precision
Bakers, manufacturing
Butchers and meatcutters
Other precision food and tobacco workers
Inspectors, testers, and graders, precision
Metal workers, precision
Boilermakers
Jewelers and silversmiths
Machinists
Sheet metal workers and duct installers
Shipfitters
Tool and die makers
All other precision metal workers
Printing workers, precision
Bookbinders
Prepress printing workers, precision
Compositors and typesetters, precision
Job printers

Paste-up workers
Electronic pagination systems workers
Photoengravers
Camera operators
Strippers, printing
Platemakers
All other printing workers, precision
Textile, apparel, and furnishing workers
Custom tailors and sewers
Patternmakers and layout workers
Shoe and leather workers
Upholsterers
Other precision textile
Woodworkers, precision
Cabinetmakers and bench carpenters
Furniture finishers
Wood machinists
All other precision woodworkers
Other precision workers
Dental laboratory technicians, precision
Optical goods workers, precision
Photographic process workers, precision
All other precision workers

PLANT AND SYSTEM OCCUPATIONS

Chemical plant and system operators
Electric power generating plant operators
Power distributors and dispatchers
Power generating and reactor plant operators
Gas and petroleum plant system occupations
Stationary engineers
Water/waste treatment plant operators
All other plant and system operators

OPERATORS, FABRICATORS, AND LABORERS

Machine setters, set-up operators, etc
Numerical control machine tool operators

Combination machine tool setters operators
Machine tool setters operators
Drilling and boring
Grinding machine setters
Lathe and turning machine tool setters
Machine forming operators
Machine tool cutting
Punching machine setters
Other machine tool
Metal fabricating machine
Metal fabricators
Soldering and brazing
Welding machine setters
Metal and plastic processing
Electrolytic plating machine
Foundry mold assembly
Furnace operators
Heat treating machine operators
Metal molding machine operators
Plastic molding machine operators
Other metal and plastic
Printing, binding, and related workers
Bindery machine operators
Prepress printing workers
Photoengraving
Typesetting
Printing press operators
Letterpress operators
Offset lithographic press operators
Printing press machine
Other printing press setters
Screen printing machine
Other printing and binding workers
Textile operators
Extruding and forming machine operators
Pressing machine operators
Sewing machine operators, garment
Sewing machine operators, non-garment

Textile bleaching and dyeing mach operators
Textile draw-out and winding mach operators
Textile machine setters
Woodwork machine setters and operators
Head sawyers and sawing machine operators
Woodworking machine operators
Other machine setters
Boiler operators and tenders, low pressure
Cement and gluing machine operators
Chemical equipment controllers, operators
Cooking and roasting machine operators
Crushing and mixing machine operators
Cutting and slicing machine setters
Dairy processing equipment operators
Electronic semiconductor processors
Extruding and forming machine operators
Furnace/kiln/kettle operators and tenders
Laundry and drycleaning machine operators
Motion picture projectionists
Packaging and filling machine operators
Painting and coating machine operators
Coating, painting, and spraying machine
Painters, transportation equipment
Paper goods machine operators
Photographic processing machine operators
Separating and still machine operators
Shoe sewing machine operators and tenders
Tire building machine operators
Other machine operators, tenders, etc

HAND WORKERS

Cannery workers
Coil winders, tapers, and finishers
Cutters and trimmers, hand
Electrical and electronic assemblers
Grinders and polishers, hand
Machine assemblers
Meat, poultry, and fish cutters and trimmers

Painting, coating, and decorating workers, hand
Pressers, hand
Sewers, hand
Solderers and brazers
Welders and cutters
Other assemblers, fabricators, and hand worker

TRANSPORTATION AND MOVING MACHINE WORKERS

Motor vehicle operators
Bus drivers
Bus drivers, except school
Bus drivers, school
Taxi drivers and chauffeurs
Truck drivers
Driver/sales workers
Truck drivers light and heavy
All other motor vehicle operators
Rail transportation workers
Locomotive engineers
Railroad brake, signal, switch operators
Railroad conductors and yardmasters
Rail yard engineers
Subway and streetcar operators
Water transportation and related workers
Seamen, ordinary seamen, and marine oilers
Captains and pilots, ship
Mates, ship, boat, and barge
Ship engineers
Material moving equipment operators
Crane and tower operators
Excavation and loading machine operators
Grader, dozer, and scraper operators
Hoist and winch operators
Industrial truck and tractor operators
Operating engineers
Other material moving equipment operators
Other transportation and material moving operators

HELPERS AND LABORERS

Freight, stock, and material movers, hand
Hand packers and packagers
Helpers, construction trades
Machine feeders and offbearers
Parking lot attendants
Refuse collectors
Service station attendants
Vehicle washers and equipment cleaners
Other helpers, laborers, and material movers

APPENDIX

Criteria for Occupational Economic Profiles

1. Annual Salary – Standard of Living Rank (Compensation Key)

   Rank 1 of 6: $70,000 and over—Superior
   Rank 2 of 6: $50,000 to $69,999—Very High
   Rank 3 of 6: $40,000 to $49,999—High
   Rank 4 of 6: $30,000 to $39,999—Above Average
   Rank 5 of 6: $20,000 to $29,999—Average
   Rank 6 of 6: Less than $20,000—Below Average

2. National Occupational Employment Change, Annual Openings, and Rank
   (Supply–Demand Key)

1996–2006 DIFFERENCE	RANK	1996–2006 PERCENT CHANGE
Less than 15,000	Very Low	Less than 3 percent
15,000–24,999	Low	3.0 percent–7.0 percent
25,000–34,999	Average	7.1 percent–13.0 percent
35,000–44,999	High	13.1 percent–19.9 percent
45,000 and over	Very High	20 percent and over

ANNUAL OPENINGS/GROWTH & REPLACEMENT	RANK
Less than 40,000	Very Low
40,000 - 59,999	Low
60,000 - 79,999	Average
80,000 - 99,999	High
100,000 and over	Very High

3. Total Replacement Rate and Corresponding Internal Labor Market (ILM) Strength (Internalization Key)

REPLACEMENT RATE	ILM STRENGTH
15.0 & over	Very Low
12.0–14.99	Low
9.0–11.99	Average
6.0–8.99	High
Less than 6.0	Very High

4. Occupational Unemployment Rate and Perceived Productivity Strength (Productivity Key)

OCCUPATIONAL UNEMPLOYMENT RATE	RANK	PERCEIVED PRODUCTIVITY*
Over 7.4	Very High	Very Low
6.5–7.4	High	Low
5.5–6.4	Average	Average
4.5–5.4	Low	High
Less than 4.5	Very Low	Very High

* Based upon the assumption that in the long run workers in those occupations of greatest productive significance to the employer will experience the lowest unemployment rates.

Annual Average Expenditures by Living Standard Group

Item	Complete reporting of income 1/									
	Total complete reporting	Less than $5,000	$5,000 to $9,999	$10,000 to $14,999	$15,000 to $19,999	$20,000 to $29,999	$30,000 to $39,999	$40,000 to $49,999	$50,000 to $69,999	$70,000 and over
Number of consumer units (in thousands)	82,629	4,660	9,279	8,974	7,661	12,554	9,830	7,528	10,772	11,373
Income before taxes 2/	$38,014	$2,121	$7,609	$12,440	$17,305	$24,547	$34,523	$44,580	$58,533	$105,756
Income after taxes 2/	34,864	1,934	7,419	12,279	16,849	23,250	32,003	40,679	53,437	94,552
Age of reference person	47.9	40.9	54.8	53.5	52.4	48.7	45.1	44.2	43.7	45.5
Average number in consumer unit:										
Persons	2.5	1.8	1.7	2.2	2.4	2.5	2.7	2.9	3.1	3.1
Children under 18	0.7	0.4	0.4	0.6	0.6	0.7	0.8	0.8	0.9	0.9
Persons 65 and over	0.3	0.2	0.5	0.6	0.6	0.4	0.3	0.2	0.1	0.1
Earners	1.4	0.9	0.5	0.7	0.9	1.2	1.5	1.8	2.0	2.1
Vehicles	1.9	1.0	0.9	1.2	1.6	1.9	2.1	2.4	2.7	2.8
Percent distribution:										
Male	60	48	32	42	56	60	65	71	75	79
Female	40	52	68	58	44	40	35	29	25	21
Percent homeowner	64	32	42	52	58	59	64	74	81	88
With mortgage	38	11	10	17	20	28	40	54	65	72
Without mortgage	26	21	32	35	38	31	24	19	15	16
Renter	36	68	58	48	42	41	36	26	19	12
Black	11	16	20	16	12	12	10	8	7	6
White and other	89	84	80	84	88	88	90	92	93	94
Elementary (1-8)	8	10	20	17	11	8	5	3	2	1
High school (9-12)	40	42	49	49	51	47	39	40	34	19
College	51	47	29	33	38	45	56	57	64	80
Never attended and other	0	1	1	1	0	0	0	0	0	0
At least one vehicle owned	86	60	60	78	87	90	95	95	96	96
Average annual expenditures	$35,591	$16,608	$15,122	$18,730	$23,563	$28,199	$33,847	$40,714	$48,809	$73,550
Food	4,913	2,568	2,539	3,275	3,587	4,109	4,929	5,576	6,411	8,260
Food at home	2,999	1,692	1,937	2,366	2,425	2,701	2,970	3,331	3,648	4,429
Cereals and bakery products	467	275	291	354	371	411	457	525	579	708
Cereals and cereal products	172	111	113	149	131	159	171	188	201	248
Bakery products	295	165	177	205	240	252	286	337	379	460
Meats, poultry, fish, and eggs	758	474	521	673	631	705	729	812	910	1,047
Beef	220	144	147	201	184	204	204	245	284	280
Pork	160	92	121	144	144	158	166	172	188	193
Other meats	101	62	67	88	75	92	94	104	128	150
Poultry	151	99	99	129	126	132	149	169	176	218
Fish and seafood	91	56	57	75	68	81	78	90	99	167
Eggs	35	22	30	36	34	37	38	33	35	38
Dairy products	330	178	203	246	259	300	349	370	407	480
Fresh milk and cream	139	82	95	117	113	139	151	162	166	167
Other dairy products	191	96	107	130	146	160	198	208	241	313
Fruits and vegetables	504	247	326	412	445	462	492	523	587	764
Fresh fruits	158	70	89	131	143	141	158	160	191	245
Fresh vegetables	148	70	101	129	132	132	143	143	162	234
Processed fruits	115	57	77	86	96	108	109	135	134	171
Processed vegetables	83	51	60	66	74	81	82	85	101	114
Other food at home	940	517	595	680	719	825	943	1,100	1,165	1,429
Sugar and other sweets	121	63	80	90	98	113	124	138	154	169
Fats and oils	87	56	71	82	77	84	86	88	102	105
Miscellaneous foods	415	224	243	288	315	358	406	499	532	646
Nonalcoholic beverages	264	147	180	198	198	238	280	310	305	385
Food prepared by consumer unit on out-of-town trips	52	28	22	21	32	32	47	65	72	125
Food away from home	1,914	876	602	910	1,162	1,408	1,959	2,245	2,763	3,832
Alcoholic beverages	333	210	126	161	193	230	369	401	365	725
Housing	10,899	5,549	5,321	6,574	7,821	8,970	10,078	11,916	14,548	21,606
Shelter	6,058	3,144	2,923	3,570	4,185	4,872	5,472	6,621	8,200	12,452
Owned dwellings	3,791	1,104	980	1,451	1,945	2,335	3,056	4,433	6,156	9,857
Mortgage interest and charges	2,139	416	268	517	673	1,049	1,684	2,709	3,777	6,308
Property taxes	922	400	352	441	699	674	728	946	1,378	2,126
Maintenance, repairs, insurance, other expenses	730	289	360	493	573	612	644	778	1,000	1,423

Item	Total complete reporting	Complete reporting of income 1/								
		Less than $5,000	$5,000 to $9,999	$10,000 to $14,999	$15,000 to $19,999	$20,000 to $29,999	$30,000 to $39,999	$40,000 to $49,999	$50,000 to $69,999	$70,000 and over
Rented dwellings	1,850	1,747	1,815	2,003	2,044	2,310	2,118	1,801	1,511	1,286
Other lodging	417	293	128	116	196	227	298	388	533	1,310
Utilities, fuels, and public services	2,359	1,427	1,560	1,833	2,073	2,196	2,397	2,628	2,865	3,490
Natural gas	290	172	202	226	248	271	278	322	330	462
Electricity	902	540	610	745	819	855	930	993	1,095	1,253
Fuel oil and other fuels	112	61	101	80	110	107	118	123	126	146
Telephone services	780	520	496	593	649	718	811	871	967	1,156
Water and other public services	276	133	151	190	248	245	259	320	347	473
Household operations	547	204	185	228	273	375	485	613	691	1,477
Personal services	274	85	48	88	97	205	283	385	415	667
Other household expenses	272	119	138	141	176	170	202	228	276	810
Housekeeping supplies	508	257	232	304	440	424	423	594	636	935
Laundry and cleaning supplies	128	58	78	99	95	128	124	182	142	182
Other household products	224	115	91	135	173	185	195	276	312	387
Postage and stationery	156	84	63	70	172	112	104	136	182	366
Household furnishings and equipment	1,427	517	421	639	850	1,103	1,301	1,460	2,156	3,251
Household textiles	78	36	31	32	70	60	78	73	115	167
Furniture	322	105	95	124	208	219	308	310	481	810
Floor coverings	110	6	14	40	31	134	85	115	214	207
Major appliances	171	54	79	87	133	147	183	173	251	324
Small appliances, miscellaneous housewares	91	23	29	48	63	78	67	65	141	212
Miscellaneous household equipment	653	293	173	307	344	464	581	724	955	1,530
Apparel and services	1,874	865	706	875	1,217	1,466	1,532	1,870	2,658	4,095
Men and boys	448	181	120	207	244	353	381	508	655	998
Men, 16 and over	351	143	78	153	198	272	294	394	503	815
Boys, 2 to 15	97	38	42	55	46	81	87	114	152	183
Women and girls	769	411	340	321	498	598	591	713	1,171	1,650
Women, 16 and over	656	378	312	274	425	505	487	588	964	1,439
Girls, 2 to 15	113	34	28	46	72	94	105	126	206	211
Children under 2	86	23	42	44	49	82	57	154	119	145
Footwear	307	138	150	181	222	275	276	316	434	535
Other apparel products and services	264	112	54	122	204	158	226	178	280	767
Transportation	6,602	3,503	2,548	2,933	4,477	5,595	6,943	7,694	9,302	13,027
Vehicle purchases (net outlay)	2,922	1,946	1,142	1,049	1,944	2,522	3,254	3,245	4,128	5,706
Cars and trucks, new	1,255	585	368	218	562	858	1,278	1,482	1,941	3,153
Cars and trucks, used	1,621	1,359	774	814	1,382	1,645	1,937	1,756	2,153	2,328
Other vehicles	46	2	0	17	0	19	38	7	35	226
Gasoline and motor oil	1,106	574	476	648	831	1,004	1,189	1,420	1,585	1,762
Other vehicle expenses	2,147	783	694	1,030	1,476	1,814	2,193	2,671	3,024	4,355
Vehicle finance charges	285	82	60	112	161	239	336	431	436	541
Maintenance and repairs	688	291	260	386	469	641	734	845	893	1,285
Vehicle insurance	717	252	245	379	577	627	771	907	1,014	1,300
Vehicle rental, leases, licenses, other charges	456	157	129	153	269	306	352	488	680	1,228
Public transportation	428	200	235	206	226	255	307	357	566	1,204
Health care	1,831	779	1,211	1,534	1,912	1,796	1,906	1,989	2,076	2,570
Health insurance	842	390	530	726	913	839	876	943	966	1,114
Medical services	559	203	328	380	528	492	617	626	673	925
Drugs	324	153	303	349	387	374	308	307	293	336
Medical supplies	107	33	50	79	84	91	105	113	144	194
Entertainment	1,940	768	616	818	958	1,346	1,749	2,865	2,710	4,398
Fees and admissions	475	201	112	159	235	262	402	477	707	1,371
Television, radios, sound equipment	580	279	310	343	438	491	593	700	797	1,001
Pets, toys, and playground equipment	364	162	117	207	167	254	384	366	524	780
Other entertainment supplies, equipment and services	522	126	77	108	118	339	370	1,323	683	1,247
Personal care products and services	540	236	238	337	363	456	551	660	678	1,009
Reading	165	77	75	87	113	133	167	179	216	347
Education	501	771	294	270	204	244	351	431	730	1,173
Tobacco products and smoking supplies	264	188	172	236	249	297	326	295	316	245
Miscellaneous	919	397	489	504	787	857	875	1,056	1,161	1,667

Item	Complete reporting of income 1/									
	Total complete reporting	Less than $5,000	$5,000 to $9,999	$10,000 to $14,999	$15,000 to $19,999	$20,000 to $29,999	$30,000 to $39,999	$40,000 to $49,999	$50,000 to $69,999	$70,000 and over
Cash contributions	1,090	455	478	465	599	786	966	1,136	1,350	2,839
Personal insurance and pensions	3,719	243	310	661	1,084	1,915	3,104	4,646	6,285	11,588
Life and other personal insurance	370	108	109	198	218	275	300	414	544	901
Pensions and Social Security	3,349	134	201	464	866	1,640	2,804	4,232	5,741	10,688
Money income before taxes 2/	38,014	2,121	7,609	12,440	17,305	24,547	34,523	44,580	58,533	105,756
Wages and salaries	29,560	1,382	1,936	4,812	8,836	16,374	26,942	37,148	51,183	88,446
Self-employment income	2,318	-599	87	158	420	867	1,345	2,266	2,754	10,379
Social Security, private and government retirement	4,334	633	3,999	5,593	6,626	5,627	4,685	3,513	2,899	3,759
Interest, dividends, rental income, other property income	761	10	76	210	302	543	681	757	1,038	2,423
Unemployment and workers' compensation, veterans' benefits	213	48	106	187	207	266	261	297	209	238
Public assistance, supplemental security income, food stamps	437	404	1,119	1,069	564	447	182	163	71	50
Regular contributions for support	243	124	150	244	211	215	297	326	259	300
Other income	148	119	136	167	138	208	130	109	120	160
Personal taxes 2/	3,150	186	190	161	456	1,297	2,520	3,901	5,096	11,204
Federal income taxes	2,372	123	119	68	286	943	1,867	2,947	3,872	8,565
State and local income taxes	665	31	41	45	98	272	544	817	1,076	2,357
Other taxes	113	33	30	48	71	82	109	137	148	282
Income after taxes 2/	34,864	1,934	7,419	12,279	16,849	23,250	32,003	40,679	53,437	94,552
Net change in total assets and liabilities	-2,242	102	-1,354	-247	-1,680	-2,076	-4,880	-4,025	-3,543	-1,370
Net change in total assets	4,142	1,001	-381	967	1,164	1,678	1,832	5,928	7,203	14,265
Net change in total liabilities	6,384	899	973	1,214	2,844	3,754	6,712	9,953	10,746	15,635
Other money receipts	377	154	160	215	123	277	181	359	541	1,085
Mortgage principal paid on owned property	-961	-326	-182	-279	-346	-534	-707	-1,168	-1,558	-2,798
Estimated market value of owned home	72,393	28,896	31,651	40,349	48,497	54,417	62,272	77,747	98,503	165,154
Estimated monthly rental value of owned home	503	206	221	310	376	392	452	565	686	1,042
Gifts of goods and services	1,175	714	546	537	932	766	940	1,123	1,568	2,724
Food	61	39	21	23	44	33	57	70	86	143
Housing	297	219	136	148	237	198	237	272	378	691
Housekeeping supplies	43	24	20	12	43	35	32	50	50	94
Household textiles	8	4	4	5	8	7	8	8	9	16
Appliances and miscellaneous housewares	33	6	10	16	32	28	32	20	40	80
Major appliances	8	1	3	2	12	4	13	7	11	14
Small appliances and miscellaneous housewares	25	6	7	13	20	24	19	13	29	66
Miscellaneous household equipment	89	44	42	33	47	56	71	97	116	224
Other housing	124	140	61	83	107	73	94	97	163	277
Apparel and services	324	170	122	121	335	243	242	294	414	734
Males, 2 and over	81	74	36	36	84	71	70	64	100	158
Females, 2 and over	108	47	42	41	107	88	90	71	156	234
Children under 2	43	6	18	17	25	33	25	85	52	95
Other apparel products and services	92	43	26	28	119	51	57	76	106	248
Jewelry and watches	53	11	4	12	92	18	32	30	54	170
All other apparel products and services	39	32	22	16	27	32	25	46	52	78
Transportation	64	31	44	28	24	25	36	66	115	169
Health care	43	5	76	15	50	51	55	22	27	57
Entertainment	122	82	47	52	70	79	126	139	175	255
Toys, games, hobbies, and tricycles	45	29	14	21	26	46	43	53	66	77
Other entertainment	76	53	34	31	44	33	83	86	109	178
Education	113	106	22	33	48	22	70	118	192	351
All other gifts	150	63	78	117	126	114	118	142	181	324

1/ See "Quintile of income before taxes" table for expenditures and income and incomplete income reporters.
2/ Components of income and taxes are derived from "complete income reporters" only; see glossary.

Note that all values have been rounded, and therefore some rounded values equal zero. When data are not reported or are not applicable (i.e., missing values), values are set to zero. Note also that some data are likely to have large sampling errors.

Consumer Expenditure Surveys

Glossary

This glossary is divided into four sections:

- **Characteristics**
- **Expenditures**
- **Income and personal taxes**
- **Other financial information.**

CHARACTERISTICS

Age - The age of the reference person.

Complete income reporters - The distinction between complete and incomplete income reporters is based in general on whether the respondent provided values for major sources of income, such as wages and salaries, self- employment income, and Social Security income. Even complete income reporters may not have provided a full accounting of all income from all sources. In the current survey, across-the-board zero income reporting was designated as invalid, and the consumer unit was categorized as an incomplete reporter. In all tables, income data are for complete income reporters only.

Composition of consumer unit - The classification of interview families according to: (1) relationship of other family members to the reference person; (2) age of the children to the reference person; and (3) combination of relationship to the reference person and age of the children. Stepchildren and adopted children are included with the reference person's own children.

Consumer unit - A consumer unit comprises either: (1) all members of a particular household who are related by blood, marriage, adoption, or other legal arrangements; (2) a person living alone or sharing a household with others or living as a roomer in a private home or lodging house or in permanent living quarters in a hotel or motel, but who is financially independent; or (3) two or more persons living together who pool their income to make joint expenditure decisions. Financial independence is determined by the three major expense categories: Housing, food, and other living expenses. To be considered financially independent, at least two of the three major expense categories have to be provided by the respondent.

Earner - A consumer unit member, 14 years of age or older, who reported having worked at least 1 week during the 12 months prior to the interview date.

Education of reference person - The number of years of formal education of the reference person on the basis of the highest grade completed. If enrolled at time of the interview, the grade being attended is the one recorded. Persons not reporting the extent of their education are classified under no school or not reported.

Housing tenure - The family's principal place of residence during the survey. "Owner" includes families living in their own homes, cooperatives or condominium apartments, or townhouses. "Renter" includes families paying rent as well as families living rent free in lieu of wages.

Income before taxes - The total money earnings and selected money receipts during the 12 months prior to the interview date. See the Income and Personal Taxes section of this glossary for a complete definition of the components.

Income after taxes - Income before taxes less personal taxes which include federal income taxes, state and local taxes, and other taxes. See section 3 of this glossary for a complete definition of the components.

Metropolitan Statistical Areas (MSA's) - The general concept of aN MSA and an SMSA is one of a large population nucleus, together with adjacent communities which have a high degree of economic and social integration with that nucleus. These are defined by the Office of Management and Budget as a standard for Federal agencies in the preparation and publication of statistics relating to metropolitan areas. The term MSA went into effect June 30, 1983, replacing the term SMSA; however, the Consumer Expenditure Survey collection process followed the old definition through 1985. Since 1986, the collection process has followed the new definition of an MSA.

Number of vehicles owned - The number of automobiles, trucks, vans, campers, motorcycles, trailers, and planes owned by members of the consumer unit, including vehicles used partially for business, but excluding those used entirely for business.

Occupation - Refers to the occupation in which the reference person received the most earnings during the survey period. The occupational categories follow those of the Census of Population. Categories shown in the reference tables include the following:

Self-employed

> Encompasses all occupational categories; the reference person is self-employed in own business, professional practice, or farm.

Wage and salary earners

> Managers and professionals--executives, administrators, and managers; and professional specialties, including architects, engineers, natural and social scientists, lawyers, teachers, writers, health diagnosis and treatment workers, entertainers, and athletes.

> Technical, sales, and clerical workers--technicians and related support workers; sales representatives, sales workers, cashiers, and sales-related occupations; and administrative support, including clerical.

> Service workers--private household workers, protective services, food preparers, health services, cleaning and building services, and personal service occupations.

> Precision production, craft, and repair workers--mechanics and repairers, construction trades, extractive occupations, and precision production occupations.

> Operators, fabricators, and laborers--machine operators and assemblers, transportation workers, handlers and laborers, and farming, forestry, and fishery workers.

Retired
> Retired persons who did not work either full- or part- time during the survey period.

All others, including not reporting
> A residual including unemployed persons, those working without pay, those not working due to illness, going to school, or caring for others, and those not reporting their occupational status.

Population - The total civilian noninstitutional population of the United States as well as that portion of the institutional population living in the following group quarters: Boarding houses, housing facilities for students and workers, staff units in hospitals and homes for the aged, infirm, or needy, permanent living quarters in hotels and motels, and mobile home parks. Excluded are military personnel living on military bases and nursing home residents.

Quintiles of income before taxes - For each time period represented in the tables, complete income reporters are ranked in ascending order according to the level of total before-tax income reported by the consumer unit. The ranking is then divided into five equal groups. Incomplete income reporters are not ranked and are shown separately.

Race - The race of the reference person of the consumer unit. All families are included in two racial groups, black and "white and other." The "other" group comprises such races as American Indians, Alaskan natives, Asians, and Pacific Islanders.

Reference person - The first member mentioned by the respondent when asked to "Start with the name of the person or one of the persons who owns or rents the home." It is with respect to this person that the relationship of the other consumer unit members is determined.

Regions - Data are presented for four major regions: Northeast, Midwest, South, and West. Consumer units are classified by region according to the address at which the family was residing during the time of their participation in the survey. The regions comprise the following States:

Northeast
Connecticut, Maine, Massachusetts, New Hampshire, New Jersey, New York, Pennsylvania, Rhode Island, and Vermont.

Midwest
Illinois, Indiana, Iowa, Kansas, Michigan, Minnesota, Missouri, Nebraska, North Dakota, Ohio, South Dakota, and Wisconsin.

South
Alabama, Arkansas, Delaware, District of Columbia, Florida, Georgia, Kentucky, Louisiana, Maryland, Mississippi, North Carolina, Oklahoma, South Carolina, Tennessee, Texas, Virginia, and West Virginia.

West
Alaska, Arizona, California, Colorado, Hawaii, Idaho, Montana, Nevada, New Mexico, Oregon, Utah, Washington, and Wyoming.

Rural population - All persons living outside of a Metropolitan Statistical Area (MSA) and within an area with a population of less than 2,500 persons. See the definition for Urban population below.

Size of the consumer unit - The number of persons whose usual place of residence at the time of the interview is in the sample unit.

Standard Metropolitan Statistical Areas (SMSA's) - See definition under Metropolitan Statistical Areas (MSA's).

Urban population - All persons living in Metropolitan Statistical Areas (MSA's) and in urbanized areas and urban places of 2,500 or more persons outside of MSA's. Urban, defined in this survey, includes the rural populations within an MSA.

EXPENDITURES

Expenditures consist of the transaction costs, including excise and sales taxes, of goods and services acquired during the interview or recordkeeping period. Expenditure estimates include expenditures for gifts, but exclude purchases or portions of purchases directly assignable to business purposes. Also excluded are periodic credit or installment payments on goods or services already acquired. The full cost of each purchase is recorded even though full payment may not have been made at the date of purchase. The order of the expenditures listed here follows the order of presentation in published CE tables.

The major expenditure categories are:

- Food
- Housing
- Apparel and Services
- Transportation
- Health Care
- Entertainment
- Other Expenditures

FOOD

Food at home refers to the total expenditures for food at grocery stores or other food stores and food prepared by the consumer unit on trips. It excludes the purchase of nonfood items.

Cereals and cereal products includes ready-to-eat and cooked cereals, pasta, flour, prepared flour mixes, and other cereal products such as cornmeal, corn starch, and rice.

Bakery products includes bread (white and other than white), crackers and cookies, biscuits and rolls, cakes, cupcakes, bread and cracker products, pies, tarts, sweet rolls, coffeecakes, doughnuts, and other frozen and refrigerated bakery products such as cookies, bread and cake dough, and batter.

Beef includes ground beef, roasts, steaks, veal, and other cuts of beef, excluding canned beef.

Pork includes bacon, pork chops, ham (including canned), roasts, sausage, and other cuts of pork.

Other meats includes frankfurters; lunch meats such as bologna, liverwurst, and salami; also lamb, mutton, goat, game, and organ meats.

Poultry includes fresh and frozen chickens and other fresh and frozen poultry (Cornish hens, turkey, duck, etc.).

Fish and seafood includes canned fish and seafood and fresh or frozen finfish and shellfish.

Eggs includes fresh eggs as well as powdered eggs and egg substitutes.

Fresh milk and cream includes fresh whole milk and other fresh milk such as buttermilk and fresh cream (including table cream, whipping cream, fresh sour cream, and fresh sour cream dressing).

Other dairy products includes butter, cheese, ice cream products, yogurt, powdered milk, condensed and evaporated milk, liquid and powdered diet beverages, malted milk, milk shakes, chocolate milk, and other specified dairy products.

Fresh fruits includes all fresh fruits.

Fresh vegetables includes all fresh vegetables.

Processed fruits includes all frozen fruits and fruit juices, canned and dried fruits, and canned or bottled fruit juices.

Processed vegetables includes canned, dried, and frozen vegetables, and vegetable juices.

Sugar and other sweets includes sugar, candy and chewing gum, artificial sweeteners, jams, jellies, preserves, fruit butters, syrup, fudge mixes, icings, and other sweets.

Fats and oils includes margarine, shortening and salad dressings, nondairy cream substitutes and imitation milk, and peanut butter.

Miscellaneous foods includes frozen prepared meals and other foods, canned and packaged soups, potato chips, nuts and other snacks, condiments and seasonings, olives, pickles, relishes, sauces and gravies, baking needs and other specified condiments, other canned and packaged prepared foods, salads, desserts, and baby foods.

Nonalcoholic beverages includes diet and nondiet carbonated drinks (cola, fruit, and other carbonated drinks), coffee (roasted, instant, and freeze dried), tea (loose, instant, and ready-to-drink), and other nonalcoholic beverages, including noncarbonated fruit drinks, breakfast substitutes, chocolate flavored powders, and other specified nonalcoholic beverages.

Food away from home includes all meals (breakfast, lunch, brunch, and dinner) at restaurants, carryouts, and vending machines, including tips, plus meals as pay, special catered affairs such as weddings, bar mitzvahs, and confirmations, and meals away from home on trips.

Alcoholic beverages includes beer and ale, wine, whiskey, gin, vodka, rum, and other alcoholic beverages.

HOUSING

Owned dwellings includes interest on mortgages, property taxes and insurance, refinancing and prepayment charges, ground rent, expenses for property management/security, homeowners' insurance, fire insurance and extended coverage, expenses for repairs and maintenance contracted out, and expenses of materials for owner-performed repairs and maintenance for dwellings used or maintained by the consumer unit. Mortgage principal repayments are payments of loans and are shown in Other financial information.

Rented dwellings includes rent paid for dwellings, rent received as pay, parking fees, maintenance, and other expenses.

Other lodging includes all expenses for vacation homes, school, college, hotels, motels, cottages, trailer camps, and other lodging while out of town.

Utilities, fuels, and public services includes natural gas, electricity, fuel oil, wood, kerosene, coal, bottled gas, water, garbage and trash collection, sewerage maintenance, septic tank cleaning, telephone charges, and other public services.

Domestic services includes babysitters, day care tuition, care of invalids, and domestic and other duties.

Other household expenses includes housekeeping services, gardening and lawn care services, coin-operated laundry and dry-cleaning (non-clothing), termite and pest control products, moving, storage, and freight expenses, repair of household appliances and other household equipment, repair of computer systems for home use, reupholstering and furniture repair, rental and repair of lawn and gardening tools, and rental of other household equipment.

Housekeeping and garden supplies includes laundry and cleaning supplies, cleaning and toilet tissues, stationery supplies, postage, miscellaneous household products, and lawn and garden supplies.

Household textiles includes bathroom, bedroom, kitchen, dining room, and other linens, curtains and drapes, slipcovers and decorative pillows, and sewing materials.

Furniture includes living room, dining room, kitchen, bedroom, nursery, porch, lawn, and other outdoor furniture.

Floor coverings includes installation and replacement of wall-to-wall carpets, room-size rugs, and other soft floor coverings.

Major appliances includes refrigerators, freezers, dishwashers, stoves, ovens, garbage disposals, vacuum cleaners, microwaves, air-conditioners, sewing machines, washing machines and dryers, and floor cleaning equipment.

Small appliances/miscellaneous housewares includes small electrical kitchen appliances, portable heating and cooling equipment, china and other dinnerware, flatware, glassware, silver and other serving pieces, nonelectric cookware, and plastic dinnerware. Excludes personal care appliances.

Miscellaneous household equipment includes typewriters, luggage, lamps and other light fixtures, window coverings, clocks, lawnmowers and gardening equipment, other hand and power tools, telephone answering devices, telephone accessories, computers and computer hardware for home use, computer software and accessories for home use, calculators, office equipment for home use, floral arrangements and house plants, rental of furniture, closet and storage items, household decorative items, infants' equipment, outdoor equipment, smoke alarms, other household appliances, and small miscellaneous furnishings.

APPAREL AND SERVICES

Men's and boys' apparel includes coats, jackets, sweaters, vests, sportcoats, tailored jackets, trousers, slacks, shorts and short sets, sportswear, shirts, underwear, nightwear, hosiery, uniforms, and other accessories.

Women's and girls' apparel includes coats, jackets, furs, sportcoats, tailored jackets, sweaters, vests, blouses, shirts, dresses, dungarees, culottes, slacks, shorts, sportswear, underwear, nightwear, uniforms, hosiery, and other accessories.

Apparel for children under 2 includes coats, jackets, snowsuits, underwear, diapers, dresses, crawlers, sleeping garments, hosiery, footwear, and other accessories for children under 2.

Footwear includes articles such as shoes, slippers, boots, and other similar items. It excludes footwear for children under 2 and special footwear used for sports such as bowling or golf shoes.

Other apparel products and services includes material for making clothes, shoe repair, alterations and repairs, sewing patterns and notions, clothing rental, clothing storage, dry cleaning, sent out laundry, watches, jewelry, and repairs to watches and jewelry.

TRANSPORTATION

Vehicle purchases (net outlay) includes the net outlay (purchase price minus trade-in value) on new and used domestic and imported cars and trucks; other vehicles include attachable campers, trailers, motorcycles, and private planes.

Vehicle finance charges includes the dollar amount of interest paid for a loan contracted for the purchase of vehicles described above.

Gasoline and motor oil includes gasoline, diesel fuel, and motor oil.

Maintenance and repairs includes tires, batteries, tubes, lubrication, filters, coolant, additives, brake and transmission fluids, oil change, brake adjustment and repair, front-end alignment, wheel balancing, steering repair, shock absorber replacement, clutch and transmission repair, electrical system repair, exhaust system repair, body work and painting, motor repair, repair to cooling system, drive train repair, drive shaft and rear-end repair, tire repair, other maintenance and services, and auto repair policies.

Vehicle insurance includes the premium paid for insuring cars, trucks, and other vehicles.

Public transportation includes fares for mass transit, buses, trains, airlines, taxis, private school buses, and boats.

Vehicle rent, licenses, and other charges includes leased and rented cars, trucks, motorcycles, and aircraft, inspection fees, State and local registration, drivers' license fees, parking fees, towing charges, and tolls.

HEALTH CARE

Health insurance includes health maintenance plans (HMO's), Blue Cross/Blue Shield, commercial health insurance, Medicare, Medicare supplemental insurance, and other health insurance.

Medical services includes hospital room and services, physicians' services, service of a practitioner other than physician, eye and dental care, lab tests, X-rays, nursing, therapy services, care in convalescent or nursing home, and other medical care.

Drugs includes prescription and nonprescription drugs, internal and respiratory over-the-counter drugs.

Medical supplies includes topicals and dressings, antiseptics, bandages, cotton, first aid kits, contraceptives, syringes, ice bags, thermometers, sunlamps, vaporizers, heating pads, medical appliances such as braces, canes, crutches, and walkers, eyeglasses, and hearing aids, rental and repair of medical equipment.

ENTERTAINMENT

Fees and admissions includes fees for participant sports; admissions to sporting events, movies, concerts, plays; health, swimming, tennis and country club memberships, and other social recreational and fraternal organizations; recreational lessons or instruction; rental of movies, and recreation expenses on trips.

Television, radio, and sound equipment includes television sets, video recorders, video cassettes, tapes, disks, disk players, video game hardware, video game cartridges, cable TV, radios, phonographs, tape recorders and players, sound components, records and tapes, and records and tapes through record clubs, musical instruments, and rental and repair of TV and sound equipment.

Pets, toys, hobbies, and playground equipment includes pet food, pet services, veterinary expenses, toys, games, hobbies, tricycles, and playground equipment.

Other entertainment equipment and services includes indoor exercise equipment, athletic shoes, bicycles, trailers, campers, camping equipment, rental of campers and trailers, hunting and fishing equipment, sports equipment, winter sports equipment, water sports equipment, boats, boat motors and boat trailers, rental of boats, landing and docking fees, rental and repair of sports equipment, photographic equipment, film and film processing, photographer fees, repair and rental of photo equipment, fireworks, pinball and electronic video games.

OTHER EXPENDITURES

Personal care products and services includes products for the hair, oral hygiene products, shaving needs, cosmetics and bath products, electric personal care appliances, other personal care products, personal care services for males and females.

Reading includes subscriptions for newspapers, magazines, and books through book clubs; purchase of single copy newspapers and magazines, newsletters, books, and encyclopedias and other reference books.

Education includes tuition, fees, textbooks, supplies, and equipment for public and private nursery schools, elementary and high schools, colleges and universities, and other schools.

Tobacco products and smoking supplies includes cigarettes, cigars, snuff, loose smoking tobacco, chewing tobacco, and smoking accessories such as cigarette or cigar holders, pipes, flints, lighters, pipe cleaners, and other smoking products and accessories.

Miscellaneous includes safety deposit box rental, checking account fees and other bank services, legal fees, accounting fees, funerals, cemetery lots, union dues, occupational expenses, and finance charges other than for mortgage and vehicles.

Cash contributions includes cash contributed to persons or organizations outside the consumer unit including alimony and child support payments, care of students away from home, and contributions to religious, educational, charitable, or political organizations.

Life, endowment, annuities, and other personal insurance includes premiums for whole life and term insurance; endowments; income and other life insurance; mortgage guarantee insurance; mortgage life insurance; premiums for personal liability, accident and disability, and other nonhealth insurance other than for homes and vehicles.

Retirement, pensions, and Social Security includes all Social Security contributions paid by employees; employee's contributions to railroad retirement, government retirement, and private pension programs; retirement programs for self-employed.

INCOME AND PERSONAL TAXES

Income is the combined income of all consumer unit members 14 years of age or over during the 12 months preceding the interview. The components of income are described below. The order of the definitions of income and personal taxes follows the order of presentation in published CE tables.

For a definition of <u>Complete income reporters</u> or <u>Quintiles of income</u>, see the Characteristics section above.

Money income before taxes is the total money earnings and selected money receipts during the 12 months prior to the interview date. It includes the following components:

Wages and salaries includes total money earnings for all consumer unit members, 14 years of age and over, from all jobs, including civilian wages and salaries, Armed Forces pay and allowances, piece-rate payments, commissions, tips, National Guard or Reserve pay (received for training periods), and cash bonuses before deductions for taxes, pensions, union dues, etc.

Self-employment income includes net business and farm income, which consists of net income (gross receipts minus operating expenses) from a profession or unincorporated business or from the operation of a farm by an owner, tenant, or sharecropper. If the business or farm is a partnership, only an appropriate share of net income is recorded. Losses are also recorded.

Social Security, private and government retirement includes the following: (1) payments by the Federal Government made under retirement, survivors', and disability insurance programs to retired persons, to dependents of deceased insured workers, or to disabled workers; and (2) private pensions or retirement benefits received by retired persons or their survivors, either directly or through an insurance company.

Interest, dividends, rental income, and other property income includes interest income on savings or bonds; payments made by a corporation to its stockholders, periodic receipts from estates or trust funds; net income or loss from the rental of property, real estate, or farms, and net income or loss from roomers or boarders.

Unemployment and workers' compensation and veterans' benefits includes income from unemployment compensation and workers' compensation, and veterans' payments including educational benefits, but excluding military retirement.

Public assistance, supplemental security income, and food stamps includes public assistance or welfare, including money received from job training grants; supplemental security income paid by Federal, State, and local welfare agencies to low-income persons who are age 65 or over, blind, or disabled; and the value of food stamps obtained.

Regular contributions for support includes alimony and child support as well as any regular contributions from persons outside the consumer unit.

Other income includes money income from care of foster children, cash scholarships, fellowships, or stipends not based on working; and meals and rent as pay.

Federal income taxes includes Federal income taxes withheld in survey year to pay for income earned in survey year plus additional taxes paid in survey year to cover any underpayment or underwithholding of taxes in the year prior to the survey.

State and local income taxes includes State and local income taxes withheld in survey year to pay for income earned in survey year plus additional taxes paid in survey year to cover any underpayment or underwithholding of taxes in year prior to survey.

Other taxes includes personal property and other personal taxes paid, including Social Security taxes for the self-employed paid in the survey year to cover any underpayment or underwithholding of taxes in the year prior to the survey.

OTHER FINANCIAL INFORMATION

The items here are not part of expenditures or income. They are provided for additional information.

Net change in assets includes changes in savings and checking accounts; purchases of securities (stocks, bonds, or mutual funds) in the year which they were held to the end of the year; sales of securities which were purchased in a prior year; changes in the balances of money owed to the consumer unit (CU); sales and purchases, and repairs and improvements to own dwelling occupied by the CU; vacation home, recreational property, unimproved land and other property owned by the CU; changes in investments in unincorporated family businesses and farms; amounts received or reimbursements from the sale of vehicles; principal amounts of trust held on own dwelling, vacation home, and other properties owned by the CU; and surrender of insurance policies. This value has a positive or negative sign to indicate increase or decrease in assets.

Net change in liabilities includes changes in mortgage principal on own dwelling occupied by the consumer unit (CU), vacation home, recreational property, unimproved land and other property owned by the CU; payments of mortgage interest due before either survey year of the survey period; money owed on purchases of cars, trucks, and other vehicles, and money owed to other creditors such as department stores, banks, credit unions, finance companies, insurance companies, doctors, dentists, and other medical practitioners. This value has a positive or negative sign to indicate increases or decreases in liabilities.

Other money receipts includes lump-sum payment from estates, trusts, insurance, sale of house furnishings, refunds from overpayment on Social Security, refunds from insurance policies, and refunds from property taxes.

Mortgage principal paid on owned property includes the reduction of mortgage principal on a mortgage obtained prior to the interview quarter for a home or any other property. This is not included in homeowner costs, but is repayment of a loan.

Gifts of goods and services includes gift expenditures for persons outside of the consumer unit: (1) clothing for females and males over 2 years of age, and infants under 2 years of age; (2) jewelry and watches; (3) small appliances and miscellaneous housewares; (4) blankets, sheets, towels, and table linens; and (5) all other gifts. These items have already been defined. Their values are given so they can be subtracted from the expenditure totals if the value of consumption within the household is desired.

Consumer Expenditure Surveys Home Page

BLS Home Page

Walter VanderHeide
Bureau of Labor Statistics
VanderHeide_W@bls.gov
Last modified: March 22, 1999
URL: http://stats.bls.gov/csxgloss.htm

U.S. Department of Labor

Bureau of Labor Statistics
2 Massachusetts Ave. N.E.
Washington, D.C. 20212

January 27, 1992

Enclosed are results from the Integrated Consumer Expenditure Survey(CE) which you requested. The integrated data from the Diary and Interview surveys provide a complete accounting of consumer expenditures and income, which neither survey component alone is designed to do. The detailed data on these listings are unpublished estimates. Caution should be exercised when interpreting these data, especially when relating averages to individual circumstances. The following points should be taken into consideration.

The expenditures are averages for consumer units with specified characteristics, regardless of whether or not a particular unit incurred an expense for that specific item during the recordkeeping period. The average expenditure for an item is, in general, considerably lower than the expenditure by those consumer units that purchased it. The less frequently an item is purchased, the greater the difference between the average for all consumer units and the average for those purchasing the item. Even if all consumer units purchased a particular item, an individual consumer unit may have spent more or less than the average for that item. The data are averages for the total population—urban and rural. Income, family size, age of family members, and geographic location are among the factors which influence expenditures. Even within a group having similar characteristics, there may be significant variation because of individual needs, tastes, and preferences.

Average expenditures of the most detailed items may be unreliable because there are so few reports of expenditures for those items. A small number of unusually large purchases or a slight increase in the number of expenditures for infrequently reported items can cause a large change in its mean from one year to the next.

Expenditures reported here are direct out-of-pocket expenditures. Indirect expenditures, which may be significant, may be reflected elsewhere. For example, rental contracts often include utilities. Renters with such contracts would record no direct expense for utilities and, therefore, appear to have lower utility expenses. Other costs are frequently paid by employers or insurance companies. Consumer units with members whose employers pay for all or part of their health insurance or life insurance would have lower direct expense for these items that those who pay the entire amount themselves.

In addition, caution should be used in interpreting changes in expenditures over a short time span. Average amounts spend on different expenditure components may fluctuate from year to year due to changes in economics conditions. For example, a decrease in the supply of food products as a result of poor weather conditions, or a decrease in the oil supply arising from political events such as an oil embargo might result in sharp price increases and short-term changes in expenditure levels. A less volatile measure of expenditure patterns is the share of total expenditures allocated to major expenditure categories over a period of several years.

For inquires please contact:

Division of Consumer Expenditure Surveys
Bureau of Labor Statistics
Washington, DC 20212-0001
(202) 606-6900

jc (4-26-94)

APPENDIX G

Cost of Living Indexes

Third quarter, 1996, selected metropolitan areas. Measures *relative* price levels for consumer goods and services in participating areas. The average for all participating places, both metropolitan and nonmetropolitan, equals 100, and each participant's index is read as a percentage of the average for all places.

Source: ACCRA Cost of Living Index, Third Quarter 1996, ACCRA, Alexandria, VA. Copyright © 1997. Reprinted with permission.

COMPONENT INDEX WEIGHTS MSA/PMSA URBAN AREA AND STATE	100% COMPOSITE INDEX	16% GROCERY ITEMS	28% HOUSING	8% UTILITIES	10% TRANS- PORTATION	5% HEALTH CARE
Anniston AL MSA						
Anniston/Calhoun County AL	90.9	97.6	80.3	103.9	89.4	88.8
Birmingham AL MSA						
Birmingham AL MSA	98.4	97.3	98.5	98.6	96.3	99.5
Decatur AL MSA						
Decatur-Hartselle AL	93.6	98.5	84.8	89.8	99.9	91.4
Dothan AL MSA						
Dothan AL	93.1	99.0	87.4	99.5	92.9	81.8
Florence AL MSA						
Florence AL MSA	94.1	96.1	85.8	98.5	97.5	95.3
Gadsden AL MSA						
Gadsden AL	92.1	98.8	80.9	100.4	92.7	90.9
Huntsville AL MSA						
Huntsville AL	95.7	95.5	84.7	90.3	96.4	104.0
Mobile AL MSA						
Mobile AL	93.9	99.1	77.1	101.4	104.7	93.9
Montgomery AL MSA						
Montgomery AL	94.3	95.3	84.4	95.7	107.0	97.1
Tuscaloosa AL MSA						
Tuscaloosa AL	101.4	97.3	98.0	104.9	97.8	94.9
Anchorage AK MSA						
Anchorage AK	124.8	121.9	133.8	84.0	109.7	173.5
Flagstaff AZ-UT MSA						
Flagstaff AZ	111.4	105.0	131.0	96.8	112.7	110.7
Las Vegas NV-AZ MSA						
Lake Havasu City AZ	100.1	108.4	89.9	92.1	105.1	114.9
Phoenix-Mesa AZ MSA						
Phoenix AZ	103.3	104.5	97.9	106.6	118.3	117.7
Scottsdale AZ	106.3	104.1	112.2	106.4	124.0	115.1
Tucson AZ MSA						
Tucson AZ	99.8	104.5	95.1	110.9	102.1	113.8
Yuma AZ						
Yuma AZ	98.9	103.6	80.4	152.6	113.7	103.2
Fayetteville-Springdale-Rogers AR MSA						
Fayetteville AR	93.1	99.5	84.5	86.8	90.3	85.9
Fort Smith AR-OK MSA						
Fort Smith AR	88.8	98.8	75.9	100.5	84.4	78.5
Jonesboro AR MSA						
Jonesboro AR	87.4	96.2	78.9	78.2	82.0	88.3
Little Rock-North Little Rock AR MSA						
Little Rock-N Little Rock AR	86.9	96.2	80.7	101.1	93.3	72.0
Bakersfield CA MSA						
Bakersfield CA	104.0	109.2	92.8	115.1	115.5	112.1
Fresno CA MSA						
Fresno CA	107.1	106.6	99.5	112.3	119.9	113.0
Los Angeles-Long Beach CA PMSA						
Los Angeles-Long Beach CA PMSA	119.7	117.1	132.0	116.0	116.2	137.5
Riverside-San Bernardino CA PMSA						
Palm Springs CA	116.2	109.6	115.6	146.1	110.1	141.0
Riverside City CA	108.7	107.3	106.1	98.7	114.7	130.3
Salinas CA MSA						
Salinas-Monterey CA	143.6	112.8	212.7	100.4	128.6	160.6
San Diego CA MSA						
San Diego CA	121.9	113.4	152.2	100.9	131.0	120.0
Santa Barbara-Santa Maria-Lompoc CA MSA						
Lompoc CA	113.2	106.9	134.0	107.4	112.0	114.5
Visalia-Tulare-Porterville CA MSA						
Visalia CA	108.6	99.6	106.2	124.2	116.4	124.8
Boulder-Longmont CO PMSA						
Boulder CO	109.5	98.9	137.5	77.5	104.4	121.3
Longmont CO	98.7	104.8	97.8	69.0	106.4	117.6
Colorado Springs CO MSA						
Colorado Springs CO	103.4	96.6	124.2	71.2	98.5	123.8
Denver CO PMSA						
Denver CO PMSA	103.4	97.6	117.4	77.5	107.5	120.7
Fort Collins-Loveland CO MSA						
Fort Collins CO	105.8	105.9	121.6	68.4	97.2	116.0
Loveland CO	95.1	101.5	97.0	74.8	100.1	102.2
Grand Junction CO MSA						
Grand Junction CO	101.4	102.3	108.5	77.7	104.3	96.9
Greeley CO PMSA						
Greeley CO	90.2	96.9	86.5	73.0	96.9	105.4
Pueblo CO MSA						
Pueblo CO	90.0	102.0	81.8	81.5	95.0	116.7

COMPONENT INDEX WEIGHTS MSA/PMSA URBAN AREA AND STATE	100% COMPOSITE INDEX	16% GROCERY ITEMS	28% HOUSING	8% UTILITIES	10% TRANS- PORTATION	5% HEALTH CARE
New Haven-Meriden CT PMSA						
New Haven CT	123.0	128.0	133.1	159.6	107.4	128.2
Washington DC-MD-VA-WV PMSA						
Washington DC-MD-VA-WV PMSA	125.4	109.0	158.7	94.2	125.3	120.9
Daytona Beach FL MSA						
Daytona Beach FL	95.9	99.2	91.5	101.1	95.8	97.2
Fort Myers-Cape Coral FL MSA						
Fort Myers-Cape Coral FL MSA	98.4	98.7	92.5	102.4	106.2	103.8
Fort Walton Beach FL MSA						
Fort Walton Beach FL	98.5	98.0	92.3	98.4	97.6	107.8
Gainesville FL MSA						
Gainesville FL	100.4	101.5	97.5	117.5	101.3	105.7
Jacksonville FL MSA						
Jacksonville FL	96.0	100.2	84.9	107.7	97.2	93.0
Miami FL PMSA						
Miami/Dade County FL	107.7	103.6	111.5	107.1	114.1	123.4
Orlando FL MSA						
Orlando FL	99.4	99.6	93.4	102.6	98.8	110.2
Panama City FL MSA						
Panama City FL MSA	94.7	98.7	86.6	98.1	95.6	90.4
Pensacola FL MSA						
Pensacola FL	95.2	102.2	83.3	95.3	97.3	99.7
Sarasota-Bradenton FL MSA						
Bradenton FL	102.9	98.9	108.5	99.5	98.8	102.6
Sarasota FL	102.0	94.8	108.5	107.0	92.9	108.1
Tallahassee FL MSA						
Tallahassee FL	102.3	97.5	104.2	116.6	99.2	98.1
Tampa-St Petersburg-Clearwater FL MSA						
Tampa FL	94.3	101.7	86.5	108.3	96.0	96.4
West Palm Beach-Boca Raton FL MSA						
West Palm Beach FL	107.7	101.9	108.9	117.6	105.6	110.0
Albany GA MSA						
Albany GA	92.8	98.1	76.1	105.7	96.8	88.4
Atlanta GA MSA						
Atlanta GA	99.5	101.9	96.4	94.4	104.9	109.7
Augusta-Aiken GA-SC MSA						
Augusta-Aiken GA-SC MSA	94.0	96.9	80.2	110.5	97.3	94.9
Macon GA MSA						
Warner Robins GA	95.7	100.4	89.1	102.6	94.8	87.4
Boise City ID MSA						
Boise ID	103.1	101.4	108.6	67.5	100.0	116.6
Champaign-Urbana IL MSA						
Champaign-Urbana IL	102.8	103.5	106.1	110.6	94.9	109.2
Davenport-Moline-Rock Island IA-IL MSA						
Quad-Cities IL-IA	96.9	103.7	91.4	101.7	98.5	93.7
Decatur IL MSA						
Decatur IL	93.9	99.6	80.1	109.9	98.7	90.1
Peoria-Pekin IL MSA						
Peoria IL	101.1	104.3	103.1	94.8	101.0	96.2
Rockford IL MSA						
Rockford IL	105.3	101.3	107.6	110.3	108.4	101.9
Springfield IL MSA						
Springfield IL	95.6	103.8	80.8	80.8	93.0	107.8
Bloomington IN MSA						
Bloomington IN	97.2	103.2	97.7	86.5	95.6	94.8
Elkhart-Goshen IN MSA						
Elkhart-Goshen IN	92.3	95.1	89.5	89.4	95.4	90.9
Evansville-Henderson IN-KY MSA						
Evansville IN	93.1	102.1	91.4	86.4	94.4	89.5
Fort Wayne IN MSA						
Fort Wayne/Allen County IN	91.3	97.6	83.9	90.0	96.1	88.7
Indianapolis IN MSA						
Anderson IN	94.7	99.2	97.2	87.9	95.9	93.0
Muncie IN MSA						
Muncie IN	96.5	98.7	101.0	79.3	100.7	91.2
South Bend IN MSA						
South Bend IN	92.1	91.8	89.1	97.2	92.9	96.6

COMPONENT INDEX WEIGHTS MSA/PMSA URBAN AREA AND STATE	100% COMPOSITE INDEX	16% GROCERY ITEMS	28% HOUSING	8% UTILITIES	10% TRANS- PORTATION	5% HEALTH CARE
Cedar Rapids IA MSA						
Cedar Rapids IA	98.9	95.0	103.0	100.4	100.2	94.2
Des Moines IA MSA						
Des Moines IA	97.7	98.6	92.9	87.6	95.2	102.9
Dubuque IA MSA						
Dubuque IA	107.6	100.0	130.0	90.8	99.3	94.2
Lawrence KS MSA						
Lawrence KS	99.5	90.5	108.0	78.6	92.0	92.9
Cincinnati OH-KY-IN PMSA						
Covington KY	90.4	95.9	84.0	88.0	92.1	98.5
Clarksville-Hopkinsville TN-KY MSA						
Hopkinsville KY	92.9	98.2	83.8	88.5	89.6	87.2
Evansville-Henderson IN-KY MSA						
Henderson KY	92.0	106.2	85.4	86.0	89.8	88.7
Lexington KY MSA						
Lexington KY MSA	97.4	97.3	94.9	82.2	96.6	100.0
Louisville KY-IN MSA						
Louisville KY	94.0	95.0	88.0	94.9	102.1	96.0
Owensboro KY MSA						
Owensboro KY	92.2	100.0	86.7	69.6	94.0	91.0
Alexandria LA MSA						
Alexandria LA MSA	92.0	87.8	88.5	93.3	93.7	76.9
Baton Rouge LA MSA						
Baton Rouge LA	100.0	101.8	98.2	107.5	103.8	92.5
Lafayette LA MSA						
Lafayette LA	96.7	96.1	90.0	107.4	101.7	89.5
Lake Charles LA MSA						
Lake Charles LA	97.5	98.0	91.3	114.8	95.8	86.4
Monroe LA MSA						
Monroe LA	96.7	93.6	83.3	131.2	94.5	89.0
New Orleans LA MSA						
New Orleans LA	94.9	97.6	83.0	132.9	100.0	79.2
Shreveport-Bossier City LA MSA						
Shreveport-Bossier City LA MSA	93.7	88.4	95.0	95.9	96.4	88.9
Baltimore MD PMSA						
Baltimore MD	100.4	101.9	99.5	112.5	105.6	95.9
Cumberland MD-WV MSA						
Cumberland MD	101.0	98.8	104.8	114.5	96.1	91.3
Hagerstown MD PMSA						
Hagerstown MD	99.0	92.5	93.9	102.0	100.3	96.5
Boston MA-NH PMSA						
Boston PMSA (MA Part)	142.5	115.0	206.6	137.2	120.3	136.2
Fitchburg-Leominster MA PMSA						
Fitchburg-Leominster MA PMSA	99.8	108.4	90.9	120.8	99.4	104.4
Benton Harbor MI MSA						
Benton Harbor-St Joseph MI	106.7	107.4	112.7	98.8	100.4	100.2
Detroit MI PMSA						
Oakland County MI	113.4	110.6	137.5	86.2	102.2	118.8
Grand Rapids-Muskegon-Holland MI MSA						
Holland MI	103.7	109.3	113.3	81.9	102.8	88.4
Lansing-East Lansing MI MSA						
Lansing MI	107.2	109.6	127.0	77.7	99.0	107.5
Minneapolis-St Paul MN-WI MSA						
Minneapolis MN	101.4	97.4	97.0	100.9	113.9	126.9
Rochester MN MSA						
Rochester MN	97.7	97.0	91.0	96.1	108.6	98.6
St Cloud MN MSA						
St Cloud MN MSA	96.7	100.5	88.1	96.2	107.7	98.3
Biloxi-Gulfport-Pascagoula MS MSA						
Gulfport MS	94.8	97.0	86.4	109.9	90.5	97.0
Hattiesburg MS MSA						
Hattiesburg MS	92.4	95.9	79.2	102.7	102.4	90.7
Jackson MS MSA						
Jackson MS	95.5	98.7	93.6	102.9	96.3	82.2

COMPONENT INDEX WEIGHTS MSA/PMSA URBAN AREA AND STATE	100% COMPOSITE INDEX	16% GROCERY ITEMS	28% HOUSING	8% UTILITIES	10% TRANS- PORTATION	5% HEALTH CARE
Columbia MO MSA						
Columbia MO	94.5	102.1	83.7	81.2	99.2	102.2
Joplin MO MSA						
Joplin MO MSA	89.9	94.4	84.1	83.5	86.1	96.7
Kansas City MO-KS MSA						
Kansas City MO-KS MSA	97.5	98.3	93.3	94.8	97.8	107.7
Lee's Summit MO	96.7	98.7	90.0	95.7	105.6	101.3
St Joseph MO MSA						
St Joseph MO MSA	94.1	88.2	96.4	82.5	95.1	95.2
St Louis MO-IL MSA						
St Louis MO-IL MSA	98.7	107.0	97.4	93.1	96.9	109.8
Springfield MO MSA						
Springfield MO	91.4	93.5	89.6	72.5	96.0	95.7
Billings MT MSA						
Billings MT	100.9	103.7	103.9	73.9	103.8	102.5
Great Falls MT MSA						
Great Falls MT	107.0	105.2	128.4	70.4	100.9	103.2
Lincoln NE MSA						
Lincoln NE	89.1	93.0	75.7	83.3	101.2	84.0
Omaha NE-IA MSA						
Omaha NE	92.0	92.9	92.0	86.7	102.7	88.9
Las Vegas NV-AZ MSA						
Las Vegas NV	104.7	110.9	106.8	75.7	116.9	119.2
Reno NV MSA						
Reno-Sparks NV	112.4	106.4	129.0	90.9	117.7	110.9
Manchester NH PMSA						
Manchester NH	106.5	99.0	103.7	147.2	102.5	117.6
Albuquerque NM MSA						
Albuquerque NM	101.9	100.0	104.2	101.6	98.2	107.0
Las Cruces NM MSA						
Las Cruces NM MSA	98.0	97.4	99.4	90.4	96.9	96.2
Santa Fe NM MSA						
Los Alamos NM	114.7	99.1	144.2	84.6	114.6	113.5
Santa Fe NM	107.4	99.5	125.8	86.8	104.3	111.8
Binghamton NY MSA						
Binghamton/Broome County NY	103.8	105.8	97.3	130.7	102.8	87.8
Buffalo-Niagara Falls NY MSA						
Buffalo-Niagara Falls NY	96.6	109.8	85.3	126.8	105.9	96.3
Elmira NY MSA						
Elmira NY	112.3	108.4	122.3	141.6	106.4	92.9
Glens Falls NY MSA						
Glens Falls NY	99.8	101.9	85.8	130.7	104.1	100.0
New York NY PMSA						
New York (Manhattan) NY	234.5	144.6	465.5	173.4	123.6	206.9
Rochester NY MSA						
Rochester NY MSA	102.2	117.0	86.9	127.9	118.9	89.2
Syracuse NY MSA						
Syracuse NY	103.2	112.4	92.7	133.6	109.1	106.8
Utica-Rome NY MSA						
Utica-Rome NY MSA	104.3	101.7	98.7	136.7	107.3	98.2
Asheville NC MSA						
Asheville NC	104.8	96.4	107.7	116.6	105.1	85.9
Charlotte-Gastonia-Rock Hill NC-SC MSA						
Charlotte NC	99.0	96.5	97.6	103.6	98.6	102.6
Fayetteville NC MSA						
Fayetteville NC	97.2	98.6	85.1	116.7	94.7	89.8
Greensboro-Winston-Salem-High Point NC MSA						
Burlington NC	91.9	94.4	86.2	104.8	89.4	90.9
Winston-Salem NC	100.9	94.9	107.8	110.1	100.3	87.7
Greenville NC MSA						
Greenville NC	97.6	96.1	88.9	132.7	92.1	94.4
Raleigh-Durham-Chapel Hill NC MSA						
Chapel Hill NC	114.5	98.1	137.9	112.3	101.4	111.2
Raleigh-Durham NC	103.0	100.9	108.2	112.3	93.7	104.7
Wilmington NC MSA						
Wilmington NC	102.6	98.1	109.8	113.8	89.3	99.8

COMPONENT INDEX WEIGHTS MSA/PMSA URBAN AREA AND STATE	100% COMPOSITE INDEX	16% GROCERY ITEMS	28% HOUSING	8% UTILITIES	10% TRANS- PORTATION	5% HEALTH CARE
Bismarck ND MSA						
Bismarck-Mandan ND	99.4	108.5	95.0	87.8	94.7	103.1
Fargo-Moorhead ND-MN MSA						
Fargo-Moorhead ND-MN MSA	98.8	101.2	96.6	90.7	91.6	103.3
Grand Forks ND-MN MSA						
Grand Forks ND	101.2	103.9	96.0	96.5	104.4	93.7
Canton/Stark County OH	97.1	100.9	100.1	83.5	96.6	91.2
Cleveland-Lorain-Elyria OH PMSA						
Cleveland OH	104.4	103.5	103.1	115.2	108.7	111.4
Columbus OH MSA						
Columbus OH	105.1	106.5	106.6	109.8	103.2	96.6
Dayton-Springfield OH MSA						
Dayton-Springfield OH	105.9	98.0	115.5	114.6	102.7	101.3
Mansfield OH MSA						
Mansfield OH	100.1	101.7	94.1	139.4	95.8	89.0
Toledo OH MSA						
Toledo OH	100.6	102.5	91.8	137.0	106.2	95.8
Youngstown-Warren OH MSA						
Youngstown-Warren OH MSA	96.3	96.8	98.2	107.0	89.0	91.9
Lawton OK MSA						
Lawton OK	92.9	95.7	86.0	87.1	94.2	92.9
Oklahoma City OK MSA						
Oklahoma City OK	90.0	89.6	77.1	92.7	92.4	94.5
Tulsa OK MSA						
Tulsa OK	93.0	93.6	83.0	100.1	91.7	95.9
Eugene-Springfield OR MSA						
Eugene OR	108.3	93.4	131.2	73.6	105.0	115.7
Portland-Vancouver OR-WA PMSA						
Portland OR PMSA	109.1	99.7	121.7	89.2	112.8	124.0
Salem OR PMSA						
Salem OR	106.0	95.1	112.9	103.6	108.4	124.8
Allentown-Bethlehem-Easton PA MSA						
Allentown-Bethlehem-Easton PA	103.4	107.2	101.9	118.5	98.2	94.4
Altoona PA MSA						
Altoona PA	96.1	101.2	95.3	118.8	87.0	88.8
Harrisburg-Lebanon-Carlisle PA MSA						
Harrisburg PA	101.7	96.6	96.5	118.4	111.2	102.4
Lancaster PA MSA						
Lancaster PA	103.2	96.7	102.5	106.8	109.6	90.7
Philadelphia PA-NJ PMSA						
Philadelphia PA	125.5	112.7	140.1	199.9	117.4	99.3
Pittsburgh PA MSA						
Pittsburgh PA	109.5	103.1	107.9	133.6	106.4	111.4
Scranton-Wilkes Barre-Hazleton PA MSA						
Wilkes-Barre PA	97.5	104.2	97.7	100.4	93.1	90.5
Williamsport PA MSA						
Williamsport/Lycoming Co PA	101.9	99.3	100.5	137.8	97.1	95.7
York PA MSA						
Hanover PA	99.8	93.6	101.9	104.9	98.4	82.7
York County PA	96.8	94.4	89.4	109.4	106.2	93.0
Providence-Fall River-Warwick RI-MA PMSA						
Providence RI	116.0	101.5	134.9	134.3	109.7	118.6
Charleston-North Charleston SC MSA						
Charleston-N Charleston SC MSA	97.1	97.5	86.0	123.5	93.9	97.9
Columbia SC MSA						
Columbia SC	94.0	97.5	88.9	111.5	86.5	88.6
Greenville-Spartanburg-Anderson SC MSA						
Spartanburg SC	94.2	97.8	91.3	103.8	91.0	87.9
Myrtle Beach SC MSA						
Myrtle Beach SC	99.9	99.2	99.7	101.3	95.2	93.9
Sumter SC MSA						
Sumter SC	94.7	97.4	79.5	115.3	93.8	94.2
Rapid City SD MSA						
Rapid City SD	96.7	100.5	93.2	103.8	98.5	92.3
Sioux Falls SD MSA						
Sioux Falls SD	95.1	97.0	93.0	92.4	95.8	102.3

COMPONENT INDEX WEIGHTS MSA/PMSA URBAN AREA AND STATE	100% COMPOSITE INDEX	16% GROCERY ITEMS	28% HOUSING	8% UTILITIES	10% TRANS- PORTATION	5% HEALTH CARE
Chattanooga TN-GA MSA						
Chattanooga TN	93.0	96.9	86.3	88.8	88.5	88.0
Clarksville-Hopkinsville TN-KY MSA						
Clarksville TN	94.5	93.2	95.3	92.4	96.7	89.9
Jackson TN MSA						
Jackson/Madison County TN	94.8	97.5	91.9	94.1	100.5	84.3
Johnson City-Kingsport-Bristol TN-VA MSA						
Johnson City TN	95.3	92.3	100.8	84.8	88.5	86.4
Kingsport TN	89.1	96.1	85.3	83.6	87.7	86.8
Knoxville TN MSA						
Knoxville TN	97.5	94.9	90.6	93.2	90.8	97.4
Memphis TN-AR-MS MSA						
Memphis TN	95.4	102.7	95.5	78.6	99.3	92.0
Nashville TN MSA						
Nashville-Franklin TN	94.2	97.1	91.3	91.1	96.8	95.1
Abilene TX MSA						
Abilene TX	92.4	88.9	84.0	92.2	102.6	100.0
Amarillo TX MSA						
Amarillo TX	90.0	92.9	86.5	62.8	102.3	88.8
Austin-San Marcos TX MSA						
Austin TX	101.3	87.6	105.4	89.2	100.0	105.5
Georgetown TX	95.9	91.8	96.3	101.3	105.3	92.2
San Marcos TX	94.0	85.4	94.1	90.9	102.7	90.4
Beaumont-Port Arthur TX MSA						
Beaumont TX	94.6	88.2	89.8	91.7	98.9	96.7
Brownsville-Harlingen-San Benito TX MSA						
Harlingen TX	88.2	83.5	77.0	96.4	104.0	93.3
Bryan-College Station TX MSA						
Bryan-College Station TX	90.5	91.5	84.3	105.9	88.2	99.7
Dallas TX PMSA						
Dallas TX PMSA	98.9	96.7	94.9	99.9	105.0	107.9
Fort Worth-Arlington TX PMSA						
Weatherford TX	92.2	86.4	76.2	119.0	100.3	95.1
Houston TX PMSA						
Conroe TX	92.2	91.8	83.0	86.7	98.7	108.8
Houston TX PMSA	93.8	92.2	82.5	98.7	106.3	104.0
Killeen-Temple TX MSA						
Killeen TX	92.2	88.0	85.7	98.9	91.1	104.5
Lubbock TX MSA						
Lubbock TX	90.5	93.0	84.5	72.2	95.9	92.9
McAllen-Edinburg-Mission TX MSA						
McAllen TX	94.5	91.1	86.5	102.5	91.5	85.8
Odessa-Midland TX MSA						
Midland TX	92.1	95.0	74.9	96.3	95.3	100.1
Odessa TX	93.0	93.0	80.7	96.0	101.1	91.2
San Angelo TX MSA						
San Angelo TX	93.0	90.3	79.9	87.4	98.8	87.0
San Antonio TX MSA						
San Antonio TX	92.2	95.2	85.1	96.0	93.0	98.3
Texarkana TX-AR MSA						
Texarkana TX-AR	88.6	90.8	76.0	91.1	97.6	95.8
Tyler TX MSA						
Tyler TX	91.2	88.8	81.4	96.9	101.3	89.2
Victoria TX MSA						
Victoria TX	90.8	85.0	88.0	95.4	93.1	92.2
Waco TX MSA						
Waco TX MSA	91.2	86.2	78.8	117.1	101.2	86.4
Wichita Falls TX MSA						
Wichita Falls TX	89.7	93.8	75.2	97.8	96.7	92.2
Provo-Orem UT MSA						
Provo-Orem UT	103.9	97.3	115.5	81.9	107.4	118.6
Salt Lake City-Ogden UT MSA						
Salt Lake City UT	96.5	102.2	96.7	76.4	96.5	105.6
Burlington VT MSA						
Burlington/Chittenden Co VT	118.2	107.5	135.2	128.9	101.6	119.9
Johnson City-Kingsport-Bristol TN-VA MSA						
Bristol VA-TN	91.9	93.6	85.5	112.3	88.9	77.4
Lynchburg VA MSA						
Lynchburg VA	95.0	100.7	91.6	89.5	89.3	92.9

COMPONENT INDEX WEIGHTS MSA/PMSA URBAN AREA AND STATE	100% COMPOSITE INDEX	16% GROCERY ITEMS	28% HOUSING	8% UTILITIES	10% TRANS- PORTATION	5% HEALTH CARE
Norfolk-Virginia Beach-Newport News VA-NC MSA						
Virginia Peninsula VA	98.5	98.0	89.5	129.2	104.1	101.5
Richmond-Petersburg VA MSA						
Richmond VA	103.0	99.4	101.9	117.7	108.4	108.3
Roanoke VA MSA						
Roanoke VA	92.5	94.4	91.1	85.2	91.8	93.6
Washington DC-MD-VA-WV PMSA						
Fredericksburg VA	108.9	105.1	111.2	125.5	105.5	106.4
Prince William VA	111.8	103.7	129.8	127.5	108.2	101.0
Bellingham WA MSA						
Bellingham WA	104.8	103.0	113.1	81.8	97.4	125.7
Bremerton WA PMSA						
Bremerton WA	111.1	102.9	116.8	109.8	107.6	134.3
Portland-Vancouver OR-WA PMSA						
Vancouver WA	106.8	97.1	113.9	73.1	104.2	127.4
Richland-Kennewick-Pasco WA MSA						
Richland-Kennewick-Pasco WA	99.5	101.5	95.0	83.7	96.3	131.6
Seattle-Bellevue-Everett WA PMSA						
Seattle WA	115.0	110.6	124.6	78.4	112.8	147.1
Spokane WA MSA						
Spokane WA MSA	107.7	102.4	125.2	61.2	101.0	119.8
Tacoma WA PMSA						
Tacoma WA	104.6	110.6	103.3	76.2	111.5	138.4
Yakima WA MSA						
Yakima WA	106.8	102.0	122.4	91.3	100.1	127.1
Charleston WV MSA						
Charleston WV MSA	100.4	106.2	100.3	109.8	101.0	91.6
Huntington-Ashland WV-KY-OH MSA						
Huntington WV	99.0	104.5	87.0	118.7	100.8	98.9
Washington DC-MD-VA-WV PMSA						
Martinsburg/Berkeley County WV	89.9	91.0	87.9	112.7	91.2	84.6
Appleton-Oshkosh-Neenah WI MSA						
Appleton-Neenah-Menasha WI	98.2	94.9	101.8	93.7	97.9	98.9
Eau Claire WI MSA						
Eau Claire WI	98.8	100.5	103.4	98.9	94.8	107.4
Green Bay WI MSA						
Green Bay WI	98.7	96.1	99.3	88.4	100.6	102.4
Madison WI MSA						
Madison WI	112.2	98.8	128.8	92.1	105.1	110.8
Milwaukee-Waukesha WI PMSA						
Milwaukee-Waukesha WI PMSA	105.4	102.1	120.8	82.5	104.3	102.1
Sheboygan WI MSA						
Sheboygan WI	101.2	103.9	114.2	81.8	100.1	90.4
Wausau WI MSA						
Wausau WI	105.5	99.6	123.1	88.5	94.6	109.2
Cheyenne WY MSA						
Cheyenne WY	97.5	106.7	91.7	89.2	96.5	95.0
Saskatoon SK CMA						
Saskatoon SK	95.9	104.4	97.1	74.4	110.1	38.3

APPENDIX

Detailed Definitions of *DOT* Aptitudes and Abilities

EXPLANATION OF DATA, PEOPLE, AND THINGS

Much of the information in this publication is based on the premise that every job requires a worker to function, to some degree, in relation to Data, People, and Things. These relationships are identified and explained below. They appear in the form of three listings arranged in each instance from the relatively simple to the complex in such a manner that each successive relationship includes those that are simpler and excludes the more complex. (As each of the relationships to People represents a wide range of complexity, resulting in considerable overlap among occupations, their arrangement is somewhat arbitrary and can be considered a hierarchy only in the most general sense.) The identifications attached to these relationships are referred to as Worker Functions, and provide standard terminology for use in summarizing how a worker functions on the job.

The fourth, fifth, and sixth digits of the occupational code reflect relationships to Data, People, and Things, respectively. These digits express a job's relationship to Data, People, and Things by identifying the highest appropriate function in each listing shown in the table on the following page.

DATA (4TH DIGIT)	PEOPLE (5TH DIGIT)	THINGS (6TH DIGIT)
0 Synthesizing	0 Mentoring	0 Setting Up
1 Coordinating	1 Negotiating	1 Precision Working
2 Analyzing	2 Instructing	2 Operating-Controlling
3 Compiling	3 Supervising	3 Driving-Operating
4 Computing	4 Diverting	4 Manipulating
5 Copying	5 Persuading	5 Tending
6 Comparing	6 Speaking- Signaling	6 Feeding-Offbearing
	7 Serving	7 Handling
	8 Taking Instructions-Helping	

Definitions of Worker Functions

Data: Information, knowledge, and conceptions; related to data, people, or things; obtained by observation, investigation, interpretation, visualization, and mental creation. Data are intangible and include numbers, words, symbols, ideas, concepts, and oral verbalization.

0 *Synthesizing:* Integrating analyses of data to discover facts and/or develop knowledge concepts or interpretations.

1 *Coordinating:* Determining time, place, and sequence of operations or action to be taken on the basis of analysis of data; executing determinations and/or reporting on events.

2 *Analyzing:* Examining and evaluating data. Presenting alternative actions in relation to the evaluation is frequently involved.

3 *Compiling:* Gathering, collating, or classifying information about data, people, or things. Reporting and/or carrying out a prescribed action in relation to the information is frequently involved.

4 *Computing:* Performing arithmetic operations and reporting on and/or carrying out a prescribed action in relation to them. Does not include counting.

5 *Copying:* Transcribing, entering, or posting data.

6 *Comparing:* Judging the readily observable functional, structural, or compositional characteristics (whether similar to or divergent from obvious standards) of data, people, or things.

People: Human beings; also animals dealt with on an individual basis as if they were human.

0 *Mentoring:* Dealing with individuals in terms of their total personality in order to advise, counsel, and/or guide them with regard to problems that may be resolved by legal, scientific, clinical, spiritual, and/or other professional principles.

1 *Negotiating:* Exchanging ideas, information, and opinions with others to formulate policies and programs and/or arrive jointly at decisions, conclusions, or solutions.

2 *Instructing:* Teaching subject matter to others, or training others (including animals) through explanation, demonstration, and supervised practice; or making recommendations on the basis of technical disciplines.

3 *Supervising:* Determining or interpreting work procedures for a group of workers, assigning specific duties to them, maintaining harmonious relations among them, and promoting efficiency. A variety of responsibilities is involved in this function.

4 *Diverting:* Amusing others, usually through the medium of stage, screen, television, or radio.

5 *Persuading:* Influencing others in favor of a product, service, or point of view.

6 *Speaking-Signaling:* Talking with and/or signaling people to convey or exchange information. Includes giving assignments and/or directions to helpers or assistants.

7 *Serving:* Attending to the needs or requests of people or animals or the expressed or implicit wishes of people. Immediate response is involved.

8 *Taking Instructions-Helping:* Attending to the work assignment instructions or orders of supervisor. (No immediate response required unless clarification of instructions or orders is needed.) Helping applies to "non-learning" helpers.

Things: Inanimate objects as distinguished from human beings, substances or materials; and machines, tools, equipment, work aids, and products. A thing is tangible and has shape, form, and other physical characteristics.

0 *Setting Up:* Preparing machines (or equipment) for operation by planning order of successive machine operations; installing and adjusting tools and other machine components; adjusting the position of workpiece or material; setting controls; and verifying accuracy of machine capabilities, properties of materials, and shop practices. Uses tools, equipment, and work aids, such as precision gauges and measuring instruments. Workers who set up one or a number of machines for other workers or who set up and personally operate a variety of machines are included here.

1 *Precision Working:* Using body members and/or tools or work aids to work, move, guide, or place objects or materials in situations where ultimate responsibility for the attainment of standards occurs and selection of appropriate tools, objects, or materials, and the adjustment of the tool to the task require exercise of considerable judgment.

2 *Operating-Controlling:* Starting, stopping, controlling, and adjusting the progress of machines or equipment. Operating machines involves setting up and adjusting the machine or material(s) as the work progresses. Controlling involves observing gauges, dials, etc., and turning valves and other devices to regulate factors such as temperature, pressure, flow of liquids, speed of pumps, and reactions of materials.

3 *Driving-Operating:* Starting, stopping, and controlling the actions of machines or equipment for which a course must be steered or which must be guided to control the movement of things or people for a variety of purposes. Involves such activities as observing gauges and dials, estimating distances and determining speed and direction of other objects, turning cranks and wheels, and pushing or pulling gear lifts or levers. Includes such machines as cranes, conveyor systems, tractors, furnace-charging machines, paving machines, and hoisting machines. Excludes manually powered machines, such as handtrucks and dollies, and power-assisted machines, such as electric wheelbarrows and handtrucks.

4 *Manipulating:* Using body members, tools, or special devices to work, move, guide, or place objects or materials. Involves some latitude for judgment with regard to precision attained and selecting appropriate tool, object, or material, although this is readily manifest.

5 *Tending:* Starting, stopping, and observing the functioning of machines and equipment. Involves adjusting materials or controls of the machine, such as changing guides, adjusting timers and temperature gauges, turning valves to allow flow of materials, and flipping switches in response to lights. Little judgment is involved in making these adjustments.

6 *Feeding-Offbearing:* Inserting, throwing, dumping, or placing materials in or removing them from machines or equipment which are automatic or tended or operated by other workers.

7 *Handling:* Using body members, handtools, and/or special devices to work, move, or carry objects or materials. Involves little or no latitude for judgment with regard to attainment of standards or in selecting appropriate tool, object, or materials.

GENERAL EDUCATIONAL DEVELOPMENT (GED)

General Educational Development embraces those aspects of education (formal and informal) which are required of the worker for satisfactory job performance. This is education of a general nature which does not have a recognized, fairly specific occupational objective. Ordinarily, such education is obtained in elementary school, high school, or college. However, it may be obtained from experience and self-study.

The GED Scale is composed of three divisions: Reasoning Development, Mathematical Development, and Language Development. The description of the various levels of language and mathematical development are based on the curricula taught in schools throughout the United States. An analysis of mathematics courses in school curricula reveals distinct levels of progression in the primary and secondary grades and in college. These levels of progression facilitated the selection and assignment of six levels of GED for the mathematical development scale.

However, though language courses follow a similar pattern of progression in primary and secondary school, particularly in learning and applying the principles of grammar, this pattern changes at the college level. The diversity of language courses offered at the college level precludes the establishment of distinct levels of language progression for these four years.

Consequently, language development is limited to five defined levels of GED inasmuch as levels 5 and 6 share a common definition, even though they are distinct levels.

SPECIFIC VOCATIONAL PREPARATION (SVP)

Specific Vocational Preparation is defined as the amount of lapsed time required by a typical worker to learn the techniques, acquire the information, and develop the facility needed for average performance in a specific job-worker situation.

This training may be acquired in a school, work, military, institutional, or vocational environment. It does not include the orientation time required of a fully qualified worker to become accustomed to the special conditions of any new job. Specific vocational training includes: vocational education, apprenticeship training, in-plant training, on-the-job training, and essential experience in other jobs.

Specific vocational training includes training given in any of the following circumstances:

a. Vocational education (high school; commercial or shop training; technical school; art school; and that part of college training which is organized around a specific vocational objective);

b. Apprenticeship training (for apprenticeable jobs only);

c. In-plant training (organized classroom study provided by an employer);

d. On-the-job training (serving as learner or trainee on the job under the instruction of a qualified worker);

e. Essential experience in other jobs (serving in less responsible jobs which lead to the higher grade job or serving in other jobs which qualify).

The following is an explanation of the various levels of specific vocational preparation:

LEVEL	TIME
1	Short demonstration only
2	Anything beyond short demonstration up to and including 1 month
3	Over 1 month up to and including 3 months
4	Over 3 months up to and including 6 months
5	Over 6 months up to and including 1 year
6	Over 1 year up to and including 2 years
7	Over 2 years up to and including 4 years
8	Over 4 years up to and including 10 years
9	Over 10 years

Note: The levels of this scale are mutually exclusive and do not overlap.

SCALE OF GENERAL EDUCATION DEVELOPMENT (GED)

Level	Reasoning Development	Mathematical Development	Language Development
6	Apply principles of logical or scientific thinking to a wide range of intellectual and practical problems. Deal with nonverbal symbolism (formulas, scientific equations, graphs, musical notes, etc.) in its most difficult phases. Deal with a variety of abstract and concrete variables. Comprehend the most abstruse classes of concepts.	*Advanced calculus:* Work with limits, continuity, real number systems, mean value theorems, and implicit function theorems. *Modern algebra:* Apply fundamental concepts of theories of groups, rings, and fields. Work with differential equations, linear algebra, infinite series, advanced operations methods, and functions of real and complex variables. *Statistics:* Work with mathematical statistics, mathematical probability and applications, experimental design, statistical inference, and econometrics.	*Reading:* Read literature, book and play reviews, scientific and technical journals, abstracts, financial reports, and legal documents. *Writing:* Write novels, plays, editorials, journals, speeches, manuals, critiques, poetry, and songs. *Speaking:* Conversant in the theory, principles, and methods of effective and persuasive speaking, voice and diction, phonetics, and discussion and debate.
5	Apply principles of logical or scientific thinking to define problems, collect data, establish facts, and draw valid conclusions. Interpret an extensive variety of technical instructions in mathematical or diagrammatic form. Deal with several abstract and concrete variables.	*Algebra:* Work with exponents and logarithms, linear equations, quadratic equations, mathematical induction and binomial theorem, and permutations. *Calculus:* Apply concepts of analytic geometry, differentiations, and integration of algebraic functions with applications. *Statistics:* Apply mathematical operations to frequency distributions, reliability and validity of tests, normal curve, analysis of variance, correlation techniques, chi-square application and sampling theory, and factor analysis.	Same as Level 6.
4	Apply principles of rational systems to solve practical problems and deal with a variety of concrete variables in situations where only limited standardization exists. Interpret a variety of instructions furnished in written, oral, diagrammatic, or schedule form.	*Algebra:* Deal with system of real numbers; linear, quadratic, rational, exponential, logarithmic, angle and circular functions, and inverse functions; related algebraic solution of equations and inequalities; limits and continuity; and probability and statistical inference. *Geometry:* Deductive axiomatic geometry, plane and solid, and rectangular coordinates. *Shop Math:* Practical application of fractions, percentages, ratio and proportion, measurement, logarithms, practical algebra, geometric construction, and essentials of trigonometry.	*Reading:* Read novels, poems, newspapers, periodicals, journals, manuals, dictionaries, thesauruses, and encyclopedias. *Writing:* Prepare business letters, expositions, summaries, and reports, using prescribed format and conforming to all rules of punctuation, grammar, diction, and style. *Speaking:* Participate in panel discussions, dramatizations, and debates. Speak extemporaneously on a variety of subjects.

	Reasoning	Mathematics	Language
3	Apply commonsense understanding to carry out instructions furnished in written, oral, or diagrammatic form. Deal with problems involving several concrete variables in or from standardized situations.	Compute discount, interest, profit, and loss; commission, markup, and selling price; ratio and proportion; and percentage. Calculate surfaces, volumes, weights, and measures. *Algebra:* Calculate variables and formulas; monomials and polynomials; ratio and proportion variables; and square roots and radicals. Geometry: Calculate plane and solid figures, circumference, area, and volume. Understand kinds of angles and properties of pairs of angles.	*Reading:* Read a variety of novels, magazines, atlases, and encyclopedias. Read safety rules, instructions in the use and maintenance of shop tools and equipment, and methods and procedures in mechanical drawing and layout work. *Writing:* Write reports and essays with proper format, punctuation, spelling, and grammar, using all parts of speech. *Speaking:* Speak before an audience with poise, voice control, and confidence, using correct English and well-modulated voice.
2	Apply commonsense understanding to carry out detailed but uninvolved written or oral instructions. Deal with problems involving a few concrete variables in or from standardized situations.	Add, subtract, multiply, and divide all units of measure. Perform the four operations with like common and decimal fractions. Compute ratio, rate, and percent. Draw and interpret bar graphs. Perform arithmetic operations involving all American monetary units.	*Reading:* Passive vocabulary of 5,000-6,000 words. Read at rate of 190-215 words per minute. Read adventure stories and comic books, looking up unfamiliar words in dictionary for meaning, spelling, and pronunciation. Read instructions for assembling model cars and airplanes. *Writing:* Write compound and complex sentences, using cursive style, proper end punctuation, and employing adjectives and adverbs. *Speaking:* Speak clearly and distinctly with appropriate pauses and emphasis, correct punctuation, variations in word order, using present, perfect, and future tenses.
1	Apply commonsense understanding to carry out simple one- or two-step instructions. Deal with standardized situations with occasional or no variables in or from these situations encountered on the job.	Add and subtract two-digit numbers. Multiply and divide 10's and 100's by 2, 3, 4, 5. Perform the four basic arithmetic operations with coins as part of a dollar. Perform operations with units such as cup, pint, and quart; inch, foot, and yard; and ounce and pound.	*Reading:* Recognize meaning of 2,500 (two- or three-syllable) words. Read at rate of 95-120 words per minute. Compare similarities and differences between words and between series of numbers. *Writing:* Print simple sentences containing subject, verb, and object, and series of numbers, names, and addresses. *Speaking:* Speak simple sentences, using normal word order, and present and past tenses.

Employment Opportunity Database Technical Note

The *Employment Opportunity Database* utilizes publicly available, government databases to demonstrate concepts presented in the *Employment Opportunity* text. Database outputs have been designed to be user-friendly, and are presented in an order meant to maximize the reader's learning experience. Detailed employment totals are *not* intended to portray official government estimates, but have been developed to provide readers with a general idea of the magnitude of jobs by significant descriptors, such as area, industry, and occupation.

Most often utilized as the base of employment is the U. S. Commerce Department, Economic Statistics Administration, Bureau of the Census, County Business Pattern series. County Business Patterns is an annual series providing subnational economic data by industry. The series is used for studying the economic activity of small areas; analyzing economic changes over time; and as a benchmark for statistical series surveys and databases between economic censuses. Most of the nation's economic activity is covered in this series. Data are excluded for self-employed persons, domestic service workers, railroad employees, agricultural production workers, most government employees, and employees on ocean-borne vessels or in foreign countries. Employment data utilized for Occupational Economic Profiles is derived from the Occupational Employment Statistics (OES) Program of the Bureau of Labor Statistics.

Occupational data have been generated through the use of national staffing patterns developed for the OES Program. The 1996 Industry Staffing Pattern data consist of separate tables for most 2- and 3-digit Standard Industrial Classification industry groups. Each table contains 100–200 occupations, with the industry's occupational employment divided by the industry's total employment and expressed as a percentage. OES also was the principal source of occupational wage data.

Since employment data are generally tabulated from universe files of administrative data, they are not subject to sampling error. However, non-sampling errors, including inability to identify all cases in the universe, definition of classification difficulties, and errors in recording or coding data may well occur. Error also may result when area industries fail to correspond to national staffing pattern characteristics. Although every effort was made to judiciously utilize and apply available data, no direct measurement of error has been obtained.

Projections included in the *Employment Opportunity Database* are based upon those of the Bureau of Labor Statistics (BLS), Employment Projections Program. This program develops information about the labor market for the Nation as a whole for 10 years in the future. The BLS projections are based upon assessments of the effect on employment of specified changes in economic conditions and/or changes in Federal programs and policies. Employment forecasts and information on occupational requirements were obtained from the BLS Occupational Projections and Training Data information.

Index